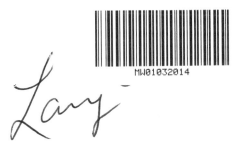

MW01032014

Thanks Anyway, Sir...
But I'll Sleep In The Tree

Larry Weill

North Country Books, Inc.
Utica, New York

Thanks Anyway, Sir... But I'll Sleep In The Tree
Copyright © 2018
by Larry Weill

ISBN 978-1-59531-059-0

Library of Congress Cataloging-in-Publication Data

Names: Weill, Larry, author.
Title: Thanks anyway, sir... but I'll sleep in the tree / Larry Weill.
Description: Utica, New York : North Country Books, Inc., [2018]
Identifiers: LCCN 2018019050 | ISBN 9781595310590 (alk. paper)
Subjects: LCSH: Weill, Larry. | Park rangers--New York (State)--Adirondack
    Park--Biography. | New York (State). Department of Environmental
    Conservation--Officials and employees--Biography. | Wilderness areas--New
    York (State)--Adirondack Mountains. | Wilderness area users--New York
    (State)--Adirondack Mountains.
Classification: LCC SB481.6.W45 A3 2018 | DDC 333.78/2097475--dc23
LC record available at https://lccn.loc.gov/2018019050

North Country Books, Inc.
220 Lafayette Street
Utica, New York 13502
www.northcountrybooks.com

To the memory of Pete Gloo, the Wakely Mountain Forest Fire Observer from 1979–1980. Even though you are gone, may your music always remain in our hearts.

Table of Contents

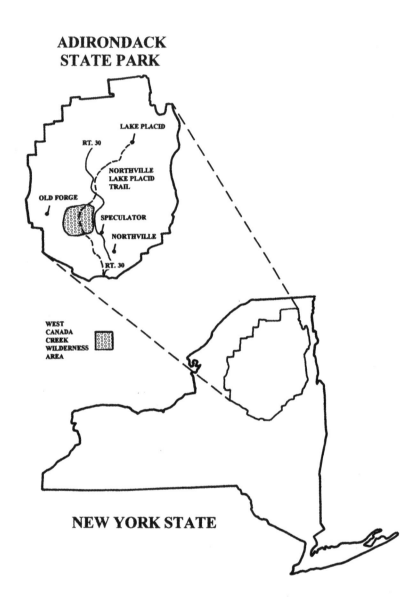

ADIRONDACK STATE PARK

LAKE PLACID

RT. 30

NORTHVILLE LAKE PLACID TRAIL

OLD FORGE

SPECULATOR

NORTHVILLE

RT. 30

WEST CANADA CREEK WILDERNESS AREA

NEW YORK STATE

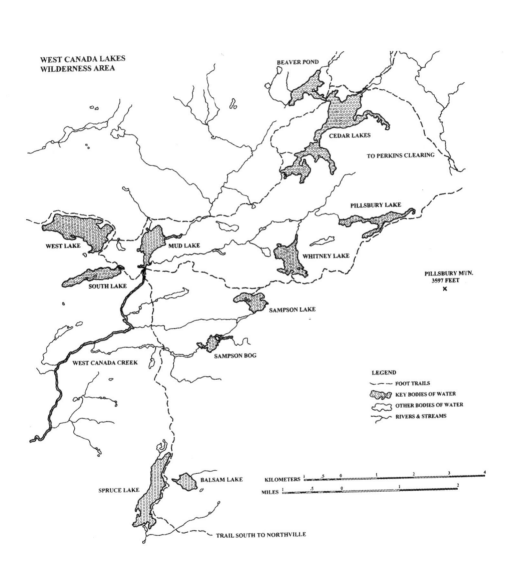

WEST CANADA LAKES
WILDERNESS AREA

BEAVER POND

CEDAR LAKES

TO PERKINS CLEARING

PILLSBURY LAKE

WEST LAKE

MUD LAKE

WHITNEY LAKE

SOUTH LAKE

PILLSBURY MTN.
3597 FEET
X

SAMPSON LAKE

WEST CANADA CREEK

SAMPSON BOG

LEGEND

— · — FOOT TRAILS

KEY BODIES OF WATER

OTHER BODIES OF WATER

RIVERS & STREAMS

SPRUCE LAKE

BALSAM LAKE

KILOMETERS   1   .5   0   1   2   3   4

MILES   1   .5   0   1   2

TRAIL SOUTH TO NORTHVILLE

Introduction – I Lied!

OK, I guess I'll admit it. I lied to you. Yup, I did. It's not something that I'm particularly proud of, but it just happened. Nine years ago, when *Forgive Me, Ma'am... Bears Don't Wear Blue* went to print, I told you that the series was complete, that I would not add a fourth book to the existing trilogy. As far as I was concerned, the series was over and the stories had all been told. I had left the woods decades earlier (twenty-eight years earlier, to be exact) and would not write about additional adventures unless I had new stories to tell—and the chances of that ever happening were remote at best.

Never say never.

If there is one thing I've learned in this lifetime, it is that your mind can sometimes push you to extremes even when your body says "no." I'm convinced this is often a matter of denial; you think you can do something, even when your bones and joints are creaking and every muscle in your body is screaming at your lack of common sense. It's OK, right? I read a story about a ninety-something-year-old gentleman who was still running marathons—and still able to smile for the camera after the race. So why not?

So much has happened in the years since I hung up my DEC Wilderness Ranger uniform for the last time in 1981. Heck, much has occurred since I returned to the woods for exploratory hikes in the early years of the twenty-first century. I underwent a total hip replacement in 2005, which is mentioned somewhere within my last book. This thankfully allowed me to resume my hiking career beyond the point where I had become a complete invalid due to arthritis. (This, by the way, is a wonderful operation for anyone in pain who is considering having it done. It works, and it will restore the freedom of mobility necessary to do as you choose.)

My time, a valued commodity I guarded carefully in order to set aside a few days to complete a walk in the woods once every few years, had become more and more restricted. With two children at home (until 2011), there were soccer games, school plays, band concerts, and innumerable other activities that restricted my freedom to pursue such frivolous endeavors. I was promoted from commander to captain in the Navy Reserves, which meant that my responsibilities increased accordingly. There were even years when I spent much of my time in Italy, working from the naval base in Naples as I fulfilled my duties to our country.

Because of everything going on in my life, I found that the time needed to just disappear into the woods had, well, disappeared. My civilian job kept me busy for a full forty-hour week. For many years, my employer generously allowed me to go away and perform my Navy work for as long as necessary and the only gaps in my schedule were filled by my obligations to my family. (My wife is the one truly deserving of a medal for all she put up with as the result of my ever-changing schedule.) It wasn't until 2008 that I fully retired from the Navy, which reduced my combined work and family obligations to a simple seventy- to eighty-hour week. Hey—life is good!

I must admit that by the time I pulled the plug on my Navy career, retiring as a "full-bird" captain, hiking was nothing more than a pleasant, distant memory. We still enjoyed hiking together as a family, sometimes climbing an easy-to-reach peak, other times strolling a flatland trail for a two- to three-hour jaunt. But I no longer desired or even thought about doing any serious backpacking into a place such as the West Canada Lakes Wilderness area and the Northville-Placid Trail.

It was a stroke of pure luck that I met my new hiking partner, Casey. I won't tell that story now, as I will write about it in one

of the early chapters of this book. But suffice it to say that anyone who is able to find a compatible hiking partner—one who has
the same capabilities and tendencies—can consider him or her-
self to be a lucky individual. Consider any two people who enjoy
hiking, and you are bound to discover differences in physical
abilities (i.e. one motors along at twice the speed of the other),
personalities, preferred destinations, and more. Finding that
compatibility with Casey was a wonderful thing, and it is part of
the reason for the re-emergence of my interest in the hiking
world. Yes, we both travel slowly, each with our own ailments
and limitations. But the joy of being there is able to overcome
most of these restrictions, and I've had a wonderful time renew-
ing my memories and immersing my senses in the places I cherished so dearly.

Our initial excursion into the woods took place in 2009, and
it was my first backpacking trip in quite a while. Because of multiple issues, I had dropped close to one hundred pounds and was
in excellent condition at the time. (That statement requires an
explanation. Not all of my weight was "bad." At various times in
my life I was a successful, competitive power lifter, in a sport
that increases your size by its very nature. I have at times
weighed in at over three-hundred pounds while still appearing to
be very fit.) Because of my reduced size and increased
endurance, I was able to maintain a respectable pace for hours
on end, even while moving uphill with a full pack. Our 2009 trip
was incredibly successful because in addition to revisiting all of
my favorite locations in the West Canadas, we ran into quite a
few colorful characters on the trail. Some of these individuals
stayed overnight in lean-tos with us, and we were able to "spin
the yarn" together around the campfire. This has always been my
favored means for obtaining stories for these books, as nothing
can beat a good tale told over a roaring blaze.

Following the success of that initial trip, I completed a pair
of follow-up trips in 2014 and 2015, with varying results. The first

was a simple, in-and-out pilgrimage of a few days in which my only goal was to reach the Beaver Pond lean-to and savor the view and fresh air. This was a success, and the experience was heightened by the presence of Casey and his teenage son. It was of no particular matter or importance that I remained fairly sedentary for the three days of our excursion. Just being at Cedar Lakes was enough for me on that trip, and I loved every minute of it.

The following year, I planned a voyage that was infinitely more difficult and complex in every way imaginable. My goal was to set forth on my own into that same West Canada Lakes area and establish a new "mini-settlement" or camping area at least a mile off any trail or other sign of civilization, where there would be zero chance of someone stumbling upon me. It would involve carrying food and supplies for two weeks of solitary exis-tence, along with enough tools and primitive building supplies to construct a shelter on my own. I pictured a small structure fash-ioned in lean-to style using the most rudimentary building mate-rials and wood I could find on the ground. The totality of these requirements resulted in a backpack that weighed in at about one-hundred pounds, which was excessive even by my standards.

Without going into all the gory details, I will admit this trip failed miserably. Although I made it to my destination, I was beset by equipment problems from the evening of day one, which reduced my chances of success to somewhere between infinitesimal and nil. I was also experiencing a physical problem—an unexplained pain in my abdomen that was restricting my mobility and making life miserable. Although I tried ignoring this malady, it continued to get worse until it required medical atten-tion. Little did I realize this would grow into a major medical issue that would keep me on the sidelines for the next eighteen months.

As I originally wrote this introduction, I was making plans to go back into the woods to complete the "mission" I had started in 2015. Two years earlier, I had done the right thing by applying for a camping permit, which involved providing the precise location of my site right down to the closest centimeter. (OK, perhaps this is the tiniest bit of exaggeration.) This time, however, I wouldn't need to make such an arrangement, as I expected to stay there only a few days at a time before taking off on side trips to some of my other favorite locations across the West Canadas.

Many of my friends and associates have asked me why I wanted to do this, and it is not an easy answer to provide—or at least, to summarize. But it is something I had always wanted to do, and it had been at the top of my bucket list for what seemed like forever. (At my age, I assume that I am afforded the luxury of having a personal bucket list, am I not?) In my mind I had envisioned the lean-to I would build at least a hundred times, and it was often the last thing I thought of as I drifted off to sleep at night. Likewise, I knew exactly how I would construct my elevated bed and table and the fireplace, right down to the placement of the grill. I had even thought of a name for my dwelling: it would be "Seymourville," in honor of the fabled local hermit Louis Seymour (aka Adirondack French Louie). I also considered the appellation "Nilsbu," the name of a hut in the mountainous wilderness that the Norwegian resistance used as a hideout while plotting to destroy Hitler's atomic bomb program during World War II; however, this seemed just a little too dark for me, so I decided to stick with Seymourville for the actual christening.

From the original conception of this idea, I knew that my intentions had caused some people (mainly family) to worry for my safety, as most folks aren't comfortable voyaging off into the woods by themselves, especially off-trail where no one could find them if needed. However, I have always thought the deep forest is a much safer location than anywhere in the city, and that my own well-being was better preserved amongst the trees and hills of the Adirondacks than it was anywhere else on the planet.

Throughout my writings, I have always chosen to tell my stories after they have taken place. Never before have I discussed my plans for the future, before I have set forth on a given adventure. However, this particular venture (which will already be in the past by the time this book is completed) is something I feel I have to do. My excitement and elevated expectations from 2015 have only served to buoy my hopes and dreams for the adventure that is to come. And as pragmatic as I have become in my advanced years, I still believe that I am up to the task of building my own settlement and then coming back to tell of it.

In the meantime, I fully expect to be on the prowl, skipping from lean-to to lean-to along the Northville-Placid Trail, encountering more people and hearing their stories. I'll be back there again, the old guy leaning on the walking stick and talking to everyone who comes down the trail. If you see me in the woods, please stop by and say hello, share the lean-to as well as your stories. Maybe you'll even read about yourself somewhere within these pages. Good luck and happy trails!

Memories of 2009

Return to the Woods

I can't say for certain whether I'm a believer in the concept of fate. Unlike many of my friends, who are of the conviction that most of life's events are preordained, I guess I've always felt as though I've drifted through a good part of my existence in a series of sequential coincidences. Either that, or someone from above must have one heckuva strange sense of humor because even now, at the tender age of fifty-five, I still haven't a clue what I'd like to do when I grow up.

I hadn't specifically planned on making a journey back into the West Canada Lakes in the summer of 2009, although I must admit that I could always be tempted into returning to that beautiful haven of wilderness. However, one very fortunate coincidence transpired about six months earlier that served as a catalyst for this journey. My wife and daughters decided to go away for a winter weekend of cabin camping with a YMCA group. As they arrived, my older daughter noticed a man sitting in a chair and reading a copy of *Excuse Me, Sir... Your Socks Are On Fire*. (This was my first book of Wilderness Park Ranger stories, published in 2005.) Needless to say, she was a bit surprised because it's not often that you see someone reading that book in public. Believe it or not, J.K. Rowling actually has more books in print than I do.

Anyway, my family members introduced themselves to the fellow, who said his name was Casey. He was from the same geographic area as we were (the east side of Rochester), and he was also an avid hiker. They exchanged contact information, and eventually Casey and I connected and traded emails about the idea of taking a four-day hike back into the woods the following summer. At the very least, we agreed to meet for lunch to discuss the possibilities.

I must admit that the first time I came face-to-face with Casey it was a bit disconcerting. I am quite comfortable meeting strangers, having been employed in many fields where this is part of the daily routine. However, when I walked into the foyer of the restaurant that day, the only person sitting there was a gentleman about the same age as me with a shaved head and sporting a completely reflective pair of wraparound sunglasses. It wasn't the shaved head that threw me for a loop, as the real estate on top of my own head is a bit sparse these days. But the sunglasses were highly unusual, making it completely impossible to see this person's eyes. I'd never before tried to introduce myself and start a conversation without making eye contact with a person, and I found it to be rather unnerving.

Casey quickly removed the glasses, and we had a chance to chat for a while before being seated at our table. I soon learned that he was a very friendly, enthusiastic outdoorsman who had already completed the entire length of the Northville-Placid Trail and was quite familiar with those sections that traverse the West Canadas. However, like many of the thru-hikers who travel that path each summer, he was curious about the many side trails that weave their way around and across the main north-south thoroughfare, and he wanted to see them for himself.

There is an interesting phenomenon I've noticed over the years since I worked in the West Canadas. When I speak with people who have read any of my books, I am often asked about the trailheads of the feeder trails I've mentioned as well as the exact location where a particular event in a story occurred. I'm always happy to encounter Adirondack enthusiasts who have decided to stray from the highest-use routes to explore some of the lesser-known lakes and lean-tos. I also enjoy showing people where various episodes took place, since a number of the structures such as bridges and lean-tos in my stories have been rebuilt in different locations.

As we sat there comparing notes and enjoying our barbeque lunches, Casey and I discovered we had another amusing similarity. Whereas, in our early days, we would have been advertising our hiking prowess and ambitious intentions, this discussion had a distinctly geriatric flavor and focused more on our various prescriptions and joint replacements. Within a short period of time we were in hysterics, wondering what crazy whiffs of nostalgia were motivating us to attempt this trip in the first place. It was nice to know that Casey was a person with whom I'd enjoy spending time in the woods, and we agreed to move forward with our plans.

After evaluating the possible routes through the West Canadas, the two of us decided on "Standard Route #1," the name I've used to describe my usual three- to four-day tour. This circuit starts from the trailhead at the bottom of Pillsbury Mountain and climbs Blue Ridge to the intersection of the French Louie Trail. It then heads north across Grassy Brook and onward another three miles to Cedar Lakes, which is where we'd spend our first night in the woods. The second day's hike would continue west on the Northville-Placid Trail (NPT) until it turned south at West Lake. (This is usually called West Canada Lake by hikers and has also appeared as such in some of the earlier USGS topographic maps of the area.) On the third day, we would leave the NPT after crossing over West Canada Creek and head northeast past Sampson Lake en route to Pillsbury Lake. The fourth day would be a short three-and-a-half-mile trek back to the parking lot at the foot of Pillsbury Mountain. This is a nice, pleasant circle that never requires more than seven miles of trail on any given day, and I enjoy the relatively flat terrain and beautiful scenery along the way. This route also takes me past the site of many pleasurable experiences and memories, which I relive whenever I return to those familiar locations.

Once we had established our intended route, Casey and I agreed on a tentative date that fit both our schedules. We also created a list that would meet all of our backpacking needs while eliminating any duplicate items. This was easy to do because we both owned almost all of the essential items for spending time in the woods. It was a simple matter of dividing up the weight and volume, which we resolved in a matter of minutes. By the time we parted ways that afternoon, we felt that we were comfortable with our decisions and could be on our way into the backcountry with little additional planning.

One of the few advantages of my new "senior" status was my conditioning. The months leading up to the summer of 2009 were some of my most successful in the great battle of the waistline, and I can honestly say that I was in my best shape in years. I had been walking five miles every day, and I had even worked in a little running from time to time. (Anyone who knows me realizes just how much I detest running, so that alone should serve as proof of my newly-attained fitness.) In addition to the walking, we took our family vacation in Vermont that June, where we spent almost every day on the trails of the Green Mountains. I was happy to see that the climbing bothered me very little, and I could motor up the tallest mountains at a pace that would have been impossible only a year earlier. All this bode well for my upcoming trip.

Another interesting lead-up to our trip was the exchange of emails I had with the Assistant Forest Ranger, Brendan Jordan, who was now stationed in the West Canada Lakes Wilderness Area. Brendan had been on the trails back there for a couple of years, and he had written to me to introduce himself some time earlier. From what I'd heard, his job was similar to the one I'd held in the 1970s and 1980s, even though the title was different, although from Brendan's description, it sounded as though he had a broader range of responsibilities than we'd been assigned thirty years earlier. Like me, he worked for Tom Eakin, who was still serving as the forest ranger out of Lake Pleasant. Tom had him doing some interesting exploratory work in addition to his patrols of the Northville-Placid Trail. On several occasions, he had been asked to spend a week or two making a complete loop around some of the lakes, including Cedars, Spruce, and West. As a result, he was able to venture to a lot of locations that I simply never had time to see.

After exchanging a few emails, Brendan and I agreed that it would be fun to meet up in the woods, where we could trade stories on our respective assignments. The only problem with this arrangement, of course, was that he'd already read my books, so there was very little that I could tell him that he didn't already know. But that made no difference to me, and I gladly supplied him with our expected itinerary, including the lean-tos where we hoped to spend each night along the trail.

The final days leading up to the trip were quite rushed because we were just returning from our vacation in Vermont, and I had precious few minutes of spare time to complete my provisioning. Thankfully, Casey and I had each agreed that we would bring our own food supplies, so I had the liberty of purchasing only those items that I knew I'd enjoy, including some old standbys such as packages of Ramen noodles, vacuum-packed tuna, breakfast bars, and dehydrated food. Actually, I was quite pleasantly surprised to see that the variety of freeze-dried trail food had expanded greatly since my days in the woods. Whereas I had been limited to a choice of four or five favorites, there were now a plethora of tasty-looking meals, each of which I'd be happy to consume as my nightly repast. I quickly stocked up on a number of ethnic selections such as Thai chicken and turkey tetrazzini. I intentionally ignored the label that listed the sodium content, knowing that my blood would be pickled for several weeks after consuming the stuff. But heck, it's not something that I'd eat for more than a week, so I couldn't see the harm in purchasing those dinners that I knew I'd most enjoy.

Perhaps the only item that I did not own, but Casey did, was a water purification pump. I never needed one while stationed in the West Canadas, as the *Giardia lambia* parasite had not yet arrived, and I would drink water straight out of any moving stream. Foolishly, this even included the West Canada Creek, which flows directly out of Mud Lake, probably the shallowest, muddiest, and most beaver-laden body of water in the entire area. If ever there was a lake that would have promised a healthy dose of *Giardia* that would have been it. However, I was lucky enough to live back there in the days when you never need-ed to worry about such a precaution.

A couple years earlier, I had purchased a filtration system for a hike I'd taken with Kelly, my older daughter. However, that pump had been defective and had quickly deteriorated within a couple days of leaving the trailhead. We followed all the direc-tions, including cleaning out the interior lines and filters, all for naught. Instead of collecting gallons of filtered water quickly and easily (as promised), this disaster required an extraordinary amount of time and energy to gather even a mere quart of safe water, and both of us returned at the end of the week with vastly larger biceps and triceps from the exercise. Lesson learned. I gratefully decided to accept Casey's offer to be the sole supplier of water on this trip.

As the day of the hiking trip approached, I made plans to head up to Speculator and see some old friends before heading into the woods. Casey couldn't make it until early afternoon, whereas I had the advantage of getting a very early start. I used the time to my advantage and stopped by to see Barb Remias, John's widow. (Barb has since passed away as well.) John had been the interior caretaker at the West Canada Lakes station prior to its destruction in the 1980s; he was my friend and mentor for most of my time on the trails. Barb made it into the woods to stay with John in the cabin from time to time, so we were all very good friends. I tried to visit her whenever I was in the area, which wasn't too often those days.

I also stopped by the Speculator post office, where I saw Debbie Remias, the daughter of John and Barb. She had been part of the trail crew when I was living in the woods, and I must say that she has changed very little despite the passage of three decades. (I am a firm believer in the restorative powers of the Adirondacks; it seems to keep people young in both mind and body.) She interrupted her mail duties long enough to chat for a few minutes, and we had a good laugh talking about old times.

By a lucky coincidence, I ran into Tom Eakin in the parking lot outside Charlie Johns' store, which was a nice surprise since we hadn't come face to face since I'd left the woods in 1981. I was amazed that he was still serving in the capacity of local forest ranger, being one of the longest-serving members of that force. Tom always was the consummate professional, and he had built a well-deserved reputation for his prowess on the job. We spoke for quite a while, exchanging news of our lives from the past thirty years. It appeared to me that the years had served to mellow him somewhat, although his passion for the job was still apparent as he discussed the changes in the state. He has since retired from his duties, at which time the department lost one of its finest members.

After saying goodbye to all my friends, I doubled back toward Barb's place in Lake Pleasant; she had given me permission to leave my car in her driveway while I spent the next four days in the woods. Casey owned a rugged, four-wheel-drive SUV, which we knew we could drive all the way up to the base of Pillsbury Mountain. My car never would have navigated that rocky dirt road, so we opted to take his vehicle.

I arrived back at her house at noon and began the thorough

preparations necessary to get my pack ready to hit the trail. I was still completely set to go by one o'clock, and Casey wasn't due for another hour. He had duties to fulfill back in Rochester and couldn't depart for the mountains as early as I could.

With the luxury of some spare time before Casey was due, I decided to relax in my car with a good book, which seemed like a pretty good idea. Unfortunately, I had slept very little the night before and was a bit sleepier than I had imagined. I must have read at least a page or two before my eyes shut, and I entered my own version of screen-saver mode. In other words, I was down for the count; zonked out.

For all I know, I might have slept for another eight hours had I not gradually become aware of knocking on my driver's-side window. My eyelids fluttered upward to discover Casey's face laughing at me from the other side.

"Want to give this a shot sometime today, or would you rather I let you sleep until morning?" he asked jokingly. Well, at least I'd made productive use of my time.

The drive to the Perkins Clearing logging road north of Speculator took us about twenty minutes, after which we turned left and headed off Route 30. The dirt lane that curves around Mason Lake en route to the trailhead is well-known to the local population, although not as familiar to the thru-hikers who start in Northville and plod straight through to Lake Placid. The road passes by a great many campsites where individuals in tents and campers pull off to spend a day or two along the shore of the lake. This has never been an official camping area, and no fees have ever been charged for staying at one of these sites. (I've heard rumors that this is changing, although I've not seen any-thing that officially alters that policy.)

In another fifteen minutes, we rumbled through the open area of Perkins Clearing, and I showed Casey where the gate had originally stood before the land swap between New York State and International Paper. This exchange of properties not only enhanced the manageability of the territory for both parties, but it also allowed hikers to drive three miles closer to the heart of the West Canada Lakes region. I must admit that I had originally been against this idea, since I'm in favor of keeping our precious wilderness acreage as remote as possible. However, in my "advanced years," I found myself quite willing to reduce the first day's hike from eight miles down to five, while eliminating the need to climb the first half of Blue Ridge. (That ridge has affectionately been dubbed "Sonofabitch hill" by the local populace.)

The final few miles of road to the trailhead were as familiar as ever, and it seemed as though I had never left. Every bend and dip in the road brought back memories of people and events in my life, and I was almost sorry that we sped past it all so quickly. I would have liked to linger, but it was the middle of the afternoon, and we wanted to get to a lean-to as quickly as possible, so we motored on up the rocky incline to the parking lot, which was surprisingly full. There are two trailheads in that spot, and the sign-in booth serves as a register for both. One trail goes west and ascends Pillsbury Mountain, while the other follows a more northerly course on its way into the interior lakes of the wilderness area. Both trails receive moderate use, and each route had several parties signed in.

After a few minutes of stretching, we were ready to don our packs and head out of the parking lot. The first mile and a half of trail would take us up the remainder of Blue Ridge and past the turnoff to Pillsbury Lake. This route was an actual road back in the days when I patrolled the woods, and it was still used by the ranger to drive all the way in to either Pillsbury or Grassy Brook, right next to the old site of Camp 20. However, all that's left today is a single path that cuts through the underbrush, with the remainder of the roadbed covered in vegetation. I've always been fascinated to see the speed with which nature overtakes and conquers what people have wrought, converting human construction back into a part of the landscape that is indiscernible by the human eye. While it is true that local outdoors people could probably pick out the original parameters of the road, most hikers would trod over the narrow trail without ever giving its origins a second thought.

At the juncture of the trail with the road to Pillsbury Lake, I pointed out the spot where I had been delayed one day due to the presence of a bear munching on raspberries. I was surprised to see that some of the bushes were still in evidence along the sides of the trail, and we we saw many more out by the wider logging road, since they tend to thrive in more open areas. Half in jest, I looked around for the bear, while Casey patiently put up with my charades.

After a few minutes of looking around, we descended the stretch to Grassy Brook and crossed over the bridge to the site of the old Camp 20. This was a cabin that was burned out even before I worked in the region, although people still used it as a campsite from time to time. Now, I noticed that there were no visible signs of the original habitation left, except the remnants of a fire ring where someone had cooked a meal. The original timbers and frame of the building were either gone or covered over with the accumulation of another three decades of debris. It doesn't take long, and I'm sure the woods are full of the remains of camps and logging operations that were once prominent structures, but have since rotted into oblivion.

Casey and I were both feeling in pretty good shape, and we managed to maintain an energetic pace as we headed north. We crossed over the outlet of Cedar Lakes, which is the start of the Cedar River, right below the site of the old dam, and headed west toward the lean-tos. The biggest change I noticed was that the dam was now completely out, which resulted in a much lower water level. I could see solid ground along the waterline that had once been part of the lake, and I was saddened to see the loss of waters that had once been the home of my favorite brook trout. I do believe that the remnants of the dam still serve to maintain a certain amount of water in the lake because the original (pre-dam era) Cedar Lakes were actually a series of smaller, barely-connected bodies of water. I truly hope that the state someday rebuilds this dam back to its original stature. Sadly, the lack of funding in the modern era of budget shortfalls may render this dream to be permanently unreachable.

Within a few hundred yards, we passed the site of the Cedar Lakes Lean-to #1. This was the smaller replacement version of the spacious structure that had stood closer to the dam. It is built in the clearing near the site of the Cedar Lakes caretaker's cabin, which was burned out in the mid-1970s. I would have loved to have stayed at the original lean-to, which held many happy memories for me, including those of my first night ever in the West Canada Lakes Wilderness Area. The newer lean-to (which is already probably twenty years old) held very little appeal to me, and we decided to risk it by forgoing the empty shelter in hopes of finding open room in the Beaver Pond lean-to, which would be another half mile along the trail.

As we headed out of the clearing and into the next stand of trees, we saw a figure approaching from the opposite direction. He was the first individual we'd seen since leaving the trailhead, and he was wearing a state uniform. Even at a distance, I could see that he wasn't carrying a backpack, which meant that he'd stashed it in a camp somewhere off the trail. He was tall and lean, with dark hair and a beard. I knew in an instant the identity of this person, even though we'd never met.

"Hey! You must be Brendan," I hollered over the short distance.

"Yes, and you have to be Larry," he replied, smiling back. "I was hoping I'd run into you today. Which way are you heading?"

"We're hoping to get the Beaver Pond lean-to for the night," I replied. "That's my favorite spot in the area, and I've been telling Casey here about it for some time now." I took a moment to introduce Casey to Brendan before continuing the conversation.

"The woods don't look too full right now, although we saw a

few other parties signed in near the dam," I said. "Do you know if anyone is in the lean-to?"

"There was a group there last night," Brendan nodded, "but I think they said they were moving on today. You could probably share the place with them even if they decided to stay."

"How about you?" I asked Brendan. "I was hoping we might be able to talk for a bit, if you have time at the end of your day."

"Yeah, me too," replied Brendan. "I've heard a lot of stories from over the years, and I'd like to compare notes with you."

We bid each other a temporary farewell and agreed to try to meet up later on, after we'd gotten settled in and had our evening meal. Brendan was heading down to patrol the route past the dam to see whether anyone was camping at the various tent sites before doubling back and possibly joining us at Beaver Pond. His words had a very familiar ring, as I'd uttered them myself on hundreds of occasions back in the 1970s and 1980s when that task was my responsibility. I must admit that I felt a bit of jealousy, as I'd always considered these to be "my" woods, even though I had lived back here for just three short seasons. I guess we are all territorial to some degree, but I had passed the torch long ago; it was time to move on.

The next stretch of trail seemed to take a little longer than I had remembered, and I was reminded that age has a funny way of making distances seem somewhat protracted. Half miles seem like miles, and one-mile climbs feel as though they've grown to two. (I am pretty convinced that the heights of most of the Adirondack Mountains have increased considerably since I was in my twenties.) Regardless, it didn't take long to traverse the northern shore of Cedar Lakes and cross the short bridge that connects the lake to the Beaver Pond. However, the bad news was that even at that distance, we could both hear and see the evidence of other people already in residence on the elevated promontory that served as the site for the Beaver Pond lean-to.

One of the few advantages of being an older hiker is that you can easily and diplomatically engage almost anyone in the woods without fear of rejection. Back in my ranger days, when I was wearing the uniform of the state, I never experienced a problem when asking to share a lean-to with another camper. This was a good thing because some individuals and groups tended to become rather territorial about their turf, especially when the woods were crowded. However, it's different when you aren't dressed like a ranger, and it's nice to have the benefit of a few gray hairs in your scalp to support your cause when asking to share the same roof for the night.

Casey and I diverted from the trail and climbed the small incline up to the path leading to the lean-to. A group of three young men, probably teenagers, was engaged in a bit of light horseplay in front of the shelter, and we exchanged greetings in a friendly manner. I noticed that their packs were completely packed, as though they were heading out, even though it was late in the afternoon. Still, I wanted to ask them if it was OK to share the lean-to with them as though they were planning on staying there overnight.

"No, that's OK, it's all yours," said one of the boys. "We're heading down to the Third Lake lean-to and meeting up down there."

"Meeting up?" I asked, confused by the statement. "Aren't you all going together?"

"No, Mac and I are taking the canoe, and Tim here is hiking the trail, since we can't fit all three of us with packs into the same boat."

I looked down at the shoreline and was surprised to see a small craft sitting in the water. I hadn't seen any signs of a wheeled cart being pulled along the trail, so they must have carried it between them. I was impressed, as always, by the energy of youth.

"Well, thanks a lot, and enjoy your trip," I said. "The Third Lake lean-to is a really nice spot, assuming that you can find it from the trail."

"Yeah, I heard that it's tough to find," said the tallest of the three. "Do you know what the trail looks like well enough to give me a description of the route?"

"Sure," I said, "but it won't be pretty. Your feet will be wet by the time you arrive. But I can get you there; that's not a problem."

I followed with a detailed description of the side trail that leads back from the Northville-Placid Trail, skirting the edge of the swampy area before gaining solid footing for the last quarter mile to the lean-to. It is a deserted place, made harder to find by the continuous efforts of local sportsmen to cover all signs of the trail. In recent years, the flooding has become so bad that the Adirondack Mountain Club has proposed creating a re-route to the site. That is perhaps the only way that the hidden lean-to will become popular once again as a resting point along the NPT.

As an afterthought, one of the other members of their group asked me if I'd heard a weather forecast for the area. I replied that I hadn't, although the conditions back in the higher lakes is usually so unstable that the standard forecasts are rendered useless. The three boys thanked us, and then departed with their gear, two by boat and one on foot. Their absence left a welcome silence in the air, which added greatly to the beauty of that magnificent camping site.

Casey and I plunked our backpacks down in the lean-to and rolled out our foam pads and sleeping bags. It took only a few minutes of unpacking to give the shelter a lived-in feel, and I savored every whiff of the woodsy scents that surrounded us. The air was laden with fragrances: the foamy breeze off the lake, the perfume of the balsam and cedar trees, and the smoky aroma from the fire pit. All of these had dominated my dreams for years, and I was unable and unwilling to clear them from my memory.

After six months of planning, we were here at last.

"That's Not Possible"

Within twenty minutes of the time the three young men departed the shelter, I regretted their leaving. It wasn't that I especially desired any additional company in the lean-to that night, because I really enjoy the solitude more than anything. But I'm also concerned about the safety of everyone around me, and this was the cause of my worries.

"If you don't like the weather around here, just wait five minutes and it will change" is a common saying in the Adirondacks, and it is never truer than in the higher elevations of the back-country. Even the West Canada Lakes area, where most bodies of water sit between 2,300 and 2,500 feet in elevation, is subject to radical changes in weather within astoundingly short periods of time. This was the case today, and I watched the transition in amazement. It was as though the very act of the boys launching their boat relayed a signal for the start of the storm, which must have been just over the horizon and waiting to pounce.

As we sat there, still catching our breaths from the hike, the skies started to darken around us. The boat with the two campers couldn't have been more than a few hundred yards down the lake, and I wondered whether they might consider turning back in advance of the adverse weather. However, they had already told their friend that they'd meet him at the Third Lake lean-to, so they may have felt locked in by their agreement.

Years of experience at this spot served to warn me about the upcoming front, and I quickly decided to use the next twenty minutes to our advantage. While Casey commenced the task of filtering a quantity of water for dinner, I sprinted down the trail in search of dry firewood. My guess was that I had about fifteen minutes of time in advance of the coming downpour, so I had to work quickly. Fortunately, I've always had a knack for finding quality wood in a relatively short period of time and today was no exception. I located a few beech and maple trees with a significant number of downed limbs and was able to pull a large pile back to the lean-to within a few minutes. I immediately made a second trip, retrieving an even larger load for the pile.

Back at the lean-to, we began to break up the wood while listening to the storm move in. Rumbles of thunder could be heard in the distance, and the sound marched closer with the passing minutes. I tried to remember whether the fellows who had just left were in a metal boat, or whether it was made of fiberglass. Regardless, I still found myself anxious at their exposed position. I knew there was no way I could have predicted the storm, but I was still a bit upset that I couldn't help them when they asked me for a forecast. Then again, the Adirondacks tend to make their own weather, which can be extremely localized, so even a regional forecast may have been insufficient for the purpose.

The only saving grace was that the storm was fast as well as furious, and the lightning and sheets of wind-driven rain lasted only about ten minutes. Once the front passed, the clouds dissipated and the skies cleared, leaving a rather pleasant evening in their wake. Neither the two boaters nor their hiking friend could have possibly made it to the lean-to before the arrival of the mini-monsoon. However, they probably escaped with only a case of very wet clothes, which they would hopefully be able to dry once they set up camp at the next shelter.

As Casey and I worked to reduce the limbs and branches into campfire-sized lengths, some of my old habits started to reappear. Casey was amused at the fact that I ALWAYS break my firewood into lengths that are about sixteen inches long. When I noticed him producing pieces that were significantly longer, I recommended that he "do like I do," because I've always found that anything longer creates waste on the ends of the pieces. I can't help it; it's just a habit that I've developed over the years, and there really isn't much that I can do to change.

As a matter of fact, the longer we worked at this chore, the more entertained Casey became, and I became convinced that he believed I have serious obsessive-compulsive tendencies. Because, you see, firewood is a serious matter to me (said tongue-in-cheek), and I pride myself on my wood-production prowess. Unfortunately, it gets even worse than that, as I'm also picky about the way that I stack my campfire wood. I seek out two longer pieces of broken-off branches, each about thirty inches in length, and then pound these into the ground about three feet apart off the right side of the fireplace. I stack all the evening's wood between those branches, which I like to fill about three feet high with pieces of wood of various thicknesses. I assemble a smaller pile of kindling materials next to the larger stack, although I move this into the lean-to if it appears ready to rain. This supply will always suffice to keep a nice blaze going from dinner time until late in the evening, until the last inhabitant of the lean-to turns in for the night.

I found myself chuckling at Casey, who quickly decided to leave the entire firewood chore to me for the duration of our journey. He claimed that I had something zen-like going on that linked me with the wood pile, and that he didn't want to interfere with the wilderness karma associated with the process. Instead, he took charge of collecting all our water, which was just as well since I had made a complete mess out of this chore with the filtration device on my last trip. I think it had been a case of trying to teach an old dog (me) new tricks. Some things just work better when you're still in your twenties.

We were in the process of getting our dinners going when Brendan Jordan arrived with his full pack, hoping to join us in the lean-to. This was a very pleasant surprise. It would be wonderful to spend time with the person who was the walking, talking, modern-day version of my own self from the 1970s, and I truly welcomed his presence in the shelter.

As we filled our respective pots with water, Brendan got unpacked and set up his gear for the night. I was interested to learn of the new responsibilities that he'd assumed in addition to what were my own duties on the job, as well as his need to educate himself on the area before coming into the woods.

"We didn't have a ranger training week like you did," he said, reminiscing about his first year on the job. "Believe it or not, I bought a copy of your first book just to see what kinds of things I could expect back here. It was pretty helpful, and it set my expectations for the job."

I got a good laugh out of that comment because I'd certainly never expected any of my recollections to serve as a training manual for someone coming to work in these woods. Yet, just by talking with Brendan for a few minutes, I could tell that he was much better prepared for the job than I had been when I started my years here. He was an intelligent, energetic man who seemed to be very at home in his environment, and he'd quickly earned a reputation as someone who took his job quite seriously.

As we talked, Brendan discussed some of the other aspects of his duties as a ranger that I never performed back when I was on the job. His boss, Tom Eakin, had asked him to completely circumnavigate several of the lakes in the area, which took him into some very rough and remote terrain. The activity was part of a land survey to determine just what did exist in those places that could not be accessed by a public trail, and it yielded some interesting results.

"You'd never believe what you run into in some of those

places," said Brendan, recalling his travels in the area. "There are some nice little camps and boats that you'd never know existed, most of which are hidden pretty well in the brush so they won't be seen. I also came across a lot of sites that looked like they'd been used in the past, but had been destroyed or fallen apart over time. I tell you, it really makes you realize how much these woods have been used by people who have avoided the typical camping sites."

"Yes, I remember finding a couple of spots like that by accident," I replied, thinking back on my own days in the region. "But I certainly never made it as far off the beaten path as you have. It's great that Tom's given you the task of getting around to all those places because I bet no one else has been there in years."

Brendan agreed, and then went on to describe some of the other items he'd found abandoned in the woods, including countless dumps where backcountry users had disposed of their trash without bothering to pack it out of the woods. The sentiment, unfortunately, used to be that nature would quickly bury any refuse beneath rapidly accumulating layers of dirt and leaves, negating the need to maintain the virgin state of the woods.

Within a few short minutes, Casey and I both found the water boiling in out stove-fueled pots, and we began to retrieve our respective dinner ingredients. Casey lifted out the massive bear container from his pack and began to unscrew the lid. He had told me about this device, which I'd suggested was completely unnecessary in the West Canada Lakes area. However, he was used to employing this container as a handy food receptacle, so he decided to bring it along anyway.

The now-common, bear-proof food container is another piece of equipment that was yet unknown in the 1970s and 1980s, so I'd never seen one in use in this neck of the woods. The West Canada Lakes Wilderness Area receives so little use that the bears are still wary of humans and remain fairly reclusive. Personally, I'd lived here for three years just hanging my food bag from a nail in the top part of the lean-to, and I had no plans to deviate from that scheme. With the exception of some minor pilferage from the local population of field mice which often cohabitate the lean-tos, my food has never been touched by any of the wildlife that surrounded me on a daily basis.

As the three of us began our meal, it struck me just how much I missed spending time in the woods like this. Living in an open shelter, out amongst the trees and waters, reduces life to its most basic essentials, away from the trappings of modern-day conveniences and luxuries. In a world of laptops and cell phones and electronic gizmos, there is nothing better for the soul than to ditch it all from time to time and spend a few days fetching water and cooking over an open fire. I've always found that it is a wonderful way to rid the mind of clutter, and I wish I had more time to spend in locations such as this.

I was in the midst of pondering this existential line of thought when we suddenly heard sounds approaching from the right side of the lean-to, accompanied by a chorus of voices. We quickly realized that another hiking party was arriving, probably looking to spend a night in the lean-to. Our thoughts were confirmed as the group of two men and a woman came into view around the corner of the shelter.

"Hello there," said the man in the front of the processional. As he spoke, he glanced toward the lean-to, seemingly sizing up the amount of available space.

"Hi," I said, trying to sound as friendly as possible. "Are you folks staying here tonight? There's room in the lean-to, if you need it."

My offer was based on my past experiences in the woods; there is room for six sleepers in almost all lean-tos, and I never wanted to send people away if they needed the spot. I've always found that the best policy was to proactively create space for any newcomer and then allow them to decide for themselves whether they wanted to stay.

The three mud-splattered hikers looked back and forth at

each other before the older gentleman responded for the group. "Yes, we're done for the day, and we'd welcome the chance to share the lean-to. And I see that we have official company with us tonight," he said, nodding at Brendan's uniform.

Brendan stepped down from the interior of the shelter and introduced himself while Casey and I finished our meals. It turned out that the three visitors were thru-hikers completing the entire trail from Northville up to Lake Placid. They had quite a few questions about the trail ahead of them, including a few about recent changes in the route after Wakely Dam. As much as I hate to say it, I was just as glad to have someone else serve as the "Shell Answer Man" (from the oil company's old TV ads) for a change. I decided to remain quiet while Brendan provided the answers to all their questions.

Shortly after we finished eating, the younger male, who introduced himself as Marty, announced that he would be putting up his tent rather than sleeping in the lean-to. He departed for a small campsite just east of the bridge over the Beaver Pond outlet and returned after setting up his tent for the night.

"I figured I might as well get that done before the sun goes down," said Marty, rearranging the contents of his backpack. "I'll bring the rest of my stuff down there before I turn in for the night. But this will give you folks some additional room in here while I'll be able to spread out inside the tent."

The conversation soon turned to the general condition of the trails, which were fairly wet due to the recent rains. The three-some had come all the way up from Spruce Lake that day, which covered about twelve miles of tree-root-lined trail that had a tendency to become rather soggy. The splashes of mud that spotted their calves and hiking shorts testified to the condition of the trails.

"It's a mess back there, especially south of the outlet of Sampson Bog," said Marty, scowling at his mud-stained apparel. "Someone ought to do something to work on the condition of those stretches of trail. It's shameful."

As he spoke, I stole a sideward glance at Brendan to see if I could catch his reaction. Personally, I felt the hackles on my neck rising in annoyance with this remark. This area of the state has no trail crew and hasn't for years. The few people who tackle the chores of maintenance have their hands full just trying to keep the trees cut out of the trail, much less struggling to convert the wet spots into virtual sidewalks. The sentiments of my former woods-mentor, John Remias, reverberated in the back of my head: "The hikers don't like to get their feet wet as they're getting their wilderness experience."

Meanwhile, as the conversation progressed, Casey noticed that the lone female, a thirty-something woman named Kim, was quiet and somewhat forlorn. He questioned her to find out how she was feeling, only to hear that she was suffering from a number of aches and pains that had depressed her spirits and tested her resolve about completing the entire trail. Casey spent some time talking to her about the rest of the route and told her how he had experienced similar problems with his own trek up the Placid Trail the previous year. His compassionate talk and his encouraging demeanor served to lift her morale, and she was soon looking noticeably happier.

As the trio prepared their meals, Pete, the oldest of the three, began to discuss his prior travels through the West Canada Lakes region. He had hiked the entire trail many, many years earlier. He turned to Brendan to describe some of his activities from those earlier days.

"You know, when I was here back in 1979, I stayed in this same lean-to, and I met one of your predecessors," Pete said. "He was another trail ranger, although I can't remember his name."

When I heard this, I instantly perked up, for I had been one of the two rangers during that 1979 season.

"Yes, I still remember this fellow well," Pete continued. "He said he had been born and raised down in New Jersey and had come up to New York to go to college. I believe he said he was studying insects, or entomology, in graduate school at the State College of Forestry at Syracuse."

WHAT? When I heard that, I almost choked on the gulp of water that was halfway down my throat.

"Pete, that was me!" I exclaimed.

"Oh, you worked as a ranger back here too?" he asked, still not catching on.

"No, you don't understand what I'm saying," I said, my voice raised in excitement. "That park ranger you met in 1979 who was the graduate student... that was me!"

Pete's eyes flew open wide in disbelief as he grasped the meaning of my explanation. "You're kidding, right?"

"No, I'm serious," I said, laughing at the coincidence. "That was really me."

"That's impossible!" he said, shaking his head in amazement. "What the heck are the chances of that happening?" We all sat around, sharing a laugh over the bizarre reunion that was thirty years in the making. It just goes to show you that if you hang around long enough, you're bound to see just about everything.

The sun was descending over the hills at the west end of the lake as I made preparations to light the evening fire. I arranged the kindling underneath some small dry twigs and applied a match, hoping that my fire-starting skills had remained undiminished. I was happy to see that I was still able to get a blaze going within a short period of time, even though much of the tinder was still damp from the afternoon storm.

Within a few minutes, everyone else had positioned themselves in front of the fireplace, falling into the hypnotic trance that tends to captivate the majority of lean-to dwellers. Even Marty, who had returned after stowing the rest of his things in his tent, seemed content to perch on the front log of the shelter and lose himself in the dancing light of the flickering flames. It was a calm and peaceful night, and it held the promise of an absolutely gorgeous evening.

As I meditated over the growing bed of orange-red coals, Marty slid a bit further back into the lean-to and lifted a pair of moccasins out of a small stuff sack. How nice, I thought, to be able to slip into a comfortable pair of soft footwear to better enjoy the nighttime fire. And while I wouldn't trade the added weight in my pack for the comfort of those soft, leather slippers, I must admit that I did envy him (and later recalculated the cost-benefit ratio of carrying that extra weight).

By now, Marty had given up on his grumbling about the wet trail conditions. However, as he removed his hiking boots, I real-ized that the soggy conditions had had more than one negative effect on him. The stench from his socks instantly filled the air and permeated the entire airspace surrounding the lean-to. They must have been wet for some time to reach that level of pun-gency, and I can only imagine that the material of which they were composed had begun to rot inside his boots. The odor inten-sified even more as he peeled off his socks, exposing his feet to the evening breeze. There isn't much in the way of scents that can compete with the honest smell of a campfire, crackling and sending off smoky tendrils in all directions, but in this case there was no contest. With each passing second, I felt that it couldn't possibly get any worse, and yet, somehow, it did.

I looked around me politely, feigning ignorance of the situa-tion. The others continued to talk about their experiences along the trail, while Brendan simply sat quietly alongside the fire-place. And yet, all the while, I thought I detected a number of sideways glances at Marty's feet, which were definitely the epi-center of the effluence, but no one said a thing about it. Thankfully, after just a short time, I was happy to see him slide his feet into his moccasins and start his journey down to his tent. His departure was accompanied by an almost instantaneous improvement in the air quality, and I once again inhaled the per-fume of the coniferous forest around us.

There isn't much that I remember about our first night in the woods, other than to say that I slept right though until morning without getting up once. At one point, I did direct my flashlight up at my food sack, startling a mouse that was dangling from the top tie strings in the back. I looked at him for a moment as he stared back at me. Then, after deciding that he probably wouldn't consume too much, I shut off the light and went back to sleep.

The following morning, everyone arose fairly early to get a head start on the next leg of their trips. Brendan and I said our farewells and promised to keep in touch via email. Likewise, Peter gave me his email address, as I had promised to send him a photograph of the Cedar Lakes interior caretaker's station from years ago. It was a reminder of the many partings I'd experienced in my younger days, as I'd said goodbye to countless hikers with whom I'd shared a campfire. To me, this was always one of the more rewarding parts of the job, and I'm sure that Brendan felt the same.

Within an hour, Casey and I had eaten breakfast and hit the trail, heading west for an early arrival at South Lake. As we started the initial climb up the first slope of trail, I inhaled the wonderful scents of the morning air. In one breath, I detected the fragrance of spruce and cedar, mixed in with the underlying aroma of the sodden earth beneath my feet. It was enough to overcome even the strongest man-made odors, even those originating from old, wet socks.

—3—

Beauty Never Changes

As we approached the west end of Third Lake, I told Casey about the running battle I'd experienced with the Third Lake lean-to due to the continuous efforts to keep campers from trying to erase all signs of the trail. This problem has apparently remained constant over the years, as some of the more frequent visitors have adopted this shelter as their own personal abode. They will go to great lengths to cover over the trail, including dragging tree limbs across the path to hide it from the Northville-Placid hikers. As if to confirm my comments, we encountered a couple who were eastbound, looking for that very lean-to. I explained to them that they had already passed it and recommended that they continue on to the Beaver Pond lean-to, which was now empty.

After about forty-five minutes of hiking, we finally ran into the spur trail that headed back towards the hidden shelter. It looked exactly as I had remembered it: no lean-to sign, no trail markers, and no clearly defined path. Whoever had been down this path last had done a wonderful job of covering their tracks, and I marveled at the near invisibility of the route. It looked exactly like the dozen or so other courses to the water that a fisherman might use to check out the local trout population.

Nothing about it suggested that a splendid shelter resided less than a quarter of a mile away.

I led Casey down the muddy path (no, change that... the very muddy path) to the edge of the water, where the trail should have proceeded on dry ground to the site of the shelter. Thirty years ago this route was frequently wet and often required hikers to submit to shoelace-deep standing water. However, this was an entirely different matter. The trail now disappeared entirely, as though it was routed through a part of the lake itself, into water that was much too deep to cross. I found this to be surprising, as the destruction of the dam had lowered the water level of the lake and should have placed this trail on more solid ground. Instead, it was even deeper than I'd remembered. I chalked this phenomenon up to beaver activity and recommended to Casey that we forego a tour of the Third Lake lean-to.

As an aside, the Genesee Valley Chapter of the Adirondack Mountain Club is considering a reroute of the trail that covers the ground from the Northville-Placid Trail to the Third Lake lean-to. They have adopted the entire West Canadas as their permanent work project and have already invested countless hours improving the trails and shelters of the region. I had made some specific recommendations to that group regarding a reroute of the trail, which would probably only require about two hundred yards of new access route plus some very sturdy (and very high!) trail signs. Time alone will see how this pans out.

We continued along the trail, heading west past King's Pond and Cat Lake. I wondered how my own private little site in the back of King's Pond had fared over the years and whether anyone had ever discovered it or used it again. However, I didn't suggest detouring off the trail as we slipped by the tiny body of water, heading west with the morning sun.

In another couple miles, we crossed over a smaller version of the Mud Creek Bridge, near where I'd met John Remias for the first time in 1979. This model was much more modest than the one I'd remembered, consisting of little more than a couple of squared-off logs accompanied by a handrail. It was the wave of the future in these parts; there was little or no money to replace anything but the most critical of structures.

Once on the other side of Mud Creek, my mind drifted back to that day in 1979 when I'd first set eyes on the man who would become like a father to me. John was up on a ladder, fixing the tenuous phone line that extended from town into the West Lake caretaker's cabin. His initial smile and greeting has never really left me, and I will forever treasure the friendship that we shared. All these memories streaked past me in a fleeting moment as we strode past that spot by the side of the trail that served as a milepost in my life.

All things considered, we were tooling along pretty nicely for a couple of gentlemen who could both qualify as AARP members. I'm sure that I wasn't moving at quite the same pace as I'd managed in my twenties, and neither was Casey. But then again, back then my right leg wasn't composed entirely of titanium right up into my hip socket. No, this tempo would have to suffice, and the two of us felt comfortable enough to maintain a running conversation as we trekked over the well-trodden soil.

One difference that I did notice in the condition of the route was that the underbrush had more or less taken over certain stretches of trail, and the ferns and witch hobble extended their leafy limbs until they met in the middle of the path. As long as the vegetation was dry, this wasn't a problem. However, it could be a bit uncomfortable in wet conditions. (Please forgive me, John, for mentioning this!)

As we approached the final stretch of trail to the eastern shore of West Lake, we came across the detour that circumnavigated the beaver-flooded outlet from West into Mud Lake. John and I had fought these beavers valiantly several decades earlier, but they had since taken over and flooded the entire area to a depth of several feet. As a result, the two hundred yards that

were once a relatively easy, straight-line stroll had been transformed into a half mile of rocky, pitted, tree-root-lined obstacles
that tested our patience and stamina. About a third of the way
around this potholed bypass, we came across a single hiker who
was a genuine throwback to the 1960s. He was tall and lean, with
a ponytail that extended almost two feet down the back of his
shirt. It was tied back with a bandana in the pattern of an
American flag, and his clothing carried a number of "peacenik"
slogans from the Vietnam era.

"Hey, dude, you're about to enter the Sanctum," he said,
nodding back in the direction of West Lake.

"The Sanctum?" I repeated, looking at him questioningly.

"Yeah, dude, I'm talking about French Louie's place. You're
almost there," he said, his enthusiastic voice attenuated in rev-
erential tones. "Have you ever been there before?"

"Uh, well, as a matter of fact, I have," I confided, enjoying
his passion for the place. "But it's been a long time."

We spoke for a minute or two before pushing on, and I
thought about the encounter for some time after we parted
ways. I guess it was this fellow's uniqueness that got me thinking
about the typical people I encounter on the remote trails, most
of them very much alike in their physical and demographic pro-
files. Over the years, I'd run into very few people I'd classify as
"hippies." Then again, I'd say that over 90 percent of the folks
on the trail in the West Canadas were in the age group between
twenty and forty-five and were Caucasian, middle-class
Americans. I don't know whether there is any significance to this
classification, but I found it to be of interest as we completed
the remainder of the trail leading into the site of the old caretaker's cabin.

As we emerged from the woods into the patch of land that
had once been John Remias' back yard, my daydreaming was
instantly shut down as a massive tidal wave of emotion washed
over me. Ahead of us lay the overgrown remnants of the house

by the shore of the lake, the birthplace of some of my fondest memories. The entire plot of ground that John had maintained around the cabin, perhaps an acre or two, was now little more than thick patches of very tall brambles. It hadn't yet reverted to a young forest, as no trees had sprouted up between the remains of the station and sign-in booth. But the tangle of raspberry bushes and other vegetation was at least six feet tall and almost impassible to hikers.

We followed a path that had been created by others, leading to the charred remains of the house. The entire foundation was still there, visible through the undergrowth. Also visible was French Louie's fireplace, although I was saddened to see that the top mantle rock had cracked and fallen from its perch. That slab had been in place for almost a century and had supposedly been brought across the lake by Louie for that very purpose. To see it broken and discarded on the ground like that saddened me greatly. I don't believe anyone intentionally vandalized the fireplace. But not everyone knew the story behind it, either, which led to wear and tear as campers may have tried to use it for cooking without knowing the significance of its origin.

Something else that was missing was the cross, which some thoughtful individual had erected on the site of the cabin a number of years earlier. It was neatly constructed, with the message "You did not conform" written on its front, a reference to the policy of not permitting any four-walled structures within territory designated as wilderness by New York State. (John liked to comment that we should tear down all the outhouses, since they have four walls as well!)

We looked around the site for about twenty minutes, as I reminisced about all the good times I'd spent there over the years. I followed the outline of the foundation around the original wall of the building, imagining where the potbelly stove had once rested. In the middle of the room, I pictured the small table where I'd joined John and Barb for the occasional meal. In the front, by the location of the window, was the spot where John would sit as we talked over the events of the week. My entire collection of memories was now represented by the concrete slab and a jumble of broken bricks. For reasons that I did not immediately understand, I picked up a couple shards of the shattered material and shoved them into my pack. They were part of the original building... and a part of my past.

After completing our tour around the ruins, we decided to head south once again, bound for our next destination. We would be spending the night at South Lake, which had always been one of my favorite stopovers. This lake was the only body of water in the entire area that had somehow been blessed with a white sand beach. Most people who spotted this phenomenon couldn't resist kicking off their shoes and wading into the warm water to enjoy a summer afternoon. However, since South Lake was never listed on my schedule as a stopover point, I very seldom spent the night camped inside that lean-to.

As we headed southward, I wondered about the condition of the lake and whether the beavers were still active down there. I had visited the same spot two years earlier, with my daughter Kelly, and we had discovered that the beavers had dammed up the outlet from South Lake into Mud Lake. This raised the level of South a couple of feet, which wiped out a majority of the sandy beach. As much as I enjoyed seeing the beavers, I hoped they'd decided to abandon this one location, thus allowing the lake level to slowly drop to its previous state. However, as we began our gradual descent from the hill that separated South Lake from West, I realized that the exact opposite had transpired, and the lake was even higher than before.

To say that the approach to the lean-to was easy would have been a gross misrepresentation of the truth. Both sides of the bridge spanning the outlet were under several inches of water, and there were places where hikers had used the planking from older versions of the overpass to construct makeshift conduits through the flooding. Even the trail well south of the bridge, the one that cuts through some fine patches of blueberry bushes, was underwater in places, and we slogged through the mess producing a series of wonderful squishing sounds.

The final yards to the lean-to were among the only dry ones we'd encountered in some time, and we happily ditched our packs inside the empty shelter. The place had changed very little since my days in the woods, right down to the graffiti, although new verses had been added with each passing season. I still wonder at the durability of this stuff; words scrawled in charcoal on the underside of roofing planks are as legible today as they were in 1960. Unfortunately, this applies to the infrequent cases of inappropriate comments as well as the rest. In an attempt to stem the propagation of new graffiti, the Adirondack Mountain Club has placed ledger books inside many of the lean-tos. These notebooks serve as a substitute outlet for the creative urges of most would-be graffiti artists, while also providing the club with some insights into the thoughts of the hikers who use these shelters.

In front of the lean-to, the evidence of the beaver activity was obvious. Whereas, years ago, there was a good stretch of beach (perhaps fifteen feet wide) leading down to the water, today the wavelets lap right up against the vegetation behind the fireplace. The waterline has moved at least fifteen feet closer to the lean-to, and all traces of the sandy shoreline have been lost.

Since we'd arrived relatively early in the day, we had some spare time on our hands, which I decided to put to good use. I quickly unpacked my foam pad and sleeping bag, and then performed a "lean-to floorboard quality examination." (This event is otherwise known as a nap.) That's one thing I never remembered doing when I was in my twenties, but have since added to my repertoire of favorite activities. Somehow, the body just seems to require a little more rest after a mere six or seven miles of trail with a heavy pack, and I found myself gladdened that I was no longer forced into covering my standard ten to twelve miles on a daily basis. I'm sure that I could still perform at that level for several weeks at a time, although I'm hardly used to it any longer.

Later in the afternoon, I took a leisurely stroll to the middle of the outlet bridge, where I gazed in amazement at the massive beaver dam. It is on the Mud Lake side of the bridge, and it is truly incredible in its size and construction. The length spans a distance of about a hundred feet, and it is curved gracefully into the current to provide the maximum degree of structural integrity. The top of the dam, perhaps a foot above the water level, is composed of tens of thousands of branches and sticks. Each piece of wood has been individually cut and peeled, and then transported to a specific location in the dam where it was woven into place. Beavers are truly some of the best builders in the world, and I am always astounded by their work.

Following my short tour, I returned to the lean-to, where I quickly recorded my own thoughts into the ledger book. I always enjoyed reading the comments of others, and I wondered why we didn't think of this idea when I was on the job in the 1970s. While signing books up in Lake Placid one summer, I had the good fortune to meet Stuart Mesinger, author of *No Place I'd Rather Be: Wit and Wisdom from Adirondack Lean-to Journals*. Stuart had collected the best journal entries from a number of locations and sewn them together in an amusing, well-written book. That's what made these notebooks so much fun. They were a form of multi-user diary that could be used to record just about anything.

As the afternoon progressed, Casey and I fell back into our already-familiar assignment of chores. I departed to start collecting firewood, while he headed over to the shoreline with his water pump. Finding wood at South Lake has always been interesting because most of the trees near the lean-to are either coniferous or yellow birch. (Yellow birch makes for very poor firewood, as it is usually too rotten to burn by the time it falls from the tree.) This has never a problem for me. I just cruise up the trail a couple hundred yards, where the wood is plentiful and of excellent quality.

Personally, I've always been amazed at the laziness of most campers when it comes to collecting firewood. Anything that sits within a few feet of the lean-to is in serious jeopardy, as most folks don't want to walk any distance to carry the stuff back. I've actually seen spots where people have expended huge amounts of time and energy trying to hack apart old tree stumps just to avoid the effort of walking down the trail. My guess is that it would have taken them less time to collect a sufficient quantity of wood, including the walk, if they'd simply moved a little farther away from the fireplace.

While breaking up the firewood, I had a chance to test another one of my out-of-practice skills, as I saw a loon floating some distance down the lake. Using my loudest loon call, I hollered across the water in the repetitious notes that I've heard on countless occasions along the lakes of the territory. Casey watched me, obviously amused, as I scowled at my own version of this aquatic bird's song.

"What the heck was that?" he asked, laughing at my cacophonous attempts. "That sounded like a critically ill duck on steroids!"

"I know," I said disconsolately. "I used to do it a lot better in my younger days. I guess that I'm not..."

My line was cut short by the sudden call of the loon, hollering back across the lake, answering my poor efforts to communicate. My God, it was working! I turned back toward the water and gave it a few more tries, alternating between a few of the different common calls. Much to my amazement, the loon answered each and every one of them.

"Well, what do you think of that?" I said, smiling smugly at my hiking partner. "I've fooled the loon; he thinks I'm a companion bird down here, and he's engaging me in conversation."

"No he isn't," said Casey, chuckling even harder. "He's probably tired of you making a fool out of yourself, and he's asking you to shut up so he can get some peace and quiet. You're probably scaring the fish away from him!"

Once the loon quieted down and began ignoring me, we settled into the routine of fixing our evening meals. As on the previous night, we decided to save the firewood for later in the evening, instead opting to cook over our gas stoves. This is something I never did as a ranger; I always cooked over a fire even if it was a tiny blaze kindled from a pile of twigs from around the campsite. It was my norm to return at the end of the week with a completely filled fuel tank. The blackened state of my two-quart cook pot is testimony to choice of fuels, and I proudly carried that vessel for years without cleaning the outside surface.

As the water boiled, I took a moment to play around with Casey's bear-proof canister, attempting to open it in the prescribed manner. I quickly came to the realization that the hardened container was effective in preventing other species from gaining access as well. No matter how I gripped the wide, outer edge of the cover, I simply could not remove the top lid from the jar. It was impossible, and Casey's instructions weren't helping.

"No, no... you've got to press here and here," he said, pointing out a couple of tabbed inserts in the cover. "Then, twist it counter-clockwise, but keep pressing down with your thumb and ring finger. Now, place your left foot on the bottom of the canister, and hold the middle of the top in place with your chin..." OK, so I've embellished this last part just a little. But still, I was glad that I hadn't purchased one of these contraptions, or I have no doubt that I'd have been forced to smash it open with a large rock, or something of the sort. (Or perhaps I could have given it to a bear, which probably could have clawed the top off in a matter of seconds!)

We spent the rest of the evening talking about the wilderness surrounding us, and Casey shared a number of memories from his trip up the Placid Trail the previous year. I had promised him that he'd probably see a very nice sunset from our vantage point on the east end of the lake, as I'd viewed some spectacular scenes in this spot when I worked back here. However, it was not to be. The sun, although not obstructed by clouds, settled down below South Lake Mountain without its usual exhibit of reds and oranges, instead displaying a much more modest palette of subdued colors. I suppose that many of the more brilliant sunsets I'd witnessed were due to the eruption of Mount St. Helens in May of 1980. That blast, which occurred in Washington State, launched a cloud of fine ash that circled the earth for over two weeks. During that time, we were treated to unparalleled sunsets that matched the most grandiose Fourth of July fireworks.

We spun the campfire conversation out longer than usual that night, as we weren't in any hurry, and we had only one night left after this one to enjoy in the woods. Tossing a few sticks into the fireplace at a time, we stayed up and traded stories until almost eleven o'clock, gazing into the flames and brewing pots of tea. This is one of the best times in the woods; resting on the simple, aged logs of the lean-to as the fire crackles in front of you. The scent of the fire drifts into the shelter along with the sounds of the Adirondack night. Loons call from down the lake, moths flutter by, attracted by the light, and the critters of the night emerge from their dens and rustle through the woods around you. It is truly enchanting, and I often wonder about those early-to-bed folks who never get to see this amazing transition to darkness.

Before climbing into my sleeping bag, I stripped off my daytime clothing and donned my new, scientifically designed thermopropyl, isotonic, insulated underwear. Yes, yes, I know, there is no such thing, so please don't go running for your dictionary or thesaurus. But I do know these garments are composed of a material that is the latest and greatest hi-tech fabric, and it is capable of performing some amazing feats of science. Both the long-sleeved shirt and the pants are very, VERY thin, yet they seem to keep the body warm in even the chilliest weather. I'm sure there is a reason for this, and the scientist responsible for the patent could write pages of formulas to explain its effectiveness. But for whatever the reason, the stuff just works, and I found myself wishing that I'd had access to clothing like this thirty years ago.

As I crawled into my sleeping bag and drifted off to sleep, I was unaware of the unique treat that was in store for me later on that night. I awoke sometime in the pre-dawn hours needing to visit the outhouse, which was about a hundred feet in back of the lean-to. As I returned, fully expecting to climb back into my bag, I heard a series of sounds coming from some distance off. First, I heard a barred owl, breaking the silence of the night with its characteristic call: who-who, who-who. Within a matter of seconds, a loon chimed in from its spot in the middle of the lake, trumpeting a long, low bellow that elevated in both volume and pitch. It called for about five seconds, and then went silent. Next, it was the owl again, calling several times from the tree to the left of our lean-to. Who-who, who-who. This was followed by another round by the loon, keeping its call to a brief ten-second soliloquy.

This concert went on for some time, alternating between the owl and the loon, their cries echoing across the water and reverberating around the hills surrounding the lake. I sat there, enthralled by it all, wondering whether the two animals of different species were really communicating with one another. I really can't say from experience, and I hardly qualify as an ornithologist. But I do know what I heard, and it definitely seemed that the two birds were waiting for one another to finish before starting their own calls. Simply amazing!

While all this was taking place, Casey remained in his sleeping bag, sound asleep. I considered awakening him to invite him to the concert, although I hastily discarded this thought and instead let him sleep. Even though he is a musical composer and might have found this unique composition to be entertaining, I decided that most people would probably rather get an uninterrupted night's sleep than be roused this far in advance of sunrise.

As the sounds of the long-distance duet finally subsided, nature substituted a light show in its place, which kept me rooted to my seat in the front of the lean-to. There hadn't been much of a moon that night, so the sky had remained fairly dark. However, it was now close to morning, and the heavens began to lighten ever so much. The rate at which this transformation took place was infinitesimally slow, and yet I noticed it happening all around me. The skies faded through a series of charcoal-colored hues, then dusky gray, followed by an eerie wash of silver, which bathed the air overhead in an ethereal glow.

Watching this scene unfold before me, I felt as though I was looking at the negative of an old photograph, developed in black and white and then left somewhat underexposed. Magically, the branches of the trees overhanging the lean-to appeared in jet black, silhouetted against the silver sky. The sides and roof of the shelter served to frame the entire scene, which was changing by the minute as the visible light increased.

Very soon, the wavelets on the lake became visible through a gap in the shoreline flora, and the dense fog that blankets the water every night magically appeared as though someone had turned on a switch. The vapor was so dense that it seemed to swallow sound, the air so quiet and muffled from inside its shapeless form.

Suddenly, from out of nowhere, came the distant sound of wings, frantically beating on the water's surface. Tap-tap-tap-tap-tap-tap-tap, as the loon accelerated, trying its best to become airborne. Within a few seconds, the tapping ceased as the heavy waterfowl lifted clear of the lake, headed in our direction. Even as it winged its way through the fog, invisible to me, I could hear its wings flapping mightily against the chilled air, growing louder with each passing second. I was wondering whether it was the same loon that had answered my call the previous day, when suddenly it burst out of the fog bank and flashed through the sky overhead, streaking east into the morning sun. It was alone, flying unescorted to some other lake in the area. As soon as it passed, the silence returned, and I was once again left alone to contemplate the morning haze.

From the back of the lean-to, I heard stirrings as Casey began to awaken from his sleep. "You've been up for quite a while, haven't you?" he said in a muffled voice, his head still inside his sleeping bag.

"Yeah, I've just been sitting here watching the night turn into day. It's been quite a show, but I didn't want to disturb your sleep," I said.

"I heard you get up the first time, but it was still dark out," said Casey. "You haven't been awake since then, have you?"

I chuckled and admitted that I had never bothered climbing back into the sack. I then told him about the wonderful duet I'd heard between the owl and the loon, along with the rest of the morning's magical scenes. It was well worth the shortened night's sleep, for these are the sights and sounds that I'll remember forever, and I treasure them all.

I glanced at my watch and was surprised to see that I had been up for almost two hours, observing the Adirondacks awaken before my eyes. I'd seen it all a thousand times before, and yet I never tired of watching it again and again, full of wonder and awe. For even as the seasons march on, and the landscape may vary slightly from year to year, there is one thing that remains constant: true beauty never changes.

—4—

Thirty's a Crowd

Sunday would be our last full day in the woods, so I wanted to make the most of it. Now that the morning fog had cleared and we were both up, we decided to get packed up and hit the road as soon as possible. It was also nice to see that the weather would cooperate, as the skies were showing the promise of yet another beautiful day. Perhaps the storm on our first night would be our only break in a string of otherwise perfect days.

After writing a few last remarks in the lean-to ledger book, we packed our things and prepared to hit the trail. As always, I gathered the last few remaining handfuls of firewood and stacked it inside the lean-to, along with some dry "paper" from a white birch tree. As a bare minimum, anyone leaving a shelter should leave behind enough to start a small fire in case the next users arrive in the rain. I, however, like to leave enough that someone could actually prepare a sustaining meal, if needed.

As we broke camp and headed south, Casey explained that he was looking forward to today's hike because it would take us off the Northville-Placid Trail, which he had already hiked once before. I explained to him that a great many trails have been cut through these woods, although many of them have been gone for decades and can no longer be traced. As we made our approach on the lean-to at West Canada Creek, a scant half-mile south of South Lake, I pointed out one of these routes.

"You'd never believe it, but there used to be a road cutting through the woods right here," I said, pointing down the north side of West Canada Creek. "There were lots of trails, even before there was a Northville-Placid Trail, but the USGS topographic map of 1903 shows a road that came in from the west and passed within a quarter mile of Mica Lakes." I pointed out where Mica Lakes were situated, on the same side of West Canada Creek as the lean-to.

"Does anyone ever camp there these days?" asked Casey, looking through the woods in that direction.

"No, not at all," I replied. "That's just the way it is. Most hikers won't leave the trail to visit someplace unless there is something there worth seeing. Mica Ponds are pretty unspectacular, and I doubt anyone's been back there in many years."

Actually, I had run into one group of campers many years ago who had come into the region by following West Canada Creek all the way up from where it crossed Route 8. It was a hike that must have taken many days, and crossed through some very rugged and remote ground. But explorers such as that are few and far between, and most of the lakes that are more than a mile from a trail are probably seldom visited.

We crossed over the large, wooden bridge that spans West Canada Creek and immediately turned left onto the side trail leading toward Sampson Lake. This was one of the routes Casey had never seen, although it was part of my weekly patrol from 1979-1981. Immediately, the width of the trail decreased, as this path gets nowhere near the usage of the Northville-Placid Trail. The vegetation once again crowded the sides of the trail until it met in the middle, and we pushed through as the witch hobble rustled against our legs. It is a beautiful trail that initially skirts the wet, marshy territory south of Mud Lake and then Whitney Creek.

As we climbed upward, ascending the first few hills towards

the ridge overlooking Sampson Lake, I was astonished to see the remains of an old trail sign on the ground from the "other" Sampson Lake Trail. About a mile after leaving the Northville-Placid Trail, it marked the spot where another feeder trail had once come in from the southwest and merged with our current route. This other trail had also originated from the Northville-Placid Trail, although a couple of miles further south, toward Spruce Lake. These two feeder trails formed a triangle with the Placid Trail, with the sign marking the point where the first two merged into a common route to Sampson Lake. What amazed me was the fact that the southern feeder trail had been abandoned in the late 1970s and hadn't been maintained in thirty years. Even then, the trail sign at that junction had been removed from the tree, so no one would venture down the neglected path and get lost. So where had the sign been for these past three decades? Surely, if left on the ground to rot, it would have been reduced to its base elements by now. I pondered that thought as we continued our ascent up the incline.

The woods along the French Louie Trail are a very special place, wide open, with lots of large hardwood trees. The morning was especially bright, with a blue sky and lots of sunlight streaming through the canopy overhead. The leaves of the beech, birch, and maple trees around us appeared especially full, their various green hues flittering in the late summer breeze. I could have imagined no better day for hiking had I been able to program it into a computer.

We stopped once for a short snack as we passed by the trail to the Sampson Lake lean-to. This was something that I was not used to, as I usually like to keep going once I get started. However, Casey was still recuperating from surgery to repair a torn ligament in his knee, and he required periodic rests along the way. Given the circumstances, he had done extremely well on it the entire week, keeping up an ambitious pace regardless of the impediment. This was due, I felt, to his superb level of conditioning, which he groomed by spending countless hours in training as a student in the martial arts. (Because of this, I had threatened to make him chop the firewood by hand, but he said that it would get in the way of my zen relationship with the wood. This was rapidly becoming the inside joke-of-the-week.)

We never did stop at the Sampson Lake lean-to, which I now regret, as I would have liked to see the shelter that was built after the original was destroyed many years ago. A huge "widow-maker" tree, which had been threatening the lean-to for years, had finally fallen across its roof. However, the site of that shelter is some distance from the trail, and it is entirely downhill—very downhill. In fact, that was the reason I dismissed the idea of the detour, although I felt somewhat remiss in doing so. But I chalked it up to old age, and said that I'd check it out the next time I was in the area. (Uh huh!)

Once we made it past Sampson and Whitney lakes, the trail broadened into the old roadbed that I remembered, and we were able to walk side-by-side instead of in line. I was amazed to see that this stretch of the route was actually drier than on my previous few visits. It seemed that some of the roadside bodies of water formed by beaver activity had receded somewhat, and I wondered whether the local trappers had discovered this haven as a convenient source of revenue during the winter pelt season.

It seemed like no time at all before we came over the last rise in the dirt roadway and spotted the trail to the Pillsbury Lake lean-to. We had been watching the lake for some time as it appeared through the trees on our left, but I hadn't expected to come upon the shelter quite so quickly. I guess time has a way of distorting distances, and I scoffed at myself for losing track of the details of something so familiar.

I steered us off the road and onto the long path that led down to the lean-to. This is a relatively open area, with little in the way of underbrush. I'm fairly certain the reason behind this lack of vegetation is the preponderance of humans who have cut down every possible bit of flora with a wooden stem in search of combustible fireplace material. This lack of undergrowth, for whatever reason, affords an unobstructed view of the Pillsbury Lake lean-to at quite a distance, and I could see that there were people already in residence at the structure.

We plodded our way down the rest of the hill and rounded the corner of the lean-to, where we came face-to-face with two young male campers who appeared to be in their late teens. They were relaxing in the shade of the overhanging roof, accompanied by a pair of large backpacks that seemed to be mostly unpacked.

"Hi there," I exclaimed in greeting. "You folks staying in the lean-to?"

"No, I don't think so," one of them replied. "We're staying here at the lake overnight, but we're thinking of putting up our tent instead."

"Great," I answered. "Then you wouldn't mind if we spread out inside the lean-to? Because this is as far as we're going tonight, and I'd rather stay inside than pitch our tents."

"Help yourself," said the other youngster. "We might cook over the fireplace with you tonight, but the lean-to is all yours."

We spoke for a few minutes and learned that they lived near Johnstown and Gloversville, and were up visiting for a few days. This lean-to represented the perfect getaway spot that they could reach in a couple hours of hiking from the Pillsbury trailhead parking lot. I must admit that I would rather have had the place to ourselves, as (once again) I enjoy the solitude of the woods more than anything. However, they seemed like nice kids, and we got along well with them as we started unpacking our own belongings into the shelter.

We took a few minutes to eat lunch, during which time Casey told the others that I had once been the park ranger in the area and that I had written three books on the subject. One of them asked about the titles, and, when I informed him of the names, he excitedly stated that his father was reading one of them. It was actually quite flattering, because he seemed to want to assign me some amount of VIP status, even though none was warranted.

After lunch, Casey and I continued the conversation we'd started earlier on the trail, a recounting of the events of our lives. He was in the final stages of qualifying for his black belt in kung fu, which I found to be a wonderful achievement. The martial arts have always interested me, even though I have no desire to participate in the activity myself.

Casey then went on to demonstrate some of the principles of his discipline, including the body control, breathing, and balance involved in even the most basic motions. It was fascinating, and the casual observer such as me wouldn't begin to understand the fundamentals behind the moves. It's no wonder it takes several years to develop the level of proficiency required to test for an advanced belt, and I admired his dedication to the task.

With lunch now out of the way, I took off once again in search of firewood. I wanted to collect a healthy supply of the stuff, since this would be our last night in the woods, and I knew we'd want to spend considerable time in front of the fire. I headed all the way back to the dirt road, and then across into the woods adjacent to the lean-to path. There, amongst the maples and beech trees, I found enough downed limbs to make a few successful loads, which I deposited in front of the lean-to. Casey decided to jump in to help at this point, and the two of us spent the next half hour breaking up the wood into "Larry-sized pieces." We filled a large area next to the fireplace, and I quickly realized that I had probably collected enough to last for two nights. But no matter; someone else would gladly make use of the leftovers after we had departed.

So there we were, relaxing in the lean-to, quite warm after the wood-gathering activity, when suddenly, from the distance, I detected the sound of human voices. The other two fellows were still arranging their campsite nearby, and I knew that these new voices were much more distant. I didn't bother getting up from my resting position, as I figured that anyone passing by would stop in to say hello sooner or later.

My curiosity increased as the minutes passed and the voices grew in volume as they approached our location. I also noticed now that there was a great diversity in tones, and my estimation of the number of people behind the sounds also grew. I listened intently as I heard the voices of numerous adults and youngsters hiking en masse. Finally, with a terminal crescendo, the pack rounded the front of the lean-to. It was a Boy Scout troop out for a weekend excursion, and this was their intended campsite for the first night. As they said hello, more of the group arrived, with additional stragglers appearing at regular intervals.

One of the leaders stepped up and introduced himself. "We're planning on making camp here, as long as you don't mind," he said.

"No, not at all," I replied, returning his handshake. "It's everyone's park, although it might get a little crowded with your entire group set up here. But we're certainly fine with that." As I spoke, Casey nodded his approval.

"Well, that's nice," said the scout leader, smiling back at us. "We'll just start getting set up, then, while the rest of the group catches up to us."

"The rest of the group?" I repeated in disbelief. "How many more do you have with you?"

The leader turned around and did a quick count of the milling throng, who were now starting to spread out over the ground nearby. "Well, it looks as though we've got the first dozen kids with us here, so that means we've got about ten more still back on the trail. Some of them were having a little bit of trouble keeping up, so we split off into two groups."

"You've got twenty-two kids in the woods on a campout!" I said, amazed at the ambitious endeavor. "You must have a phe-nomenal amount of patience."

"Yeah, I know," said the gentleman, who seemed resigned to

his fate. "And some of these kids have never been in the woods before, so it's bound to be an adventure."

"Well, there are only two of us in the lean-to tonight, so you're welcome to share the space. But they really don't hold more than about six, so I hope you've got arrangements to sleep the rest of your kids someplace else."

"Oh, that's not a problem," he replied, looking back at the crowd. "We've got enough tents to sleep all of us, just in case the lean-tos were full. But, if you don't mind, I think a couple of the leaders would enjoy staying with you inside the lean-to. Also, I see you've got a nice pile of wood collected. Would it be alright if the kids came down and toasted some marshmallows on your fire tonight? We're planning on making s'mores after dinner."

I smiled at the idea, and remembered some of the intriguing foodstuffs I'd carried into the woods when I was a lad. "Of course, they can come down whenever they're ready," I said. "As long as they don't leave anything around that would attract animals tonight, I'm fine with it."

"Please don't worry about that," he replied. "We read all about bears, and we're completely ready for that. We have a number of bear containers for the food, and we also have rope to hang our food in the trees, so we shouldn't run into any difficulty there."

"Believe it or not, you don't have to hang your food in these woods; not in this area, anyway," I explained. "The bears just aren't that used to people around here, and they've never been a problem."

"You seem like you've spent a bit of time in this area," said the gentleman, who identified himself as Scott.

"Well, I used to be the park ranger in this area, although that was thirty years ago. But yes, I am still quite familiar with this region, and I can assure you that the bears won't bother you."

"OK, but I think we'll hang our food up just to be safe," said Scott. "Plus, it will teach the kids how to do it, just in case they ever hike into an area where the bears do go after the food." As he spoke, Casey unpacked his own pack, and Scott noticed that Casey was also carrying a bear container. I hope he didn't think that I was putting him on, because he looked at the gear suspiciously, as though I was trying to play some sort of a practical joke on them. But he never said anything to that effect, so I let it go at that.

True to Scott's word, the second half of the troop arrived within about thirty minutes of the first, joining their counterparts at the bottom of the hill. These boys tended to be a bit younger and perhaps not used to the rigors of carrying a pack with an overnight load. Accordingly, they were somewhat quieter as they caught their breath and rubbed their sore backs and legs. However, within a relatively short period of time, they had regained their energy and were soon scooting around the lean-to, making mad dashes down to the lake for water before zooming back to their friends.

It was quite a sight. The regulation for the maximum camping party had always been ten people; once that number was reached, it required a camping permit signed by the forest ranger with jurisdiction over that territory. I had no idea whether this troop had bothered with this formality, or whether they even knew of the requirements, but they were here, and I certainly wasn't about to ask. Besides, what would I have done—used my cell phone to report them for failing to obtain a camping permit? We decided to make the best of it and enjoy our last night in the woods. The two teenagers from Gloversville apparently decided the same thing, and we all braced for a long night with predictable interruptions in the solitude. After years of camping by myself in solitude in these woods, I had definitely decided that thirty's a crowd.

As we progressed through the hours of the late afternoon, the area around the Pillsbury Lake lean-to underwent an amazing transition. What been a relatively quiet and secluded site a short time earlier grew into a virtual tent city of colossal proportions. The conversion progressed relentlessly as bustling streets and neighborhoods of tents popped up from the ground, sometimes overlapping one another. They were not of uniform shape or color, which was probably a good thing, or the residents might have experienced difficulties in distinguishing their own tent from that of a fellow camper. The megalopolis extended up the hill from the lean-to, presenting the appearance of a rather hastily constructed refugee camp from a third-world country. For all I know, there may have been suburbs of this urban scene extending over the horizon and down the trail toward the West Canadas. It was very disconcerting, and I decided to try to ignore the scene as much as possible.

I can't say that I remember the other scout leader's name, although both of them asked to share the lean-to that night. We readily agreed, and they moved their packs into the shelter as we prepared our evening meals. One of them eyed our large wood pile, which we were saving for the nightly fire, and asked once again whether it was OK for the scout troop to use while heating their s'mores. "We'll tell them that wood pile is yours; they'll leave it alone as long as they know."

"That's fine," I said, smiling at his seemingly apologetic request. "I remember being that age and being out in the woods for the first time. They're all welcome to join us."

"Thanks," he said, relieved at our acceptance. "We may even have some extras, if you want to toast a marshmallow or two for yourself."

The next surprise of the evening came after the boys had finished cooking and cleaning up their dinnerware. Even though I had advised them that there was no bear problem, they all decided to hang their food for the night. All of them. Individually. It was a sight to behold. It started with a solitary stuff sack, lifted by a single cord over a thin maple tree. After attaining a height of about twenty feet, the boy made certain that the sack was at least eight or ten feet from the tree trunk before tying it off with a square knot. It was simple and efficient, although definitely not necessary.

The next youngster to attempt this feat must have decided that the first fellow's was too close to a bear-accessible branch, because his rope spanned the gap between two trees, with another cord tied to the middle that held his food supply. Once again, it was a workable arrangement that would probably have defeated a hungry bear, had one been present to care enough about the challenge.

From that point on, things got out of hand, with each successive food bag hoister attempting to outdo his predecessor. I don't know whether any of these kids had bear proof canisters inside their food bags, nor would it have mattered. The arrangement of ropes and knots was becoming more complex by the minute, with some of the final versions resembling the hemp-equivalent of intricate origami. I was beginning to wonder whether a new species of six-foot-long spiders had populated the woods, spinning their webs amongst the trees of Pillsbury Lake. It was a sight, and the local bird population chirped their approval as they eyed the many new places to perch. Had a bear actually wandered through our site that night, I imagine it would have been laughing too hard to attempt a theft after eyeing the elaborate precautions taken by the scouts.

As the sun went down, several of the kids from the troop went down to the water to watch the sunset over the west end of the lake. Pillsbury always had wonderful sunsets, and tonight would be no exception. The entire tree line to the west turned a fiery orange, and the loons called their songs over the expanse of calm water. However, the serenity of the scene lasted only a few minutes, until the youthful energy of the scouts took over and anarchy returned in full force. Several of the older boys discovered that the younger, lighter members of the troop made wonderful splashing noises as they were thrown into the lake, and that became the activity of the hour. I must admit that even I was amazed at the altitude attained by some of these young-sters as they were flung skyward by their older counterparts. I was happy to see that no one was intent on doing any fishing that night, as every trout in Pillsbury Lake was probably a half mile away by now.

As the shadows lengthened and darkness took over, I lit the kindling underneath the small piles of sticks in the fireplace and gently nursed the small flame into a healthy blaze. It took a rel-atively short amount of time to build up a glowing bed of coals, which instantly attracted several of the scouts. I knew that they were interested in getting their s'mores cooking, even though most of the troop was still setting up bedding or getting thrown into the lake.

Within about thirty minutes, nighttime preparations were done and the swimmers had been retrieved from the lake and sufficiently wrung out to dry. A long procession of them began appearing from alternating sides of the lean-to, each boy bearing a long pointed stick on which he would toast his marshmallows. Still others decided to toast the whole concoction, using forked branches that could hold a graham cracker on a relatively hori-zontal plane and in turn, support the chocolate and marshmallow on top. These were the most interesting to observe, and I mar-veled at some of these fellows' hand control as they maintained a rock-solid position until the entire s'more was perfectly toasted.

Within a few minutes, the airspace over the fireplace was filled with marshmallow-laden sticks and twigs, as the boys com-peted for the best place over the coals. Some of the older kids had it down to a science, turning the stick until the fluffy white candy turned a perfect shade of brown. Others, however, allowed their marshmallows to catch on fire, which rapidly converted the outside surface to a black, shiny substance that is probably a mystery to scientists. One of the youngest scouts seemed to enjoy this metamorphosis, and he watched in fascination as the melting sugar dripped from his stick and hissed its way between the logs of the fire. But hey, no one said that they actually had to eat the stuff, and I'm sure that his lack of proper cooking skill was more than offset by an improved level of dental hygiene.

Given the hoard of scouts preparing their evening treats, the process seemed to go rather smoothly, and it wasn't long before the group began dispersing for the comfort of their tents. They all thanked us for the use of the fire, and I must admit that I was highly impressed by their manners while sharing the communal fire pit.

Within a half hour, the only people left in the lean-to were me, Casey, and the two scout leaders. Even the teenagers from Gloversville had decided to turn in early, leaving us to tend the fire by ourselves. Since it was our last night in the woods, we had decided that we'd stay up and talk for a while, expending most of the wood in the pile next to the fireplace. The four of us traded stories of our times in the woods and watched the onset of the Adirondack night. I was happy to see that the two troop leaders were in no hurry to turn in early, as would have been their right, since I wouldn't have wanted to keep them awake with our conversation.

By the time we threw a last pile of wood onto the coals, the final vestiges of dusk had been erased from the sky, replaced with a twinkling blanket of bright stars. I had warned Casey in advance about the chilly temperatures we would experience at Pillsbury Lake, which I'd always felt was colder that any of the other lakes in the area. I suspected that this was due to the elevation, as it is a bit higher than most of the nearby bodies of water. It also might have been the lake's close proximity to Pillsbury Mountain, as the cold air may have rolled directly down the slopes from the nearby peak. Whatever the reason, I was glad that I had my full set of thermopropyl, isotonic, insulated underwear (there's that word again!) and my matching hat and gloves to keep me warm. These new scientifically-designed garments do make quite a difference, and I noticed their warmth as I hunkered down into the depths of my sleeping bag.

In contrast to some of my previous visits to the Pillsbury Lake lean-to, I was very comfortable throughout the entire night, and I slept uninterrupted until morning. We arose quite early in order to get a good start on the final leg out of the woods. Unlike in my earlier days, there were now chores to be done at home, business to attend to at work, and a slew of other responsibilities calling from afar. Casey shared the same concerns with his own work schedule, so we didn't dally once we arose from our slumber.

Casey did have one idea which I hadn't considered. He proposed having a light snack as we packed, followed by a full breakfast once we hit town. The King of the Frosties restaurant was an old favorite of mine, and I had eaten breakfast there often before entering the woods as a ranger. The place had changed very little in that time, and it is still extremely popular with both tourists and local residents.

Casey noticed my initial hesitation and immediately set about the task of convincing me to join him for the post-hike meal. "Can't you see it? A neat stack of pancakes with pure maple syrup, accompanied by some nicely browned sausage links, with a heap of hash browns on the side, just for good measure," he said, painting a mental image of the feast. "Add a steaming mug of coffee, and we'll be good to go for the trip home."

I was trying to avoid consuming more calories than necessary, as I'm always fighting the battle of the bulge, but it didn't take long for him to overcome my resistance. "That sounds pretty good," I agreed, trying to sound coolly amenable to the suggestion. The truth be known, though, I was positively drooling at the thought of the hot breakfast food, served fresh off the griddle, in the nice cozy restaurant down in Speculator. By the time Casey had finished his description of the meal, I could almost smell the griddle cakes browning on the stovetop.

"Oh, no, that's OK, you don't have to join me," chided Casey.

"You can eat those wonderful looking cold breakfast bars instead. Yummy, they sure do look, uh... nutritious."

"OK, OK," I cried, ceding to his idea. "I'll have breakfast with you at the restaurant. Just stop with the descriptions of the pancakes and sausage, alright? You're making my stomach growl like crazy."

We bid farewell to our shelter mates and saddled up our packs before most of the scouts had emerged from their tents. True to my prediction, every one of the food sacks hung undisturbed from its lines, and the entire area rested in a peaceful (although crowded) haze. I scanned the woods around the lean-to one last time, never knowing when I'd be back for another visit.

The rest of the trip back down to the parking lot was short and uneventful. The Pillsbury Lake lean-to is inside of four miles to the trailhead, and most of that is downhill, so the trek went by quite quickly. It seemed like no time at all before we were unloading our packs into Casey's SUV. We signed ourselves out in the register booth and were on our way back to our lives in the real world.

Overall, I felt that the trip went wonderfully well, and my "advanced age" did little to diminish my enjoyment of the hike. (The many hikers I've met who are ten or twenty years my senior would probably roll their eyes at this last line.) Despite the passage of time, I was pleasantly surprised to see that I felt fine, with fewer aches and pains than I'd noticed on some earlier trips. As a matter of fact, the only unpleasant sensation I experienced at all came from my midsection, where my stomach was still churning in anticipation of those pancakes. Thanks, Casey. I owe you one.

—5—

Return to the Mountain

Poor Pillsbury Mountain. It had been my home for three full months in the fall of 1979, when my boss pulled me out of the woods at the end of the ranger season and extended my employment as a forest fire observer. I had lived on it, adopted it, and made it my home. And now it appears as though the authorities don't even know its official height, or even its relative order in the top one hundred peaks of New York State. It deserves better.

Pillsbury is a very large mountain considering its location; it dominates the skyline in the West Canada Lakes Wilderness Area, although there are a few other taller peaks (including Snowy Mountain) in Hamilton County. What baffles and annoys me are the inconsistencies of the listings for this prominent summit, which are easily researched on Google or other search engines of today. According to the various online references, Pillsbury's summit is 3,557; 3,579; 3,597; or 3,602 feet high. Its order in the Adirondack top-one-hundred list is slightly more defined, but it still toggles between number eighty-one and eighty-two depending on the source.

Even when I lived in the cabin at the top of the mountain as the observer there had been some disagreement on the precise altitude. The trail sign at the bottom of the mountain read 3,597 that entire summer. However, just before I was assigned to the job at the summit, a replacement sign was posted that transposed the last two figures, and the altitude became 3,579. I always wondered whether that meant I had eighteen feet less to climb, although the logic of my own musings escaped me on that matter.

The very bulk of Pillsbury Mountain is an overbearing part of the scenery to anyone who is visiting the West Canada Lakes from the Perkins Clearing entrance. From the moment you emerge from your vehicle at the trailhead on the Old Military Road, it looms over you as you commence your hike into the woods. Climbing Blue Ridge is always a task, with the rocky road winding its way up and up, then seemingly up again. However, all you have to do is turn your head to the left and look up and you'll quickly appreciate that at least you don't have to go up and over "that!"

In mid-August of 2009, I had a day off from work in Rochester and noticed the forecast of perfect blue skies and warm temperatures. Since I not been up on Pillsbury Mountain since 1981, I decided that a drive to Hamilton County was in order for an ascent of the old fire tower. Not that I was in shape to make the climb; time and inactivity had added greatly to my bulk and reduced my aerobic capacity. But it was something I just wanted to do, and I packed my daypack the night before in order to hit the road by five.

Somehow the alarm seemed to awaken me earlier than I planned. I looked at the dial and it did read 4:00 AM, which accurately reflected my intentions of the previous evening. It only felt earlier, and I debated with myself mightily regarding my degree of sanity. My Larry-of-old side prevailed, and I dragged myself out of bed and through my routine of showering and dressing.

The four-hour drive to the Mason Lake access road went by more quickly than I anticipated, and I soon found myself making the turn from the relatively well-maintained logging road onto the steep uphill leading to Sled Harbor and the Old Military Road. I have always seen a few normal two- or four-door sedans parked all the way up at the barrier to the trail system, which coincides with the trailhead to the Pillsbury Mountain Trail. Granted, most of the vehicles that had successfully navigated the rocky incline were SUVs with significantly greater ground clearance (at least twelve inches), but some of the smaller, lower cars somehow manage to make the grade. So can I, I thought resolutely, even though of all the cars on the road at that time, I believe that my Dodge Charger had perhaps the least clearance.

As I downshifted to low gear, my car's rear wheels dug in and began pushing the auto up the first grade, with steeper and rockier inclines coming into view. It wasn't long before I heard the first grating noise as it ominously sounded somewhere beneath the front end. I ignored the metallic sounds and continued onward, the bottom touching ground every ten or fifteen feet. The "road" (using that term loosely) leveled off briefly, and I was able to gain a bit of speed until it once again reverted to the rock-strewn route of before, only worse. I noticed with increasing concern that some of the boulders protruding through the gravel were becoming progressively larger and more angular, with little or no way to pass around their muffler-removing crowns. I soon decided to give up on making it to the parking lot. A quick-and-easy parallel park job to get me off the main tracks of the road would have to do.

I was able to find a grassy plot off to the side that would permit other vehicles to circumnavigate my Dodge en route to the trailhead. My starting point would add a couple miles to the overall length of my climb, including the first couple hundred feet of incline up Blue Ridge, but since my intention was to take a hike and my daypack was light, it didn't concern me that I'd have a one mile "warm-up" prior to starting the fire tower trail.

The hike in didn't take long, and I was soon signed into the register book on the edge of the parking lot. I noted with some concern that the upper ridges of the mountain looked extremely tall and distant, much more so than when I could scamper to the top without losing my breath. I've heard that altitudes and distances double with age, and I was ready to agree before I even took my first step.

Something that has always bothered me when climbing is that you are often required to go down in the process of going up. I've always felt that once you ascended to any height on a mountain you shouldn't have to give it up and retreat to a lower position before resuming the climb. But of course, I know this is something that can't be helped. Each mountain has its own topography, complete with dips and hollows, and the trails must follow those topo lines accordingly. Still, it doesn't make it any easier.

In the case of Pillsbury Mountain, the steep downhill hike at the start of the climb is one of those required descents. From the parking lot one can hear the babbling waters of the Miami River as it flows beneath the trail. Its volume increases gradually as it follows the route of the Old Military Road downhill. Getting to the river crossing requires a descent of forty to fifty feet, which is quickly regained on the other side of the stream.

Climbing this mountain will always be a sentimental return to the past for me, in the same way as my trips to the interior lakes of the adjacent wilderness area are, and as I climbed the well-worn path, I noticed many details from the past. I also missed a number of landmarks I'd expected to see. The last remnants of the telephone poles that ran through the woods to the tower cabin were now gone, rotted and returned to the soil. Perhaps I'd have spotted some of the insulators if I'd known where to look, but chances are they were buried beneath thirty years of downed leaves and other forest litter.

Even though I'd looked, I did not spot the side trail that joins the main route halfway up the mountain. This alternate trail had long been abandoned when I served as the observer, but it could still be located and followed by the skilled woods person. I remembered back to the day when one of the local folks had become turned around on this seldom-hiked path, only to be rediscovered the following day. I had never hiked it myself, but I had used it as a distance marker to judge my progress as I ascended the peak.

The climb was much harder than in my earlier days, when I could take the mountain at a brisk hike from bottom to top in less than an hour. The distance is only 1.8 miles, but the altitude gain is impressive—over 1,500 feet in that short stretch. This translates to about 850 feet of altitude per mile, enough to slow down any aging hiker, much less one who is not used to a dedicated exercise program.

As I moved slowly up the mountain, my steps decreased in length and speed, and I noted wistfully that the duration of my climb had passed through the two-hour mark. I needed longer and more frequent rest breaks, during which I listened intently to my heart beating loudly in my chest. Likewise, I felt continuously out of breath, unable to keep up with my need for air. "Altitude doubles with age," I recited, all the while cursing myself for all those extra pasta and pizza dinners. It shouldn't have been that hard.

I was approaching the final inclines of the summit when I recognized the specific rock I'd used to mark the location of a freshwater spring. This was at a point about two hundred yards beneath the actual peak, and it signified the place where I had refilled my water jugs every night back in 1979. The water flowed from a pipe that had been tapped into a crevice in the rocks, and it continuously filled a crystal-clear pool of water that spilled over into the vegetation below. I was happy to identify that spot, and I quickly stepped off the trail as I removed my canteen from my belt clip. It wasn't hot at that altitude (as a matter of fact it was now a bit on the chilly side), but I was still thirsty and had only about a third of my water supply left.

I was disappointed to see that the previously free-flowing spring had long since become filled in with sediments, with a fine mat of vegetation sprouting from the soggy patch of soil. Almost all springs must be dug out annually in order to maintain access to a reliable source of water. The last year I knew of the Pillsbury Mountain fire tower being staffed was 1981, although I've seen reports saying it officially closed in 1985. Regardless, the spring had been abandoned for at least a quarter century, rendering it useless for my needs.

The final stroll to the summit became easier as the slope of the incline decreased until the top flights of the fire tower came into view. To say that the experience was sentimental would be an understatement. Even though I felt rather exhausted, I still wanted to see everything immediately. It had been my home in the woods that season, and now I was back. So what had changed?

My first observation was that some parts of the cabin were in better shape than I'd expected, while other portions had fallen into severe disrepair. The structure itself looked OK, as did most of the roof and the shutters covering the windows. However, the front porch was a complete shambles, with some of the stairs and many of the floor boards missing. I was wondering who would do such a thing, disassembling the cabin in such a way that it would never be used again, when I recalled the final hundred yards of my hike. The ground had been extremely wet, with numerous pools of standing water deep enough to cover my hiking boot to a point above the ankle. Someone had removed a number of the porch flooring boards and carried them down the trail, constructing a walkway over the flooded areas. I wasn't sure how I felt about that, as the wood would absolutely rot away on the ground within a few years, whereas the front porch would never be repaired. As I debated the merits of this recycling, I at least felt the comfort of knowing that the disassembly of the porch had not been an act of vandalism.

The next feature I noticed missing was the outhouse. It had been in terrible shape while I was in residence and needed to be replaced even in those earlier days. The "pile" inside the structure at that time reached almost all the way to the seat; rather than solve the problem, I used a large stick to push it to lower levels, thus clearing room at the top. I know I should have moved the entire assembly and shoveled it out. But I was only up there for a matter of months, and I simply wanted to avoid the messy task. (Wouldn't anyone?)

In addition to being overfilled, the entire outhouse leaned at a distinct angle that was rather unsettling. It wasn't enough of an angle to render it perilous, but it was enough to make me consider just what would happen if the thing toppled while I was inside. How would I get out? What would end up where? It was a matter that I did not wish to focus upon, and I quickly changed the topic of my thoughts. It never did collapse or tumble on its side, which is all that mattered.

The tower itself impressed me as I climbed one flight of stairs after another. This sixty-foot-tall tower had originally been constructed out of wood in 1918, but it had been rebuilt in 1924 using steel. Its rework had transformed it into one of the "heavier-type" towers with an integrated staircase and a nine-foot-tall, window-enclosed cab on top. The condition of the stairs always depended upon the year of the most recent replacement steps. From the solid footing I felt as I ascended the staircases, I would guess that the replacement boards were relatively new. Every once in a while I felt an excessive degree of sag to a step, which made me grasp the handrail even tighter, but for the most part the footing was solid up to about the fifth or sixth platform, which was as far as I would go.

My reticence at moving to the top two platforms of the tower had nothing to do with the sturdiness of the stairs. Instead, it was the fierce intensity of the wind blowing through the tower, coupled with the cool air temperature, which was somewhere in the low-to-mid forties. The wind speed must have been at least thirty knots, resulting in a wind chill factor that felt well below the freezing mark.

The severe cold made it difficult to perform several tasks, most notably maintaining a grip on the angled, metal handrail. I found this to be rather disconcerting, as the chicken wire that had been fastened around the outside of the stairwell as a safety guard was missing from the upper levels of the tower. This meant that one missed footstep resulting in a fall could send the unlucky individual plummeting down the outside of eight flights of stairs to the solid rock base below.

The other disadvantage of the wind at the higher reaches of the tower was that it made it more difficult for me to take photographs of the cabin and clearing and to capture the views looking west towards South and West lakes. Instead, I modified my plan and retreated to the third or fourth platforms on the tower, where the wind was not quite as severe. The only drawback to that was that the west side of Pillsbury Mountain itself obstructed the views of some of the closer lakes. But I still got what I wanted before completing my return to the ground.

The clearing itself had changed little since I'd lived there, although a new crop of softwood saplings appeared to be making headway toward providing summit coverage. Smith Howland (known as "Smitty" to his Speculator friends and neighbors) had cut down the trees around the cabin in the early 1970s as a means of obtaining firewood and providing a ground-level view of town. Smitty was a well-known personality in his day, and signs of his woods craftsmanship remained in evidence while I filled his shoes as the fire tower observer. I sat in his three-legged, tree-stump chair every night while I ate my supper, and I used his rigged system of gutters and fifty-gallon drum to collect water for doing dishes and other cleaning around the cabin. He was a resourceful man, and I proudly wore the heavy Johnson wool jacket he'd left in the cabin once the cooler days of September and October arrived. The garment had been worn threadbare and all of the buttons were missing off the front. Still, I was pleased to be able to extend the life of one of Smitty's favorite jackets.

I noticed sadly that the blueberry plants that used to proliferate in the clearing near the cabin had been overgrown as well.

Perhaps there were still a few of these small shrubs remaining, hidden down amongst the thicker, taller vegetation, but I failed to notice any during my brief inspection. I used to love collecting the small, sweet-tart berries and sprinkling them into the morning pancakes or baking them into loaves of fresh lemon bread. (Smitty had even built a small baking oven, complete with a heat gauge on the front door, to enable the occupant of the cabin to bake his own breads and cakes.) It was also possible that the blueberries were now out of season, but to the best of my recollection I was harvesting the fruits until at least the end of September.

I remained on the mountain summit for a couple hours, checking out signs of recent activity in all directions. For some crazy reason, I even tried making a cell phone call from the lower platforms of the tower, just to see if it could be done. After all, the fire towers were built for other functions than simply reporting smokes; they also served as communications relay stations when there was a medical emergency or other critical issue in the backcountry. Portable VHF radios and, later on, cell phones alleviated the need for manned fire towers with their heavy radios and tower-mounted antennae. These thoughts and more ran through my head as I waited to see whether my card-sized phone could reach out from the tower on Pillsbury.

As expected, my call went through with no problem, even further proof of the advances in communications since my tenure on the mountain. Even though cell coverage in the Adirondack lowlands (between the various mountain ranges, valleys, peaks, and gulches) is still limited in many areas, newly constructed cell towers and advances in technology are closing in on those blacked-out areas. I fully expect that in another twenty years we will have full coverage in all locations, thus eliminating yet another function for which the fire towers were originally built.

By three o'clock, I had nothing left to do on the summit, and commenced my descent back down the old trail. Although I am a fairly social creature, comfortable with my communal environment and cadre of friends, I was more than pleased that I had the summit to myself for the entire day. Not as many people climb to the top of Pillsbury as the mountains located in the High Peaks as it isn't on the list of the Adirondacks' highest summits. You don't get a badge or patch for reaching the fire tower on the peak, and there are no clubs or gatherings for those who accomplish the feat. Then, as today, it is just you and the mountain, which is the way it should be. Still though, several groups each day sign into the trail register as they prepare to start this journey.

I remembered fully the thoughts I used to have as I made this trip every week, how I felt returning to the rest of the world from my perch up high on the mountain. I would be lying if I said that I didn't feel somewhat supercilious to everything that existed down below. It was a strange sentiment back then, but one I could not shake. I lived in a place that on many days was above the clouds, alone, just me and the mountain. True, it was a different era in 1979, and so much has changed in the past four decades. Then again, much hasn't, and I felt some of those same attitudes as I descended the trail today, complete with my heavy walking stick and head of gray hair.

To say that I flew back down the mountain as in days of old would have been yet another tall tale. My trek back down the flanks of Pillsbury took another couple of hours, as my balance isn't what it used to be, and I can no longer count on my boot soles "one-timing" the tops of boulders in rapid-fire succession. Instead, it was another round of slow, methodical steps, using my walking stick to provide stability between each rock. Even with my caution, I still managed to take one full-scale backward dive, ending up with my feet down a muddy slope and the seat of my pants in a four-inch deep pool of water. It took some effort but I was able to raise myself back to a standing position with only my pride being injured. Still, it wasn't pretty.

By the time I made it back to my car it was getting on into dinner hour, and the sun was dropping back toward the top of the peak from which I had just returned. My sentiments were a bit mixed; part of me (including my still-soaked posterior) was thinking that I'd been crazy to make this trip today for the sole purpose of "being there" once again. On the other hand, the rest of me was simply happy that I could still make the grade. Yes, it had taken me double or triple the amount of time I used to allot for this hike. Then again, as my friend Casey had once asked, how many of your friends are still doing this at your age?

At least I was there, and I will be for as long as I can manage to put one foot in front of the other until I reach my destination— even if it was just a 3,600-foot-tall mountain with a well-marked trail. I smiled as I thought to myself: Smitty would have been proud of me.

Memories of 2014

—6—

Preparations

September 12, 2014:

For reasons unbeknownst to me, it's been five years since I've ventured back into the West Canada Lakes. I can't say why it's been so long, and I don't know if it will happen again, but it's time I've lost that I'll never retrieve. This is all the more reason why I'm blessed to have at least one friend who is willing to poke and prod at my tired old body until my resistance crumbles and I finally say, "Yes, I'll go," even if I wonder how the bag of bones underneath my creased exterior will hold out.

Those were my sentiments as Casey and I first commenced our conversation about "The Trek of 2014." It wasn't to be a long, extended trip up the Northville-Placid Trail, or even a full loop through the West Canada Lakes area. Constrained by time, this was to be a simple, three-day, in-and-out visit to the Beaver Pond lean-to on Cedar Lakes. Since the demolition of the original Lean-to #1, which was situated by the old dam, Beaver Pond has become my favorite spot to plunk myself down for just about any weekend-length excursion into the woods.

Our previous venture had been both smaller and simpler, as there were only the two of us. Since we were both born in the same year and had both attained "senior" status, this time it seemed wise to invite at least one person of younger age and greater endurance, just in case anything happened to one of us. Of course I didn't admit this to Casey, although I'm sure the same thought must have crossed his mind as well. Within the past ten years, I'd had my hip fully replaced and he'd suffered a mild heart attack. We all have to face facts—we're not as young as we used to be. (Well, maybe I am, but no one else is, of course.)

Within a week, Casey got back to me and said that his son, Gino, a strapping young man of sixteen, would love to join us. Tagging along would be Gino's friend, another teenager in prime condition who had already enlisted in the Marine Corps. This trip would be one of his last activities before reporting for basic training in the fall. The addition of these two youngsters would add a bit of entertainment and a lot of security to our trip. (Remember, though, that's not why they were invited!)

After one last meeting to finish our planning (and also do another BBQ lunch), we parted ways for the last time prior to starting our hike. After this, we also started the process of packing, which is much more complicated than it used to be back in my ranger days. For one thing, anyone who has gone five years between overnight trips into the woods knows that hiking apparel and equipment grow legs of their own. Mine had performed this disappearing act, and hours of searching turned up only a fraction of my insulated undergarments, socks, pants, and gear. I was amazed, however, at the number of one-of-a-kind socks that were filling the drawers of my dresser. I firmly believe that there is a black hole in the center of our universe that is completely filled with the odd socks from every wardrobe on the planet. It's just got to be true.

Shopping for a hiking trip is also much different than it used to be, with new technologies available to suit almost any need. The clothing is entirely new, with space-age fabrics and breathable, zipper-laden outfits galore. These marvelous tops and bottoms, most of which are worn in layers, enable your heat and sweat to escape while you maintain an even body temperature inside your clothing. A salesman proudly told me that one of the items I'd selected to try-on was "fifth generation" of some wonder fabric or another. OK. I'm not sure whether I missed generations one through four, but I did trust his sales speech and went on to purchase the recommended sweatshirt. Hey, it was pretty too. He also presented another garment for my inspection—a wonderfully soft, elegant sweater made out of lamb's wool that felt like silk in my hands. When informed that this too was "fifth generation" fabric, my mind conjured up a vague image of a techno-lamb, with printed wire circuitry and other gizmos woven into its fleece. Regardless, once the sales guy informed me that the sweater was "reduced" to $159, I quickly decided that my existing low-tech, fleece sweatshirt was good enough for camping in September.

I also got involved in purchasing techno-geek survival gear. Even though I'd never gone for the high-tech gadgets in the past, I was now attracted by the high beam LED flashlights and the germ warfare water filtration systems. I didn't purchase the latter, as Casey had a good water filter system to protect us from the *Giardia lambia* microorganisms that became a plague on hikers in the ten years after I left the woods. But I did give in and pick up a bear-proof food canister, even though my gut feeling was that these were still unnecessary in the lightly-traveled West Canadas region. I'd never hung a bag of food in a tree in my entire career, and I really didn't feel like starting a new tradition now. So I don't know why I bought one; perhaps it can be blamed on old age.

One thing that hadn't changed much was the stock of available dehydrated trail food. The breakfasts, lunches, and dinners really didn't appear any different than they had five years ago, or for that matter, thirty years before that. Dinners still consisted of the standard array of beef stroganoff, chicken a-la-king, lasagna with meat sauce, and chili mac. Lunches were based around skillet wraps, biscuits and gravy, and "just-add-water" western omelets. Yummy. I decided on a combination of dehydrated trail food and some of the old standards I'd enjoyed back in the 1970s. Regardless, I knew that it probably didn't make a difference, as almost anything tastes good in the woods, especially if you've been on the trail for most of the day. I'm sure there's a reason for this, although it's probably just due to hunger and the allure of eating around the campfire at night.

In addition to the selection of dehydrated, freeze-dried, sterile, chemically-enhanced packages of lunch and dinner entrees, I also decided on a tasty array of snacks and beverages to complement my food bag. Being a dedicated tea drinker, I picked up a variety pack of English breakfast tea and Earl Grey, along with a package of tea biscuits, Fig Newtons, and a massive bag of GORP ingredients. I realized as I was purchasing the ingredients for the GORP that I was buying enough to last for a trip that was several times the length of our current excursion; however, I also knew that I love to feed the squirrels and chipmunks, so I planned accordingly. Additionally, if I thought my supply would be more then I desired to carry out, the two teenagers in our party would gnaw though that bag in less time than it takes to heat a can of soup.

GORP is another thing that has undergone multiple evolutions since my prior life in the woods. Once upon a time, the term "GORP" was an acronym that stood for "good old raisins and peanuts," to which people added candy (M&Ms), other dried fruits, and a variety of nuts and seeds as desired. However, as the years progressed and culinary preferences matured, the contents of this high-calorie snack evolved as well and progressed into the GORP we know today, which can be almost anything. My own version came mostly from our neighborhood grocery store, where I acquired a combination of jelly beans (cherry and eggnog), candy corn, cashews, sesame snacks, dehydrated pineapple chunks, more cashews, yogurt-covered peanuts, macadamia nuts, shredded coconut, and even more cashews. (I like cashews.)

The result was a wonderful mixture of everything sweet—plus cashews—that probably weighed in around 1,500 calories per cup, but tasted great nonetheless.

The other problem I had while assembling the GORP was that I threw all caution to the wind regarding portion sizes. I picked up one or two cups of each ingredient, but neglected to consider the extraordinary number of choices I was adding to the mix. The resulting mountain of fully-assembled GORP filled a massive pasta bowl in our kitchen, far more than I'd consume in any full month in the woods. Then again, there would be two active teenagers with us, which meant that it would probably last through the first day and perhaps into the afternoon of the second.

Other issues came up while trying to get ready for this trip. For example, my old Svea white-gas stove hadn't been used in at least five years. It was one of the most reliable pieces of equipment in my collection, but it was still over thirty years old, and it showed its age on every surface. And the old can of white gas in my garage was over five years old, which meant that I didn't know if it was still useable. (Does gasoline degrade over a period of years?) Rather than investigate any of this scientifically, or research it online, I decided to do the typical "guy" thing, which was to fill the stove with fuel and apply a match. This probably wasn't very smart, as I had visions of a fireball and ensuing mushroom cloud that would be visible for miles, after which my face (or what was left of it) would be seen on the evening news across much of the state. However, much to my amazement, there was no explosion. It took a few tries, but the fuel in the primer ring flamed up and created the pressure inside the burner valve to start a fiercely hot blue flame. It worked! Like me, it was old and tarnished and cranky, but it worked.

There were a few other items in my backpack that I decided had progressed beyond the end of their service life. My sleeping bag fell into this category. It was the same bag I had used as a ranger in the 1970s, which meant that the thirty-five-year-old "space age" material that had been used in its construction had worn down considerably. Additionally, it had been kept tightly rolled in my pack, which reduced its loft even further. I had used this bag on our trip five years earlier, but that had been during the summer months when the temperatures weren't so chilly. I obviously needed a replacement for this fall season trip.

If the number of varieties of sleeping bags was large twenty years ago, today it is positively astounding. There were various kinds of artificial fillings versus down, along with a vast variety of outer shells, linings, configurations of tubes and baffles, ventilating zippers, stitching, hoods, compression ratios... and more. And in addition to that, there was also an enormous range in price and temperature ratings. By the time I'd finished browsing the websites my head was spinning. In the end, I opted for a nice, roomy, down bag that was rated to about minus fifteen degrees. My last bag was a narrow "mummy" version with a tapered configuration from the waist to the feet. However, that bag was purchased in 1979, when my body was tapered from my waist to my feet. Since I'm now much larger and lacking the taper, I thought it wise to purchase a sleeping bag that matched my body type. Also, the extra filling on the bottom would go a long way towards softening the feel of the lean-to planking below my bag. It was a wise choice, as my artificial hip (and the rest of my bones) would have felt the lean-to floor much more easily without the extra padding.

The only other item I decided to add to my oversized Kelty backpack was a pair of comfortable slippers. This is one luxury that very few hikers are willing to carry, but one that had come to have great appeal to me. After wearing great, big, heavy hiking boots on the trail to reach our destination, the last thing I wanted to do was to have them on my feet for the rest of the day. A visit to my local L.L.Bean store turned up a pair of fleece-lined, leather moccasins that featured a Vibram-like sole. They were still subtle and flexible, with enough "give" to allow my feet to slide in and out without requiring extra effort. Yet the rugged exterior bottom sole looked tough enough to stand up to performing double duty on the trail if the need arose. It was a wonderful combination, considering the downy-soft feel of the fleece against my bare feet, and I knew that the extra pound of weight would be more than justified by the added comfort once we set up camp in the lean-to.

With the shopping and packing done, we set our sights on an early take-off for a Friday morning. Our plan was to hit the trail as early as possible in order to increase our chances of getting space inside the Beaver Pond lean-to. When Casey suggested that we leave by seven that morning, I asked if he'd be OK with a five o'clock departure instead. The drive would be between three and four hours, and I wanted to be on the trail by nine. Casey seemed to be OK with that alteration, although he wasn't sure how big of a crowbar would be required to lever Gino out of bed at that early hour. Gino's friend had already backed out of the trip, so it would be just the three of us heading down the Thruway, looking for the sunrise.

After navigating the turn off Route 30 north of Speculator, we cruised along the six miles of dirt logging road to Perkins Clearing, where we turned right and continued on to Sled Harbor, which is another two miles down the road. I never had the benefit of driving those two miles, as my tenure as a ranger took place before the land swap between New York State and the International Paper Company, and this territory was all behind locked gates back then. As we drove over those miles that I used to cover by foot, I could see and recall each dip and incline in the road. Even nicer was the last mile after Sled Harbor, where the road turns to the right again and begins the climb up Blue Ridge. Those people who own SUVs with significant ground clearance can drive right up to the trailhead, located at the base of the Pillsbury Mountain fire tower trail. It's a very rugged road, with large boulders protruding from the rocky base and areas of washout cropping up after heavy rains. It always amazes me to see the occasional passenger car up there, and I wonder how much damage was done to the undercarriage in order to save that final mile of hiking.

Once we pulled into the dirt plateau that formed the parking lot, I was confronted by the biggest surprise of the day. As we climbed out of the high seats of the SUV, we were hit smack in the face with a blast of seemingly arctic air. It was quite a shock, as it was still the first half of September, and the leaves on the trees had barely begun to turn. Yet there was no doubt about it, the temperature felt a good twenty degrees cooler than when we had departed Rochester earlier that morning. A quick check of the digital thermometer on the instrument panel of the car read 38 degrees. I was astounded. This was in the bright sunshine, at least three to four hours after sunrise. It just didn't seem as though it should be that cold, and I thanked my lucky stars that I'd over-packed on the cold weather apparel. Between my new high-tech hiking shirts, my thin layer of thermal long underwear for top and bottom, my Under Armour sweatshirt, and the heavy fleece jacket, I knew that I'd be warm no matter what the weather. But I just hadn't planned on it being so cool during the day, and I knew that the next two nights would be much colder.

I've never been one to hike with multiple layers of insulation, as I tend to overheat quite rapidly. So I quickly did my stretching and got ready to heave my pack onto my shoulders. It was then that I discovered that I'd left my trusty walking stick back in Rochester. This didn't sit well with me, as I'd carried that same stick since I pulled it from a beaver dam on Cedar Lakes back in 1981. Thankfully, I was able to quickly locate a suitable stick left behind by another hiker, which I quickly adopted for my own. (At my age, I don't fare well taking a major slip or fall, and my walking stick always saves me from such a mishap at least once or twice a day.)

Even though Casey and Gino were still getting their gear

together, I decided to get a short head start on them, as I knew that they were both capable of hiking much faster than me. Five years earlier, I had been a bit quicker on the trail than Casey, because I had been lighter back then and he was still recovering from knee surgery. Today would be different, and I knew that I really didn't want to hold them up. So we agreed that we would meet at the top of Blue Ridge, unless they caught up to me beforehand, as I was certain they would. The top of Blue Ridge sports a split in the trail where you can turn left and start down the French Louie Trail, taking you past Pillsbury, Whitney, and Sampson lakes, then on to the merger with the Northville-Placid Trail at the head of West Canada Creek. On the other hand, if you remain straight at that juncture on Blue Ridge, it will take you in to Cedar Lakes.

Hiking alone up the first inclines of wooded pathway felt exhilarating. For much of that distance you can look to your left (westward) and see the towering bulk of Pillsbury Mountain, where I had served as fire observer for a few months in the fall of 1979. It is still a popular hiking destination, and many of the people logged into the trailhead register had listed that as their destination. I didn't know how much of a lead I had on my two companions, so I tried to maintain a decent pace for as long as possible. As the elevation increased and the sloping old road became steeper, I paused for an occasional breather and sip from my canteen. Years ago the thought of stopping along this route would have been sheer nonsense. It would have taken me just one rapid, sure-footed sprint to the top, where perhaps I might have stopped to check out the traffic based on the footprints leading down one trail versus the other. But not now. Out of shape, with forty to fifty pounds of pack on my back, I stopped every time I felt my heart rate increasing beyond a certain comfort level. This was no race, and I knew my limitations. Still, I was pleased with my progress and even more surprised to find myself on top of the ridge without coming in contact with Casey and Gino. Hooray—chalk one up for the old timer!

—7—

Balance Beam Gymnastics

Once at the top of Blue Ridge, I paused for my compatriots to catch up, which took just about five minutes. I'm sure they were plodding along at an intentionally slow pace in order to give me some breathing room up ahead, but no matter. I was simply enjoying the scenery, with the familiar trail signs and leaf-covered paths leading off into the woods in various directions. I noticed to my chagrin that the extensive thickets of raspberry bushes were no longer evident by the side of the trail. I used to stop there often to grab a quick snack as I passed that spot every week. (That was, of course, assuming that I beat the local bears to the fruit.) However, being an early seral-stage plant, they had probably disappeared decades ago as the vegetation in the area matured and grew back from earlier disturbances.

Other things had changed as well, some for the better and some for the worse. The farther I hiked in from the parking lot to the higher ground, the more the old road now resembled a simple path. A true, rugged, four-wheel drive vehicle could still make it through most of the route, although there were spots where the road had completely washed out and reverted into a rocky streambed which no vehicle could circumnavigate. But for the most part, the residual vestiges of the original road were fading into oblivion.

Another surprise awaited me when I completed the descent on the backside of Blue Ridge where the trail crosses Grassy Brook at the site of the old Camp 20 ruins. The bridge was never replaced, and the brook crossing must be made by hopping from stone to stone. Well, this might have been fine for me thirty to forty years ago, but it's a bit different today. The sense of balance fades over time, and what was normal in my youth is pure trickery today. Providing additional adventure to the crossing was the fact that none of the rocks had smooth, level surfaces that could serve as easy stepping stones. Nope. Instead, there was a continuous array of pointy, slippery, ever-rocking stones that seemed to say "I dare you!" However, I didn't have much choice, so I carefully selected my path and gave it my best effort. I even managed to remain fairly dry throughout my thirty seconds of maneuvering to the other side of Grassy Brook, while Casey and Gino patiently waited for me to complete the transit. After we were all across, I was able to point out to them the outlines of the old camp that once stood there, although there was little left but the remnants of the clearing where it used to stand. Back in the late 1970s, you could still see charred timbers sitting in the weeds, their skeletons forming the outline of the original building.

Other paths through the woods indicated where there had been dirt roads down which old trucks had chugged as they transported passengers into the camps that dotted the hillsides. But even then, these primitive roads were closing in with vegetation and saplings, so today they would be hard to locate unless you knew their original positions in the woods. As John Remias used to say, "Nature reclaims her own quite quickly."

The next few miles of trail were quite challenging, as Casey and Gino set a fast pace that I struggled to match. It was perhaps the most out-of-shape I'd been in many years, and it didn't feel good. On top of that, Gino was simply itching to gallop ahead, and Casey (being a good dad) wanted to keep up. That left me. Ugh. I have many colorful descriptions for old age, and all of them applied over the next three to four miles. It simply wasn't pretty. Every time we reached an incline of any significant degree, my progress was cut in half. It made me wish that I'd spent some time on a stair-climber machine over the past few months.

Things got even worse when we arrived at the bridge crossing over Grassy Brook. (The trail crosses this stream several times en route to Cedar Lakes.) The bridge had deteriorated into a virtual obstacle course, and unfortunately there was no way around it. The brook at this point was about fifteen feet across, at least five or six feet deep, and straight down to a muddy bottom. There wasn't a rock or other useful foothold anywhere, so if you had to select an alternate method for crossing other than the bridge, it would have to have been swimming.

The rickety structure was suspended by a single log on only one side, the other one having given up the ghost long ago. There was a single handrail left on that surviving side, and the entire walkway tilted at a thirty- to forty-degree angle to the left. This meant that you had to hang on for dear life with your left hand while you shuffled your feet, one after the other, to cross to the other side. Even this description fails to match the true precarious nature of the route, as the handrail felt as though it would fracture with a single "snap" if too much pressure was exerted on its frail timbers, and with every step you could feel the springing and sagging of the single log that still spanned the distance from one bank to the other. As thick as it was, the thought hammered away in my brain that this thing could go at any time, and I fervently wished that I'd reduced my weight by at least ten or fifteen pounds before ever setting foot on the construction.

Once the three of us made it across the bridge (feeling something like contestants on American Gladiators), we continued along the path towards Cedar Lakes. At least for a couple hundred yards. That's when the next obstruction became evident.

The balance beams.

Somewhere, at some time, I am convinced that all trail crews are instructed to hire at least one sadistic individual whose sole purpose in life is to make part of each hike pure hell, if only for a short period of time. Unfortunately, the trail in to Cedar Lakes employed at least one such builder-designer who deviously decided to construct a device to test the balance and endurance of anyone over the age of fifty.

As I stood at the start of the obstacle course, I realized that this wasn't the normal example of a coordination test. No, this was going to be much worse. I understood the need to build such a structure to transverse the trail-turned-waterway, which had long been submerged due to beaver activity. Those creatures were experts in turning dry land into water-filled marshes, and this large parcel was just another example of their handiwork. It was impossible to judge the depth of the flooding, but it appeared to be at least a couple of feet, with additional muck and mud beneath the bottom. However, what concerned me was the construction of the walkway. It was made up of what I've referred to as "stringers"—logs split in half and supported by other logs, designed to carry hikers over the water that now covered the trail beneath. Perhaps six inches across, they stretched across the water for hundreds of yards. In some places there were two of these logs, side-by-side, so that it was possible to stroll in a normal manner without altering your stride. I found this to be no problem, and I was able to cross those sections with relative ease. But the other sections narrowed to a single beam, and it was here that I started having problems.

Stepping onto these stretches of balance-beams, I experienced multiple emotions. Part of me felt like Rambo as I plunged ahead into the jungle. Another bit of me emulated Nadia Comaneci, the famed Romanian gymnast who at the tender age of fourteen became the first athlete in Olympic history to attain a perfect score of 10. (Heck—in addition to the balance beam, I would compare the bridge to the uneven bars!) I even felt like attempting a quick, one-legged hop as a dismount when I got close to the other side. However, since I'd almost plunged face-first into muddy water on at least three occasions, I decided to forego the theatrics and simply settle for a safe crossing. That would suffice as my "10" for the day.

Over the course of the next mile, we ran into three additional lengths of stringers. Whenever I see trail work of that magnitude, I scream internally over the amount of sheer effort and muscle power required to undertake such a task. The labor alone—to split, lift, and position those logs before hammering them into place—is enormous. Unfortunately, those same logs will deteriorate into a slippery, slimy pulp within a decade, leaving the hiker to perform the "balance-beam ballet" down a hundred yards of home-grown gauntlet that is more slippery than any freshly-cleaned ice rink. It won't be pretty, but at least it was fairly secure for the time being.

Within a couple miles of descending the Blue Ridge, we settled for a time onto trail that was drier and more stable. But the end of the hazardous bridges was still nowhere in sight. It seemed that whenever we arrived at a crossing of any stream or outlet, we had to balance, dance, and prance to find our way to the other side. It made me feel no better to realize that we'd have to retrace our steps over these same obstacles in just a few days. And if I thought we were home-free from the obstacle course, I was sadly mistaken.

The bridge over the outlet below Cedar Lakes wasn't in very bad shape. However, it wasn't much of a bridge, either. Instead, it was a single layer of planking – perhaps two inches by six inches—with a single, wobbly handrail alongside for encouragement. The dangerous part (besides the flimsiness of the whole affair) was the fact that there were nails sticking out through the lumber, posing a definite hazard for anyone who happened to take a spill. Fortunately, I managed to cross without impaling myself on any of these protrusions.

The next bridge, which was the crossing over the moderate-sized flow between Beaver Pond and the main body of Cedar Lakes, was tilted precariously on one broken base log. This ruptured support, which was located on the northeast side of the bridge, allowed the entire structure to dip to the waterline on that end, requiring hikers to once again display advanced levels of agility. To complicate matters, there was also a large step down to get to the uneven surface. Thirty years earlier, I would have leapt off the upper shoreline surface and landed deftly on the bridge, whereupon I would have bounded effortlessly to the other side, my body automatically correcting for the degree of list as I perambulated thoughtlessly on my way. But not today. Once again, I managed the crossing, albeit more slowly than surely, until I reached the safety of the gravel on the other side. Things are so much easier for the young. (I am happy to report that this bridge has since been replaced in its entirety by a wide new structure that is a joy to cross.)

Within a minute or two we found ourselves scrambling up the brief incline leading to the side trail of the Beaver Pond lean-to, otherwise known as Cedar Lakes #2. I was happy to see that even Gino breathed a sigh of contentment as he slung his pack to the floor of the then-empty lean-to, more than happy to reach our destination at such an early hour. This was not an accident. Since this is my favorite lean-to in the entire West Canada Lakes territory, I like to get there early in the day to "stake our claim" as the primary residents on any given day. I'm always happy to share with folks arriving later in the afternoon, but I want to make sure that I'm "in" as well.

OK, I had successfully completed one more transit into Cedar Lakes under full pack without passing out. Then again, there was always time for that later.

—8—

Fifty-Eight is the New Seventy

We've all heard the expression "Sixty is the new Fifty," but as far as I'm concerned, it just doesn't hold water. At the time of that hike, I was fifty-eight, and damn it, I felt every day of my age. As soon as my pack came off, my body went down on the floor of the lean-to, with the only intermediate step being the unraveling of my foam pad and sleeping bag. These I dumped rather unceremoniously on the bottom planks of the structure, mostly to serve as a cushion to break my fall as I collapsed downward onto the floor and fell immediately asleep. No roundhouse punch from Ken Norton or Muhammad Ali could have accomplished the trick quicker, and I'm told my snores soon reverberated about the lean-to, competing with the honest sounds of the woods in a most disruptive manner. Casey and Gino later informed me that every loon on the lake was answering my call with music of their own. (I didn't believe them.)

If I thought that I would escape into slumber until it was time to gather wood for dinner, I was mistaken. I had completely forgotten to account for the early September chill, which had never permitted the temperatures to rise much above the low forties. As my shirt was still damp from the perspiration of the hike, I found myself chilled to the bone within a relatively short period of time. With record speed I removed my saturated shirt and replaced it with my new wonder-fiber sweatshirt, which quickly delivered everything it had promised in the small print of the advertisement. Hi-tech certainly does have its advantages, right down to the clothes we wear.

Upon levering myself into an upright position, I quickly observed the difference between myself and our teenaged accomplice. Gino hadn't bothered to take a nap, or even to reduce his forward motion in any way. He had snagged the ball I sometimes carried into the woods and was tossing himself forward passes across the bare area in back of the fireplace. His friend, who was originally supposed to tag along for the week, had unfortunately cancelled, leaving Gino as the only youngster in our group. For Gino, the mere stroll of six miles was apparently not enough exercise for the day. And so, as I groggily observed his movements through partially open eyelids, he sprinted this way and that in our clearing, leaping several feet in the air to spear each successive toss. It was impressive, although I must admit that part of me was silently cursing him out for having the audacity to possess such a stockpile of excess energy. It just didn't seem fair.

As for myself, I stirred my own mental resolve so as not to be reduced to a sleeping hulk for the remainder of the trip. I pulled myself up, and with purposeful strides, headed out to collect wood for the coming evening. This has always been one of my favorite activities, which was duly noted by Casey on our last excursion into the woods, and remains so today. I found myself quite surprised at the abundance and quality of downed wood that was available within a couple hundred yards of our camping site. I have always said that most campers aren't willing to look more than fifty to one hundred feet from their fireplace to collect their supply and thus end up with the "reject limbs" that were left behind by previous residents of the lean-to. This is usually true, as most of what is left behind at campsites is either too green or too rotten to serve any use other than stacking for photographic purposes. I also ventured a short distance down the trail to the old spring, just to see if it was still flowing. It was, but it was only a trickle, and the original pipe that had carried the clear, pure water from the ground had long since vanished.

Within fifteen minutes, I had as large a bundle as I could carry. This I trudged back to the lean-to, where Casey and Gino were now reclining. Ok... my turn! Rather than gently lowering my load to the ground, I went for the full-out theatrical version: I lofted the large bundle of sticks and branches as high into the air as possible (as long as I wasn't being watched) and allowed them to crash to the ground as noisily as a small tree dropped by a logger's ax. Yeah, yeah, I know; it was kind of childish. But it made a big impression, and at my age that's getting tougher to pull off. So... crash!

Gino jumped up from his prone position, obviously startled. Casey merely lifted a shoulder and turned his head around. "Sounds like you've chopped down half the forest," he murmured, one eyebrow raised as he assessed the pile.

"Nah, just a few twigs picked up along the trail. I'll go out for the real load as soon as I break up this bunch."

Well, that's what I said, anyway. My real desire was to get some help in reducing this load to fireplace-sized sticks, and that is exactly what Gino did. He sprang from his position on the floor of the lean-to into an action position on the front edge, and from there to the ground in a single bound. I can't even remember if I used to possess that kind of energy and agility, but it was fun to watch nonetheless.

After a couple minutes of rapid-fire wood-breaking, Gino decided that he was going to go after bigger game. There was an old log left over from some previous inhabitant of the lean-to that was sitting in front of the fireplace. It was a piece of softwood that looked as though it had been tested once before, as a piece of its length had been sawed off the end, leaving a clean-cut surface of exposed grain. Another part of the log appeared to have been burned at some point, with the charred bark bearing witness to the heat. How this occurred I can only guess. Perhaps a camper laid the entire log across the top of the fireplace, hoping to burn it in half? (Your guess is as good as mine.)

Regardless, once Gino had got it in his mind to further saw this log into usable pieces, he would not be dissuaded. There was an old saw inside the lean-to that had been left behind by another group, so Casey quickly befriended this dull-looking tool and went to work.

And work... and work... and work.

Gino had been exercising his muscles for about ten to fifteen minutes when he paused to inspect the results of his efforts. The cut had only progressed about one to two inches into the water-logged timber.

"I think you need a sharper saw," I remarked as I commiserated with the teenager. "That thing's probably been back here since the days of French Louie!"

"It'll work," he grunted as he returned to the attack. "I've just got to get a better rhythm going."

Unfortunately, I think that any sharp edge this particular saw once had was completely worn away over its years in the woods, because the faster Gino moved the blade across the log, the less it appeared to cut. I eyed the progress skeptically as I noticed that little or no sawdust was falling from the log to the ground. Additionally, whereas the teeth should have produced a grating noise with each stroke, instead there was a smooth "whooshing" noise, as though a dull, flat edge was being run over a smooth surface. Not good.

After about twenty minutes of this, Gino put down the saw and placed one end of the log on top of a nearby stump that had been cut off close to the ground. He then proceeded to step on one end of the log while stamping the heel of his hiking boot onto the cut he had made. Nothing. He repeated this exercise numerous times in an attempt to break off the section of spruce log, all to no avail. Finally, with a most dissatisfied groan, he kicked the log off the stump, allowing it to thump to the ground in its original state.

"Oh well, I'll get that thing cut up after dinner," said Gino, looking wistfully at the timber. "It'll make a nice, long-burning log for the campfire tonight." Somehow I didn't see that happening, and my twisted sense of humor could almost detect a chuckle coming from the log. At least for now, the log was winning.

Over the course of the next few hours, we had a couple hiking parties come through, none of whom decided to stay at the Beaver Pond location once they saw that the lean-to was already partially occupied. Many folks would rather surrender the gorgeous view afforded at that location for the solitude of a less picturesque but unoccupied spot. I can't say that I blame them for their preference.

It was around five o'clock, as we were beginning our preparations for dinner, when a group of three male hikers arrived and announced that they were going to stop over for the night.

"That's fine," I said, already starting to move my sleeping bag and pad to the other side of the floor next to Gino's and Casey's gear. "We've got plenty of room."

"No, that's OK," said the tallest of the three, a bearded gentleman in his mid-thirties. "We've got tents and tarps and everything we need. We'll just set up shop on that little bluff to the side of the lean-to."

The group was another bunch of recreational campers who were only in the woods for a few days and not attempting to complete a significant portion of the Northville-Placid Trail. They were from Batavia, which is between Rochester and Buffalo, and near the town where my wife was raised. Trying to be neighborly, I invited them to join us for a campfire later that evening.

"We've got plenty of wood," I said, nodding at our impressive woodpile. "We usually like to stay up for a while at night and listen to the loons."

"Sounds like a great idea," said another of the group. "We'd be happy to join you once we finish our own meals and get things cleaned up."

Over the course of the next hour, the three of us lit our respective stoves (saving the firewood for our evening communal blaze) and got water boiling for dinner. It was very interesting observing the differences between Casey and me as we undertook this task. Casey, being a modern hiker with all the knowledge of the contemporary tools and devices, set up his butane fuel tank and Jetboil stove and simply pressed a button. Presto! In an instant, he had a roaring blast of incredible heat, which had his water boiling in almost no time. I, on the other hand, removed my ancient Svea stove from its bag and began the ritual of filling the internal tank with liquid white gas, which was always a dicey proposal. I wasn't really all that worried, since (as I mentioned earlier) I had tested the device only a few weeks prior to our hike. After spilling some fuel into the priming ring at the base of the nozzle and then re-sealing the main fuel can and moving it a safe distance from the stove, I was ready for ignition. Except this antique contraption didn't work with a pushbutton. Instead, it had to be lit from a match or lighter, which was always an interesting proposition. The lighter caused a miniature eruption of bright flames all about the stove, after which the operator (that's me) had to allow it to heat the brass shell until the primer flame had almost gone out. Then, and only then, I could turn the key that released a small spray of vaporized white gas from the top nozzle, creating the cooking fire.

Once upon a time, this stove worked very well, and I could get it to operate in almost any temperature, even with the gas tank mostly empty. But it was now thirty-five years old, with significant deposits of carbon that I had negligently allowed to accumulate on the nozzles and surrounding burners of the apparatus. My first attempt to light it was met with a sputtering, popping ignition that made several attempts to self-extinguish, and it was only with a significant amount of adjusting and "fiddling" that I could get it to function. Finally, after a few minutes of endless turning and tweaking, I was able to coax a steady blast from the stove that boiled my water, although in about double the time of Casey's stove.

Note to self: replace stove soon!

As we ate our meals, the conversation turned to other topics. It's always amazing the variety of subjects that come up around the evening meal. On this occasion, the banter was about the surrounding forest and its similarity with the wooded battle-grounds of some Civil War sites. As we launched into this topic, I was vaguely aware that Casey was a participant in some Civil War re-enactments, which is a popular hobby and activity for many Americans. However, I did not know that he had engaged his entire family in the same pastime.

"In a way, the woods surrounding this campsite remind me of the area around Chancellorsville," I stated. "There isn't a lake there like this one, but the woods look the same."

As I spoke, Casey cast an appraising eye around the nearby woods without saying anything. So I continued. "I visited Chancellorsville a couple years ago on a field trip. It's an interesting place. They erected a monument at the very spot where Confederate General Longstreet was shot and eventually died. It's a really solemn setting."

This last statement caused Gino to shoot a glance in the direction of his father, who silently returned the look without comment.

"Actually, Longstreet wasn't killed at Chancellorsville," said Gino in a halting tone. "I think you're getting him confused with Stonewall Jackson, who was accidentally shot by his own troops and died about a week later." As he spoke, he sounded apologetic for correcting me, but confident in his expertise on the subject.

And of course he was correct, which was confirmed by Casey

and even by me once I dug further into my own memory bank. I quickly deduced that they were experts on the subject, having travelled to many of the actual Civil War sites to participate in the battle reenactments. But I still felt a bit inadequate, with my misstatement coming right on the heels of my cooking debacle.

As the sun went down over the next few hours and the sky darkened, I made the shift from my heavy hiking boots into my fleece-lined slippers. Ah, yes! Some folks might look quite skeptically at my choice of items to pack, but this was one for which I had no regrets. Even though I would never have carried such a luxury in my days as a ranger, I'd come to believe they were worth their weight in gold (although weighing in at only one pound). They are lined with the softest fleece imaginable, and I sighed as my feet slid into their caressing interiors. An amazing sense of relaxation instantly came over me.

Before the skies darkened completely, we lit the campfire, which soon grew into a respectable blaze. The three hikers from the group nearby strolled over and took their places around the fireplace, happy to share the warmth of the flames. The temperature hadn't climbed out of the low forties all day, and the chill was quickly returning to the air as the sun retreated. It would be another cold night on Cedar Lakes.

The men introduced themselves as Mark (the tallest of the three), Tony, and Carl. All were experienced hikers, and we quickly fell into a conversation about our travels. One of the beneficial tidbits I learned from the three was the name of a small but excellent company that produces gourmet-like dehydrated food for backpacking.

"I heard about them from a friend," volunteered Mark. "He was tired of the same old pork and beans in a bag, so he did some searching and found this company online. Their stuff is prepared by a retired professional chef, and it's a lot different than the stuff you get off the shelf in the camping store."

"Yeah, but don't get the 'Hot Italian Sausage' dinner unless you really like it HOT," said Carl with a wide-eyed expression.

"Oh my God, yes," laughed Tony, recalling the scene. "You should have seen him the first night out trying to get this stuff down. His eyes were as red as a stop sign, and he had tears running down his face."

"It wasn't that bad," argued Carl. "But I will admit it was very hot."

"It wasn't that bad?" exclaimed Mark incredulously. "You must have swallowed your entire canteen and half of mine trying to get the stuff down. And then you ended up farting half the night!"

"I did not. You're making that up," argued Carl, ready to fully deny this last accusation.

"I am not," said Mark, returning to the attack. "After you fell asleep, you had the entire lean-to filled up with explosive methane gas. Tony and I jumped out of our sleeping bags to put out the campfire, since we didn't want you to cause a major explosion way back here in the woods and blow up the lean-to!"

The laughter grew along with the merriment until Tony and Mark decided that their companion had suffered enough, after which the conversation returned to more conventional topics. It's always fun swapping tales around the evening fire.

Once our visitors returned to their tents, we sat around for a few more minutes before turning in ourselves. The night was cold, which meant that there would be no bugs and the sleeping bags would remain zipped shut. We were awakened only when the loons decided to put on their nightly chorus.

The next morning was one of those times when the frost clings to the leaves on the ground like frosting on a thin wafer. The air was nippy and sent a chill quickly through my body, which served to expedite my dressing process exponentially. I hopped into my pants and laced my shoes quickly en route to the fireplace, where I was able to find enough glowing embers remaining from the previous evening to quickly ignite a small fire. This wasn't a cooking fire, and it wouldn't require much fuel. Instead, I'd rather refer to it as an "old man's fire," with the sole purpose of providing a little bit of heat to neutralize the glacial air. I was just plain cold.

The fire had only been crackling for a few minutes before Casey joined me in front of the stone fireplace, with both of us rubbing our hands together over the flames to get our joints working. Gino, of course, was still in his sleeping bag, oblivious to the activity surrounding him. At his age, he simply needed the sleep more than the heat.

On the agenda for the day was a trip down Cedar Lakes to find the cave of French Louie. It was (and remains today) a legendary landmark of the territory, but one that many people are unable to find. It really isn't tough to locate, being situated in a very recognizable outcropping of stone. Yet more often than not, hikers leave without ever setting foot in its entrance. The plan was for Casey and Gino to head out with their daypacks while I held down the fort at the lean-to. By this point, my fleece slippers and I were way too comfortable for a day hike.

The word "cave" is actually a poor description for the formation, which is simply a square room formed by a large plate of rock that fell on top of a few vertical walls during some prehistoric upheaval. The result is an extremely regularly-formed room that has been utilized by many trappers and hunters over the years as a temporary shelter. At one time, it even contained a wooden bed frame, although I don't know if that feature remains there today. French Louie himself used this natural shelter as a stopover point when caught between lakes at night, as do local fishermen to this day.

Although I worked in these woods for three years, I seldom had time to do much exploring off the beaten path, so I had only visited the cave once during my tenure as a ranger. I did my best to explain to Casey and Gino where they could locate the geologic formation, including the direction of approach. My memory wasn't clear on this subject, but I thought I could get them there.

"Once you walk past the end of Cedar Lake #3, you will start to see an elevated formation of gray stone rising up on your right, which is to your north and slightly west," I explained. "It's only a hundred yards at most from the trail to the rock. Once you are over there, detour to the right and follow the contour of the rock around the base until you find yourself standing at the entrance of the cave. It's not very big and it shouldn't take you long."

As I spoke, I truly hoped that I was providing accurate directions, as it had been over thirty years since my last visit, of which I remembered little. But I spoke with confidence that, at worst, they would not find the cave but also not get lost in the woods. That would be difficult to do in the location I'd described. Still, I felt some misgivings at not accompanying them on their journey.

Over the course of the next hour, the air warmed a bit, but the sun never made an appearance. Instead, the gray skies remained in place under a heavy cloud cover that threatened to release a downpour on short notice. I was more than happy to remain in place, comforting myself in the thought that I was performing a valuable function by maintaining our "reservation" in the lean-to for the following night. Why of course... yes! That's exactly what I needed to do that day.

Gino and Casey took off about the same time as the other group of three hikers, with my companions heading west while the latter dispersed to the east. Left alone to myself, I simply decided to gather wood and get it under the roof before any rain commenced for the day. Within an hour's time I was able to collect a respectable pile of wood and tinder, which I stowed beneath the overhanging shingles of our lean-to. I still can't explain the simple joy I experience in collecting firewood for a campsite. I look forward to the activity so much that I cannot honestly refer to it as a chore.

After finishing this task, I took a stroll down to the lakeshore, which is only about thirty yards down the slope from the lean-to. It looks quite a bit different than it did three decades ago. The dam had washed out many years ago and never been replaced, and the resulting waterline was now several feet lower than in the past. Many areas that were previously submerged are now dry land, which has changed the topography of parts of the lake. Across the expanse of water from Beaver Pond lay the remnants of Noisy Inlet, which used to be navigable by canoe but now boasts only a dried mud flat bisected by a thin trickle of water. I often wonder how many trout have been lost to the lake due to its reduced depth and volume.

While I was spending some time rebuilding the fireplace (which is always in a state of disrepair), I noticed a couple of friendly chipmunks who were busy observing my work around the lean-to. I like chipmunks; I can't help it. They weren't completely tame, as they still appeared skittish as they approached me from across the clearing. But they did approach me, which I enjoyed. I opened my bear-proof food vault and extracted my bag of GORP, which was full of almost everything I could find in the snack-food section of my local supermarket. It was a junk-foodie gourmet treat in a bag.

The first couple trips, the small creatures were quite reluctant to approach my feet, which is where I deposited the goodies for their reward. However, within a few minutes they became much bolder as they became used to being in close proximity with my body. They seemed to favor the cashews and peanuts, jockeying between themselves for the biggest and best pieces. I got a good laugh out of their attempts to stuff the banana chips into their pouch-like mouths, as the large and elongated shapes stretched the walls of their cheeks out to comical proportions. I also quickly decided that chipmunks are smarter than people in their culinary preferences, as they appeared to reject the candy corns for other more natural and healthy selections.

On their first visit to "Larry's Wilderness Diner," the chipmunks nibbled on a few of the nuts rather than carrying them immediately back to their nests. However, this soon changed, and my furry friends reverted to filling their cheeks and immediately disappearing across the clearing to dump their goods at home. They repeated this process time and time again until about thirty minutes later, which is when I noticed that my supply had been reduced by about a third. At this time, I decided to close the restaurant in order to preserve my dwindling stock for the remainder of the trip. The chipmunks stayed with me for a short period of time, nosing about for additional treats before realizing that I had suddenly turned stingy, after which they vanished to their lairs to inspect their newly-acquired stockpiles. (Talk about being fair-weather friends!)

Over the course of the next hour, I completed a number of chores around the lean-to such as breaking up the rest of the wood, filling all the canteens, and neatening up the site. As I worked, I noticed that the clouds had thickened even more, and a fine mist of rain began filtering through the trees. This slowly intensified until it became a gentle shower, which was rather unpleasant due to the cold temperatures. I wouldn't have wanted to be spending time on the trail that day, as the combination of cold and wet can have a rather nasty outcome. Having completed my chores, I hopped back into the lean-to and retrieved my writing pad from my pack. True to my expectations, it wasn't long before Casey and Gino came rambling back up the path and joined me in the shelter.

"We weren't able to find the cave," Casey reported, getting right to the point. "We looked around for about twenty minutes or so, but then it started raining and we decided to postpone the hunt for another time."

"Did you find the outcropping at the end of the lake?" I asked. "Once you start circling around that formation, it's not too tough to find."

"Yeah, I know," said Casey ruefully. "But I think we'll wait until the weather is a little better before trying it again."

During the course of the next few hours, the weather remained fairly constant, with the mist drifting down and the skies maintaining their hazy, gray hue. With little else to do, Gino decided to continue his battle with the log, which was still sitting at rest near the stump on the right side of the lean-to. Retrieving the battered old saw, he returned to the attack with renewed vigor. Rarely have I witnessed such energy expended by anyone in this pursuit. Gino's right arm drove forward and backward, over and over and over again, as he tried to deepen the cut. However, the dull edge of the cutting device never seemed to make progress, and the blade still hadn't reached the center rings of the timber.

Gino was getting frustrated and upset, struggling with each movement. It was getting personal. Before long, the saw became "wood bound" in the log, meaning that it was stuck and could not be moved against the grain at all. I observed silently, wondering just how many others before him had made futile attempts at cutting this very same limb.

Gino's next move reflected even more desperation. He moved the branch back to the same stump, adjusting it so that the cut was about six inches above the ground and about eighteen inches from the flattened surface of the stump. I thought he was going to try stomping on the exposed length with his heavy hiking sole, but I was wrong. Instead, he launched himself high off the ground, landing with a double kick onto the top of the log. It was an impressive combination samurai-kung fu move that looked as though it would have served to penetrate through a thick layer of concrete. I was aware that, had I tried the same maneuver, I would have snapped every bone from my hip down to my ankle and ended up in traction for about a month. But Gino seemed to find the move natural, and he repeated it a number of times, regardless of warnings from his father. Even under the continued heavy assault with the saw and the leg kicks, however, the log still resisted breaking. Gino's resolve had yet to falter; he quit for the time being, but insisted the battle wasn't over.

The rest of the day was pretty uneventful. I took another stroll back along the old spring trail, which is the path that hikers see branching off to the right as they pass the lean-to spur trail when hiking west from the Beaver Pond Bridge. The spring is almost two hundred yards down the trail, which runs directly into the spot where the spring pipe used to sit. Below this rests a pool filled with what was always the best drinking water around. So pure was the spring's output that I used to fill my canteen right from that pristine pool of water without bothering to hold it under the flow of the pipe. But today I noticed that the supply has been reduced significantly from the old days. The flow just isn't what it used to be, with barely a drip leaking from the crack in the rocks, and a shallow film of brackish fluid sits on top of the mud. There was no way I'd trust that water for consumption unless under the most desperate circumstances. It's probably still good to drink, but only after adequate filtering, and there was barely enough fluid in the pool to submerge the filtering device. Very sad.

Continuing past the spring, I strode into the woods beyond the path's terminus, enjoying the feel of finding my own way through the woods that surround Cedar Lake's northern extension. Several camps used to populate the land around Beaver Pond, although that was long before my earliest days as a ranger. I'd heard stories about some of these primitive buildings, although I was never able to locate any of their structural remains even back in the 1970s.

After my exploration, I returned to the lean-to, carrying a small load of additional firewood for the evening. No one had joined us this second night, so we prepared to cook dinner and spend the evening by ourselves. I lay down for a few minutes, resting on my sleeping bag and enjoying the comfort of its soft filling. And I suppose that I enjoyed it a bit more than I expected, as I drifted unknowingly into a quiet, restful, blissful slumber.

Crack!!!

The sound was an ear-piercing, penetrating blast that made me wonder whether one of my shelter mates had carried in left-over fireworks from the Fourth of July.

"Yes!" cried Gino, his voice proclaiming success. But success in what endeavor, I wondered. I sat upright and peered out from the lean-to to see our young accomplice holding up a piece of wood, about two feet in length, with a freshly cut (but still soggy-looking) end.

"Got it!" he cried triumphantly. "This will burn for a long time tonight, a lot longer than all that small stuff you've been collecting."

Remaining silent, I eyed the length of wood suspiciously. While I was impressed by the amount of sheer force and labor required to obtain this piece of wood (which in my estimation was less than one percent of a face cord of firewood), I was seriously doubtful that it would ignite unless subjected to the most intense heat, and even then only marginally. My years of experience in the woods has taught me that old, waterlogged limbs such as this often sap as much heat from a fire as they contribute and simply aren't worth the effort to collect and process.

Over the course of the next few hours, we prepared our meals, stoked the evening fire, and did a bit of organizing for the next day's hike out of the woods. We chatted as we worked, exchanging thoughts on our visit and the changes we'd seen since our previous excursions into the West Canadas. One of the things I mentioned was the passing of Barb Remias, the wife of John Remias, the caretaker at West Lake. John had been my companion and mentor throughout my three-year tenure in the woods, and I had missed him ever since he passed away about thirty years earlier. John had brought Barb back into the woods several times a year, and I always enjoyed her company and her caring demeanor. They had raised a family of three talented and devoted daughters, each of whom held positions with the Department of Environmental Conservation in and around the West Canada Lakes. Barb had passed away quite unexpectedly since my last visit, and I always regretted not stopping by to visit one last time. But hindsight is always 20-20; now all I can do is recall my fond memories whenever I pass their clearing in the woods, which is now reverting to its original state of wilderness.

The night was cold and clear, and we were treated to the best-ever orchestra of loon calls from up and down the lake. I know this sounds impossible, but I am convinced that I always hear the best loon concerts on nights prior to my departure from the woods. On this particular night, at least three separate sessions were presented at various proximities along the body of water from the dam to the narrows of second and third Cedar Lakes. All the familiar loon shrieks and cries were incorporated into the performance, with other members of the species responding from different locations on the water. I awoke with the first tones of each concerto, my ears tuned to enjoy the soulful calls as they reverberated over the misty surface of the lake. I smiled to myself, happy to be here in one of the most beautiful and secluded regions of the Adirondacks.

We broke camp the following morning immediately after breakfast. We had a few hours of hiking followed by a five-hour drive, so we didn't linger once our packing was complete. Casey and I quickly surveyed the campsite to ensure that we weren't leaving anything behind, either personal property or trash of any kind. We then departed on the trail back to the parking lot.

The only sign of our three days at the site was the single length of Gino's sawed log, which had ultimately survived the previous evening's campfire unmarred and now rested in its near-virgin state in back of the ashes in the fireplace. My guess is that it still resides there today.

—9—

The Stroll Home

The hike back out to the car had the same traditional feel as any march out of the woods. Your time is up, and the calendar says that you've got to get back to work. Or home. Or appointments. Or, well, fill in the blank with whatever you desire. Regardless, you can't stay any longer, and it's time to head home. It never feels good, regardless of how wet or hungry or bug-bitten you've become over your length of stay. When it comes time to leave, you always want to stay.

We headed down the half mile of Northville-Placid Trail that flanks the northwestern side of Cedar Lakes, the early morning sun illuminating the path with darting rays of sunlight that turned each leaf and blade of grass into a sparkling crystal ornament. It wasn't so cold as to require us to wear outer garments, as long as we kept on the move. So hustle we did, at least until we arrived at the site of the original lean-to, which was within a couple hundred yards of the dam. There, we encountered a hiking party that needed some assistance with directions and recommendations. Casey was more than happy to oblige, and he stepped in to provide some sage advice.

I know that I should have joined the conversation because I was more knowledgeable about the exact details and distances from point-to-point within the territory. But I had already walked about fifty yards beyond the intersection where Casey was chatting, and I found myself itching to get on down the trail. Finally, after a few minutes of pacing, I hollered back that I would get a head start, as I was anxious to keep up with the others and not hold anyone back. I motored on down the trail, looking back only once when I stopped to sign the trail register at the site of the old dam. As far as I could see, neither Casey nor Gino had disengaged from their conversation, so I was on my own.

Without the additional load of my food or other expendables, I was able to make good speed over the next three miles, arriving at the crossing of Grassy Brook within about eighty minutes. Nothing slowed my progress, and I traversed the balance beam stringers and the wobbly first crossing of Grassy Brook (with the tilting bridge) without difficulty. I even tiptoed across the angled, wobbly stones of the second Grassy Brook crossing in fine fashion, avoiding a cold dunk in the creek. My final ascent of the back side of Blue Ridge (still affectionately known as Sonofabitch Hill) was also uneventful, although that climb is less than a quarter mile and can be performed without undue stress by most folks regardless of their condition.

I had been at the crest of Blue Ridge (where the French Louie Trail branches off to Pillsbury Lake) for less than ten minutes when my two companions caught up with me, looking a bit worse than I. Gino had taken a bit of a spill crossing the short bridge below the Cedar Lakes outlet and had been gouged by the pointy end of an exposed nail. Not good, but certainly not a game-ender either. I found myself wondering how he of all people had managed to fall at that intersection when both of us senior citizens had avoided a similar fate. My guess was that he was not paying attention, or he had crossed without using any handholds or some other bit of carelessness. Regardless, it was a minor injury that would cause him no harm, so we continued on our final mile of the trek together.

At the parking lot, we removed our backpacks and exchanged high-fives, happy to be back and ready for our customary post-venture breakfast. A few other hiking parties were arriving to begin their trips, so of course we asked them to take a couple photographs of our trio as mementos of our expedition. Casey was already talking about the following year and his ideas on where to go and what to do. But never mind; I had my own thoughts on the matter. I was already planning a solo adventure into these same woods, but one of much greater scope that would test my mettle as never before. I would share this concept with Casey when I was ready. In the interim, however, I wanted to savor it for myself for a while, taking time to plan and antic-ipate my every move. It would be a challenge for someone my age, but I felt up to it.

Little did I know how many unplanned events and mishaps I'd encounter that would turn the dream into a nightmare.

The Nightmare—2015

—10—

Ill-Prepared Dreams

I suppose I'm like most people in that I don't enjoy talking about my failures. For the most part, I've been able to accomplish almost everything I've set out to do in life, especially in my more mature years. However, my most recent venture into the woods, which was to fulfill a "bucket list" dream, was not one of my more successful voyages.

I've always had a dream of going into the woods and finding my own piece of wilderness, far away from not only the roads and cities, but also from the trails themselves. I've longed to establish my own encampment, to build my own settlement and live in total seclusion, if only for a couple weeks. It would be somewhere totally removed from everything, where there would be a zero percent chance of encountering anyone, even if I was to remain for a century of more.

I cannot say just how long I've had this vision, but I've pictured the site in my mind for years. It would have a nice snug lean-to with an elevated log cot and enough protection to shield my wood pile, with extra space for my belongings and perhaps a guest, although the guest would impede on my quest for solitude. A stone fireplace with a rock base (to prevent starting a ground fire) would sit immediately in front of the lean-to, and perhaps some roughly-fashioned stools and tables would adorn the outside. I would build this site within eyesight of a lake, although I would comply with the regulations and keep it one hundred fifty feet from the waterline. I'd also want to keep it out of view of anyone either hiking or camping on the other side of the lake or stream, to preserve my own peace and solitude.

Although I had thought about the expedition for years, I didn't tackle the mission until 2015. Then, at the tender age of fifty-nine, I set out to literally go where no man had gone before. (That's not entirely true, as these entire woods were logged at least once, so there are no genuine plots of "virgin wilderness" left to be explored.) But the allure of the trek was overwhelming, and I found myself planning the entire trip throughout the winter of 2014-15. It was something that I had to do, and the vision crowded everything else from my mind.

There were problems with my planned adventure that I knew beforehand but chose to ignore. My desire to undertake this excursion overcame my normal common sense. The first of the obstacles was the sheer amount of supplies and tools I would have to carry into the woods. Food for two weeks alone is a load, even when much of it is dehydrated. A shovel and axe and saw would contribute their share of the weight, and the various tarps and lines I'd need to waterproof my lean-to pushed the needle on the scale even higher. I should have put it all together in one place and weighed it ahead of time, but I was afraid to know the total sum.

Physical space was also an issue, as my pack has become "bulked out" with items I never carried as a ranger, such as a bear container for food. Since there had never been a bear problem in the West Canada Lakes, I'd never needed one, but I do carry one now (although I'm still convinced it will only be needed to keep out mice).

I addition to the weight issue, I was leery about the state of my health. I knew I was out of shape, which I should have addressed earlier in the year. However, there was something else that I could not pinpoint, and it was disconcerting. For at least three years leading up to the summer of 2015, I had experienced an unusual sensation in my right side, about halfway up my abdomen. It was never much of a bother, and it didn't hurt under most circumstances. However, there were many times when something bumped into me at that spot, perhaps a screen door swinging into my side or brushing against a car door handle, and caused me undue pain. I often thought, "That shouldn't have hurt as much as it did." But nothing ever came of it, and my physical exams never hinted at anything out of the ordinary.

There would be other considerations leading up to this trip that I had never before addressed. Since I would be camping in the same spot for two weeks, I would need a camping permit. I contacted the ranger of the West Canada Lakes, Dave Kallen, who jotted down some notes on the location of my expected campsite. He wanted to get the exact coordinates for my lean-to, as he needed to be able to check up on the distance from water and other requirements for campsites in the Adirondacks. I must admit that it felt a bit different being on the other side of the equation—I was used to being the one checking other people for compliance, not vice versa. Regardless, I was now a "civilian" camper and this was part of the process, so I filled out the application and submitted it as required.

Part of my problem in providing the exact coordinates was that I really didn't know the precise location of my site. I could give the latitude and longitude right down to the square foot, but what happened if the site was uninhabitable? What if there was a forty-degree pitch to the land, or if it was submerged by six inches of water? So I did my best to approximate, based on the topographic maps available and any satellite images I could pull off the Internet. But I really didn't want to be nailed down to a specific set of coordinates. Anywhere within a few hundred feet should be fine, right?

The area I selected for my hermitage was on Cedar Lakes, in a spot between the second and third main bodies of water. Following the shoreline from the Beaver Pond lean-to, the waters narrow several times en route to the third lake. It was at the last of these narrows that I planned to build Seymourville. It looked to be fairly flat, with clear access to the water and a great view in either direction. The heavily-wooded area should have at least a few open clearings, from which I would select the location of my lean-to. I also hoped that the areas of thick forestation would provide a nice mix of downed hardwood and softwood material I could use to build my structure without undue travel for construction material.

Looking at the satellite images, I could imagine most of the voyage from the nearest lean-to. The plan was to hike in to Beaver Pond lean-to the first day, then strike out through the woods on day two. I wouldn't have far to go; it was actually less than a mile from the lean-to to my declared campsite. The topographic lines on the USGS map were close together on the side of the hill between the lakeside and the top of the ridge where the Northville-Placid Trail lay. The bottom of that ridge, closest to the water, looked fairly easy to traverse. In fact, I had stumbled around that area often during my days as a ranger, and the area near the lean-to was relatively open with little undergrowth. Yet the majority of the route to my final destination was an unknown, and I was quite cognizant of the fact that the make-up of a forest can change in a blink of an eye. At one point, the woods are wide-open, with easy footing and visibility of a quarter mile. Then, suddenly, it all changes to a tangled thicket of intertwined softwood and undergrowth that is simply impassable. It can and does happen, and I'd only know whether it had when I got there.

The final few months leading up to my voyage seemed to fly by. Supplies mounted in an ever-increasing pile, and all the while I felt the pain in my side become more and more pronounced. There is no doubt that I was living in denial at this point. The discomfort still wasn't enough to cause me to consider postponing the trip, but it was enough that I should have sought specialized testing.

The date for my anticipated launch was July 11, with a return set for July 23. I checked into a hotel in Utica on the night of Friday, July 10, to get a decent night's rest before a three-thirty wakeup, as I wanted to be at the trailhead and commencing my hike at six. Most of my pack was already together, although there were large parcels that I couldn't fit inside. They would have to be tied onto the top or back of my pack for the walk in. This was alarming, as I had never had to do this. As a matter of fact, one sign of inexperienced hikers is often the ragtag assortment of stuff dangling from the outside of their packs, so I was still hoping that I'd be able to cram most of the overflow equipment into one compartment or another at the trailhead.

Three-thirty came all too quickly that morning. To save time, I passed through an all-night McDonald's in order to eat as I drove. I had rented an all-wheel drive SUV in order to avoid hiking from Sled Harbor, and I thanked myself for that decision the entire drive up to the Pillsbury Mountain trailhead. I knew the pack would be excessively heavy, so every step I could save would be worth its weight in gold—and steps leading uphill were worth twice that amount.

By the time I reached the trailhead at the base of Pillsbury Mountain, the sky was getting pretty light. I would be able to start on the trail whenever I completed the process of assembling my pack. And that was quite a task. The bear container and day food (breakfasts and lunches) filled up the main compartment of my pack. I stuffed my extra underwear and socks in with my sleeping bag and the stove and extra fuel tanks in the side pockets, and I crammed the rain gear, tarps for shelter, water filtration kit, et cetera, around it all. I also had the standard emergency equipment, including a full first aid kit and everything else I'd need for two weeks of living in the woods. Meanwhile the saw, axe, shovel, and grill were tied onto the outside equipment loops. Just what I needed!

There is one piece of equipment that I shoved into my pack under duress, and that was a satellite phone. This device is sort of like a cell phone on steroids; it will work from anyplace in the world where you can see a mostly clear sky overhead. (Thick tree cover will impede its use.) Since cell phones are useless due to the surrounding mountains, I had assumed that I'd be completely out of touch for those two weeks. However, the constant urgings of my entire family finally broke down my resistance, and I rented one of these expensive devices that would provide what I'd hoped to avoid in the first place, which was a connection to civilization. If there's one thing I've learned in my sixty-plus years on this planet, it's that no matter how old you get, mothers and wives still get their way.

After about an hour of pushing, shoving, and knot-tying, I was finally ready to mount up and hit the trail. I stood the pack up on the rear door of the SUV, using it as a platform from which I could slide into the shoulder straps without having to heave it up from the ground. That proved to be a good choice, for as soon as I had the thing on my shoulders I realized the insanity of my plan. Being a former competitive power lifter, I was pretty accurate when it came to estimating weights, and my guess was that I was carrying about one hundred pounds, no exaggeration. I knew for a fact that it was much heavier than the sixty-pound pack I usually hoist, and I wondered about my ability to transport it all the way in to my campsite.

To this day, I thank my lucky stars that the ascent of Blue Ridge (aka Sonofabitch Hill) came within the first mile of my hike, or I doubt that I would have gone on. My steps came in measured counts; I'd go up for a tenth of a mile, and then take a breather; then another tenth of a mile, and another stop. It probably took me an hour to reach the top of the ridge where the Pillsbury Lake (French Louie) Trail branches off to the left. But at least I made it, and I gratefully started my descent to the crossing of Grassy Brook.

A further indignation came about thirty minutes later, as I was entering some of the more wooded lengths of trail en route to the Cedar Lakes Dam. I was strolling along, pleased at myself for my progress, when I heard a sound behind me on the trail. I turned around to find that I had been overtaken—by two senior citizens carrying a canoe! Well, it doesn't get much more embarrassing than that, and I stopped to say hello. (Actually, the real reason I stopped was to give them an excuse for passing me while I wasn't still moving.)

Realizing the absurdity of the situation, I stepped to the side of the trail as the two gentlemen approached.

"Well good afternoon!" I called in salutation. "Nice to see someone else out here that can match my fifty-nine-year-old bones."

"Fifty-nine?" replied the hiker in the lead. "You're literally a babe in the woods. I'm seventy-two!"

"And I'm not quite that old, but I did turn sixty-five last month," volunteered his partner, who was carrying the back end of the canoe. "I do have a hard time keeping up with this guy," he added as he nodded to his accomplice.

They stopped to chat for a short period of time, and it turned out the older man had also worked for the Department of Environmental Conservation for a number of years. I had to find out a little more about this duo, as I seldom encountered folks willing to transport such an unwieldy item as a canoe into the woods.

"Oh, we've been coming back in here for many years, doing a little fishing and a little camping," said the older gentleman. "It really depends on how the fish are biting. A lot of times we fish for the day and then carry the boat back out of the woods before it gets dark."

"Why don't you just stash the boat in a hidden spot for the summer so you don't have to lug it in and out each time?" I asked.

The older hiker scratched his chin and replied with a forlorn expression. "Well, we used to do that many years ago. But it's tough to get away with these days because the brand of hikers has gone downhill over the last twenty or thirty years. These days, if some young kid finds your boat stashed in the bushes somewhere, he's bound to take a hatchet to it and rip the bottom out. Either that or he'll take it for a ride and leave it someplace else on the lake where you'll never find it again. It's just not worth it."

As he spoke, his friend remained quiet but nodded his concurrence. And I agreed—it's a shame, but things just aren't the way they used to be a long time ago.

"Did you know John Remias, the caretaker on West Lake?" I asked.

"Yeah, of course I knew John," he replied. "But I knew him back when he had the caretaker's cabin up here on Cedar Lakes."

"That was before my time by a few years," I said. "I wish I'd seen it at least once. It looked like such a beautiful place."

"They were all beautiful. The people working for the State who made the decision to burn them all out were out of their minds. But then again, I only worked there; I can't say that I often agreed with them."

Listening to him talking about the politics of the Adirondacks, I felt like I'd never left. The discord between the local population of the Adirondacks and the State's policies appears to be just as strong today as it was forty years ago, and I could sense the frustration in these old-timers' voices.

After a brief chat, we said our goodbyes and the two of them started back down the trail. There were one or two stream crossings when I caught back up to them as they needed to re-configure their carrying device in order to ford the waters with the canoe. But it wasn't long before they'd put enough distance between us that I lost all contact with everything but their footprints. My only comfort came from reminding myself that I was carrying a one-hundred-pound pack, and all they had was a light canoe and a couple of daypacks.

At least that's what I told myself, but it wasn't much consolation.

—11—

Checking Out Early

July 11, 2015:

I hadn't counted on staying at the first lean-to on Cedar Lakes my first night, but that was as far as my legs would take me. By the time I arrived at the bridge over the Cedar River below the wreck of the old dam, I knew I'd go no farther. My calves were cramping up with each step, and I felt pain even going up the few feet of rise from the bridge to the junction with the Northville-Placid Trail. I signed in at the booth, and then limped the remaining distance to the lean-to. Thankfully it was empty.

After gratefully relieving myself of the weight of my pack, I immediately spread my sleeping pad and bag on the floor of the lean-to and was asleep within a matter of minutes. I cannot say just how long I was out, but it seemed like mid-afternoon by the time I raised myself to a sitting position. Given the way I felt, it would have been very natural to just remain reclined for the rest of the day, but I knew there was work to be done. There was wood to be gathered and water to be filtered, plus other bits of lean-to and gear maintenance. And so I set about levering myself up and out of the shelter, all the while creaking from every joint and bone in my body. I just hadn't counted on feeling so run down after a few short hours on the trail.

I was about to start feeling sorry for myself when I detected the sound of footsteps approaching from behind the lean-to. These were followed by the appearance of a pair of male hikers, on the younger side of middle-aged, who briskly strode around the front of my humble abode. They both looked chipper and in good spirits, which was quite welcome in my current mood.

"How are you?" the first one ventured, nodding in my direction. "Nice day to be in the woods."

"It sure is," I replied, repressing my opinion that I felt pretty darn beat up. I don't think I even had to volunteer that information, however, as it was taking me a long time to take even the shortest steps. My muscles were tightening up, reminding me that I needed to stretch.

"Are you by yourself in here?" asked the same hiker, nodding to the inside of the lean-to.

"Yes," I laughed, "although I'm sure that it looks like there's enough gear here for a party of six. I got carried away with the packing process and tried carrying in half the stock of an L.L.Bean store."

The two gentlemen got a chuckle out of that. They introduced themselves as Josh and Jason, from the town of Trumansburg on the eastern shoreline of Cayuga Lake, one of the state's more scenic Finger Lakes.

"It's pretty down there, but nothing compared to the Adirondacks," said Jason as he removed his pack. "Josh and I have been coming up here for years; each trip we try to find someplace nice where we've never explored. This is exceptional."

"It is," I agreed. "I used to live back in here for a few years, way back in the 1970s."

That comment drew a lot of interest, so I explained to them how I used to patrol the trails from April through September, basically getting paid to camp and backpack in the prettiest wilderness area of the state's prettiest park. It's a concept that leaves most people wishing they could have done the same.

"Did you used to have to tote all that gear around with you?" asked Josh. "It seems a bit excessive, if you ask me." As he spoke, he eyed my pile that included the saw, shovel, axe, and other implements of destruction.

"Ha; no way," I countered. "I was a lot smarter back then and only carried what I needed. This stuff is all part of my devious plan to set up a place to stay for a week or two. I always wanted a place of my own back here, and now I'm going to build one."

"You're going to what?" cried Jason, not believing what he'd just heard.

"Yeah, I've always wanted to do this," I explained. "It's not like I just hatched the idea yesterday. I've actually wanted to build something like this for a long, long time."

This time the quiet interlude lasted even longer as they both considered the scope of my plan. It was Josh who broke the silence.

"Well, it sounds interesting, although I'm not sure I'd want to tackle a job that size by myself. But it sure does sound peaceful. I bet you won't see a single person as long as you're back there."

I agreed with him that I most certainly wouldn't, and that this was the lion's share of my intent—peace, quiet, solitude, and the opportunity to construct a "village" of my very own.

As we spoke, I detected a few more glances from the two men into the interior of the lean-to. "Hey, do you folks want to crash here for the night?" I asked. "There's plenty of space, and I'd enjoy the company."

"We wouldn't want to intrude."

"No, really," I offered again. "Most of the lean-to is empty."

"Thanks anyway, but I'll sleep in the tree."

"Huh?" I grunted in reply. I couldn't have heard that correctly.

Josh smiled and nodded in the direction of his backpack. "We've both become quite used to sleeping in hammocks, which are really comfortable and can be set up almost anyplace. We'll probably head down closer to the lake after dinner and find a place to set up there."

OK, that was one I'd never heard of before. But nothing surprised me anymore. Old traditions and equipment were being replaced by a flood of new ideas and products on an ever-accelerating pace. Everything was newer, faster, higher-tech, and made of space-age materials. I myself had carried my cell phone into the woods that week, not to make telephone calls but to take advantage of the ability to shoot some pictures. It was indeed a new world, and these two modern hikers were certainly born into a different generation.

Interestingly enough, I had also packed in my new, lightweight digital camera, complete with a data card that could store literally thousands of photographs. I smiled as I thought back to the antique I had attempted to lug through the wilderness decades earlier. It was bulkier and heavier and could only capture fuzzy, low-resolution shots for printing out on rectangles of rapidly-fading photo paper. There was no doubt that newer was better in the photo world.

Jason and Josh stuck around the lean-to long enough to cook their dinners, which they consumed as I worked to clean my pot from my own evening meal.

"After we eat, we'll go out and collect some wood for you," Josh said.

"Thanks, but you don't have to do that," I answered, measuring the size of my own wood pile and calculating its longevity for an evening blaze.

"That's OK" answered Jason. "Well come up and join you for your evening fire. This way you'll have enough to last for a few hours."

"Great!" I exclaimed. "Campfires are always better when you've got a decent-sized group of storytellers."

"Oh, you've picked the right people for that," smiled Jason. "Josh has at least one story for every occasion." I wasn't going to say anything about that declaration, as most people say that I fit into precisely the same category.

True to their word, Josh and Jason cleaned up their dinnerware and then set out to bring in some firewood. And what a load it was. After breaking it down into fireplace-sized pieces, the pile was about four feet tall. It would be some fire.

Once the two men lifted their packs and headed down to the lake, I was surprised by the late arrival of yet another group. This one was younger than the duo from Trumansburg and consisted of two women and one man. (Or perhaps I should say two girls and a boy, as I doubt any of them were out of their teens.) They didn't really stop, but only stepped in front of the lean-to long enough to survey the grounds. Once again I tried to be hospitable and offered them room inside my shelter. Their answer came much more readily than that of the first group.

"No, that's OK. We all have hammocks with us, so we'll just find some trees and get ourselves rigged for the night."

You've got to be kidding me! I know that coincidences are bound to happen, and I believe that events both good and bad tend to arrive in bunches. But this was strange indeed! I had never heard of campers sleeping in hammocks strung up above the ground, and now suddenly there were two groups within the span of a couple hours. I could just picture the jousting for prime tree sites along the shoreline. In my day you looked for a clearing in the trees, hopefully with a fire ring already in place.

As I sat there pondering this odd turn of events, I decided that I was in the mood for a cup of tea, which is my drink of choice in the woods. The small fire I had used to heat my dinner had already died down, and I didn't want to dig into the supply we'd collected for later that evening, so I unzipped the pocket of my pack containing my trusty old Svea stove and removed it from its stuff sack. I was carrying two full fuel tanks, which I'd hoped would last me the entire two weeks. I seldom used the stove in the woods, as I preferred cooking over wood, but this would just take a minute.

I quickly removed the top of the fuel can and poured a little

white gas into the priming ring on top of the stove. After returning the fuel can to my pack, I applied a lighter to the fuel in
order to build up a bit of heat pressure inside the brass body of
the stove. Nothing happened. The small flame flared for a
moment, and then went out without producing the hissing sound
I was used to hearing. Well, this wasn't good. Next, I used the
key to open the valve to release the pressure, and very little gas
vapor came out. Very unusual; this really was not good. I had
tested this stove just a week earlier inside my garage at home
and it functioned just fine.

I next tried expanding on my efforts to ignite the stove by
pouring a much greater quantity of gas into the priming ring. As
a matter of fact, the ring filled to overflow and beyond and was
dripping fuel down its sides, which glistened in the early evening
sunlight. I prudently moved the stove from the lean-to onto the
rocks of the fireplace due to the amount of flammable liquid
involved. Surely this had to work. I carefully applied the match
to the fuel in the priming ring.

Then all hell broke loose.

An audible "fffwump" sound was issued from the fuel in and
around the base of the stove as the entire assembly was instantly
engulfed in its own miniature fireball. Blue flames shot up from
around and under the brass base tank as every bit of the white
gas caught fire, creating an instant inferno. The flames produced
a significant amount of heat as the seconds rolled by, with the
blaze becoming almost colorless against the gray background of
the fireplace rocks.

I tried turning the release valve to allow some of the pressure
in the tank to escape, but the heat was too great on my hand to
apply any torque on the metal key. Worse yet, the stove was
beginning to produce a series of sputtering noises, and jets of
liquid fuel began spurting from the pressure valve itself, which
was something I had never seen before. The longer I stood watching the phenomenon, the more pronounced it became. The

hissing was getting louder, and fuel was squirting in all directions in a heat and pressure-induced geyser. This was already out of hand and getting worse. The gasket lining the bottom of the fill cap must have decayed along with the deterioration of the pressure valve. That was the only thing I could figure, and I knew it was about to get very bad, very quickly.

I gave up. By the time I grabbed my large water bladder, leaves next to the fireplace were starting to burn, the result of being sprinkled with ignited fuel. I quickly dumped about a gallon of water over the entire stove, much of which gushed down the fireplace rocks and into the ashes of the previous fire. Thankfully nothing else erupted, and the menacing stove was instantly extinguished. For the next few minutes it sat on the rocks, still emanating a high-frequency hissing noise as the excess pressure bled from the bottom storage tank. Then that too fell silent, and the stove slowly began to cool. I knew right then that the old Svea had reached the end of its life; I would never again trust it sufficiently to attempt lighting it for any reason. It would be carried out, drained, and discarded.

But this created a huge problem. Could I (or would I) go the next two weeks relying entirely on wood fires for cooking everything? That could include in the rain, possibly even in a prolonged rain. I wasn't so sure. I definitely preferred cooking over a fire, and there were times in my ranger days when I would exit from the woods with a still-filled gas tank. However, that was then and this was now. The convenience of preparing a meal without the effort of collecting a woodpile was more than appealing; at times (like at the end of a long hike), it was a lifesaver. I vowed to go on, but this was a game changer.

True to expectations, the campfire that night was memorable, as Josh and Jason joined me at the lean-to for tea and more tall tales. I've always found it to be rather an amusing phenomenon that when stories are told around a communal bonfire, no one ever questions anyone else, but instead simply listens while gazing sightlessly into the roaring flames. It's really quite hypnotic, and I've often felt that I could state authoritatively that I was the king of Denmark without anyone challenging my declaration. I've never been able to determine whether people are just being polite, or they're tired, or hypnotized, but that seems to be the code of the campfire.

I stayed up rather late that night, burning through an additional quantity of wood even after Jason and Josh returned to their hammocks. We had offered the other group the opportunity to stop by and share the fire, although they decided to remain down by the waterfront. They appeared to be enjoying themselves, as bursts of laughter pierced the evening air throughout our conversation. And although we could not see them through the thin veil of trees protecting their campsite, we could tell that they had decided to forego a fire of their own, as we would have been able to see the light of the flames if nothing else.

I turned in early, expecting to rise at a decent hour and push off down the trail. My hermitage awaited, silently demanding to be built and to serve as my residence for the next two weeks. It would be a stove-less encampment, but an encampment nonetheless. And since I knew *exactly* the size and shape of the fireplace I would build, the survival of my Svea would be a non-issue. I was sure of it.

—12—

Final Straws

July 12, 2015:

Old age is a miserable thing. It can pick the most inconvenient of times and places to remind you of your years, and there is little or nothing you can do to avoid it. (Perhaps being in better shape would have helped.) But I have often joked that the height of many of the local hills and mountains had doubled since my tenure in the West Canadas, and I was to discover that a similar phenomenon would extend to the wood floor planks in the lean-tos. Perhaps it was the age of the structures, but the wide planking certainly felt harder than it had in my youth. Much harder.

I also learned during that first night at Cedar Lakes that rising up from those same floorboards was much more difficult now than it was thirty years earlier. I couldn't just push up to my knees and bounce to a standing position. Nope. Instead I had to rock myself into a four-point stance, slightly resembling a sprinter about to launch upward with the start of the starter's pistol. Except my "launch" was much less dramatic and sometimes ended with a failed attempt that landed me back on all fours. I was glad there was no one around to observe my futile efforts.

Making matters worse was the fact that I couldn't remain in my sleeping bag for more than a few hours at a time due to a certain old age syndrome. (I won't dwell or expound on that matter. Suffice it to say that men my age often require a number of side trips throughout the nighttime hours.) I truly envied the days of my younger self, when I could zip myself into my sleeping bag at nine and snooze uninterrupted until the sun came out in the morning. That was simply no longer possible. No further explanation is necessary.

It was with some degree of relief that I awoke to a sky that was lightening in the east, and I pulled myself up in order to pack my equipment and get an early start down the lake. After downing a couple sterile-tasting breakfast bars and a few gulps from my canteen, I began the loading process. All was going well until I tried folding my large, one-gallon water bladder. (This was one of the new-fangled bits of gear that didn't exist in my early days. I had brought it into the woods in lieu of the five or six canteens I'd need in order to filter water only once a day.) As I folded the large, flexible container, my fingers caught on some rough material at one of the bottom corners, which puzzled me, as the entire bladder had been very smooth the day before. I examined it closely and found something quite disconcerting. One of the local lean-to mice had chewed the bottom corner of the plastic right through to the inside, rendering it useless. Perhaps if I'd carried a healthy supply of duct tape into the woods, I might have been able to affect a repair. But the closest I had to tape was my supply of Band-Aids, and I knew for a fact that was a non-starter.

Great. I was one day into the woods, half-paralyzed with cramps; I'd lost my ability to cook on a stove, and now I had no way to store significant quantities of filtered water. Things were going south at an astounding pace, and I wondered about my ability to continue with the rest of the trip. I could do it, I felt, although the inconveniences would be multiplied significantly, and I hoped that I wouldn't run into rain that lasted longer than a day or two.

After a brief period of stretching, I headed out onto the trail southwest toward Beaver Pond, which would be my launch point off the trail and the beginning of the bushwhack to my campsite. It was a pretty nice day, and my cramps of the previous day were gone, so my spirits were up at last. Better things were in store, I felt, and I made great time getting down to the Beaver Pond lean-to. From there, I'd have all day to reach my destination (even though I felt that I could get there within an hour or two, even if the brush was very thick).

As I rested at the lean-to, I decided to try out the satellite phone, which I'd neglected to attempt the night before. If nothing else, I could call my family and let them know that I was almost to my site and that all was well. The good news was that the phone performed better than I'd expected. I was able to reach home and hear my wife's voice even though I wasn't standing beneath an "open sky that was clear of all trees and overhanging obstacles." (As the phone company asserted I needed to be.)

That was the good news. The bad news was yet to come.

My wife, my partner for the past forty-plus years, went on to inform me of the death of a very dear friend who had been suffering from cancer for the past several years. He had made several comebacks during that time, and at times it looked as though he would beat it. But it was not to be. He slipped into a coma and passed on within a week. The funeral would be conducted sometime during the coming week.

The news hit me like a ton of bricks. It was as though my entire world was crumbling around me, with one disastrous event coming on the heels of another. My body was not cooperating, two major pieces of gear had been destroyed, and now I'd lost one of my best friends in life. It was the final straw, and I knew I had to leave the woods without even starting my adventure.

One consolation I decided to award myself was a look at the spot I'd selected as the setting for Seymourville. Even though I wouldn't be building a shelter or staying a single night, I just had to get there, if only once. With more gusto than common sense, I began a push through the woods in the direction of my selected coordinates. The going wasn't terribly hard, but it wasn't easy either. I found that I had more trouble with the ups-and-downs of the rocks on the hillside than with the vegetation. I finally decided that I'd make better time if I moved ahead without my pack, which I removed and stashed beside a large yellow birch tree.

Continuing on with only my canteen and a small, belt-mounted ditty bag, I marched through the woods until I arrived at the second narrowing of the waters between second and third Cedar Lakes. It was around noon, and I was here. Finally.

With some degree of wistful disappointment, I looked around the site and was surprised to find much of it looked as I'd expected—fairly flat with a mixed deciduous and coniferous forest, especially moving away from the shoreline and slightly uphill. It was drier than I'd thought, although there was no shortage of mosquitoes and other biting insects. Also, there were fewer downed trees than I'd have desired for building my lean-to, which would have complicated matters had I been able to stay.

I spent about an hour looking around the area, never wandering more than a few hundred feet from my initial arrival point. The purpose was to find a spot that could have been "ground zero" of my settlement—the location of my own personal lean-to. I finally decided on a parcel of ground between two spruce trees, about two hundred feet from the lake. The slope of the land was a bit more graded than I'd have wanted, but it would have sufficed. I moved a few yards further up the hillside and sat down on a downed trunk, just to observe the land and breathe the air.

Failure. It didn't feel good.

After a brief interlude, I walked over to a pile of downed limbs from a dead hardwood and pulled out a sturdy branch that was about twelve feet in length. I carried this over to the two spruce trees that would have served as the supports for the rear wall of my lean-to. Without a conscious thought, I placed the limb between some of the lower notches on the trees, thus erecting a ceremonial crossbar for my shelter.

This act completed, I turned and commenced my walk out of the woods. But I knew I would be back.

—13—

Dark Days

2015-2016:

These next few pages record events that took place completely outside the woods, and they represent some of the lowest times of my life. For that reason, I shall try to keep this section relatively short. However, the misfortunes of 2015 and 2016 were central to my abstinence from all hiking and camping activities, indeed to physical exertion of any kind. For that reason alone, I shall provide an explanation of these unfortunate years.

When I left the woods unwillingly in July, 2015, I was already in a depressed state. Besides sustaining critical equipment failures and the loss of a dear friend, I knew that I was suffering from an unknown physical ailment. As I dropped my insanely heavy backpack to the ground at the trailhead the day I left the woods, I felt the shoulder strap cruelly spin me towards the ground, and my entire front section ached unnaturally. I tried to ignore it, although it just felt horribly wrong. I crawled into the front seat of my vehicle and promptly fell asleep for the rest of the afternoon.

Upon returning to my home in Rochester, I took a day off to attend my friend's funeral and then immediately returned to work. I have a desk job which requires no physical movement of any kind, so I could rest as much as I desired to recover from my physical ordeal. And rest I did, sitting in front of my computer screen without moving a muscle for weeks. However, the more I rested the worse things got. The pain in my side became more pronounced and more intense with each passing week. I went on vacation with my family in August, visiting the Azores islands off the coast of Portugal. For two weeks, I attempted to attenuate the pain with a continuous diet of over-the-counter pain remedies, often combining two or more varieties while doubling the recommended dose of each. I augmented these pills with a wide, elastic compression band, which I wore around my waist to support my abdominals. (This was in case the underlying cause was a hernia or two, which was my belief.)

Nothing helped. I started taking hot showers daily at two or three in the morning, as that provided enough short-term relief for me to fall back asleep, at least for another hour or two. But the end result was always the same. I'd be up by four, rolling onto my right side in an attempt to stop the pain.

The return to New York after the two-week trip was something I welcomed. I would check in at my doctor's office and demand an immediate examination, to be conducted in a hospital by specialists and internists who were trained in this kind of thing. No matter what it took, we would find out the problem and fix it. I couldn't live like this, and the pain kept getting worse.

Over the course of the next few weeks, I underwent multiple rounds of imaging, including ultrasounds, MRIs, and various other procedures that I can't even recall. All the while, I expected the results to indicate a serious hernia (or multiple hernias) that would require extensive surgery. I didn't look forward to the diagnosis, but I had to know.

Finally, while driving home from work one afternoon, I got a call from the physician's office. She didn't beat around the bush. "You have gall stones," she intoned, her voice lacking in any emotion.

"Well, that's good," I replied, relieved that I wasn't suffering from cancer or being ripped in half by hernias. "So what's the next step? How do we get rid of them so I can get back on track?" At this point I was still hoping for a quick fix.

There was a long pause on the other end of the line, and I sensed my physician carefully measuring her words. "You can't get rid of them," she stated. "According to the report, your gall bladder is completely filled with stones, with no chance of clearing them. The only option is surgery to remove the entire organ. It's the only way."

OK, I could accept that. After all, the gall bladder is not a necessary accessory in the human body, so I'd have it removed and then get on with life, right? However, once I spoke to someone at the hospital, I learned that scheduling my surgery was not an immediate priority on everyone's calendar. At first, the hospital just said that "they'd get back to me." I kept waiting for the call, but it never came.

Days turned into weeks, and weeks turned into months. They prescribed some heavier-doses of pain killers, which graduated into oxycodone pills and other prescription remedies that have less than stellar reputations on the secondary market. Then, once I received my surgery date, October 2015, my physician's office played a cruel joke, severely restricting my medications and leaving me writhing in pain while waiting for an operation that was still weeks away. Those were very darks days, and I took them one at a time. I slept on a couch downstairs in our recreation room, as I knew I would have kept my wife awake for hours on end with the grunts and groans I emitted on an ongoing basis.

I'd love to report that the operation to remove my gall bladder solved the problem, but the pain persisted in the weeks and months following the operation. When I reported this to my physician and to the surgeon, they recommended waiting to see if it would get better on its own, which it never did. Another round of imaging early in 2016 determined that a large stone had been retained by my body and remained lodged in a tight location that may have been causing the discomfort. By the end of January, I was back on prescription painkillers, which they soon replaced with fentanyl patches. Although leery of the strength of this drug, I meekly accepted it and tried to move forward with my life, which didn't work well.

In addition to the pain, I found that I was chronically tired. Sitting in a chair offered partial relief, but I was also in need of several naps interspersed throughout the day. On weekends this was no problem; I could simply collapse on the bed or couch whenever necessary. This was harder in the office, where snoozing is not considered a "better business practice," especially for one who snores with as much volume as me. (Co-workers, while empathizing with my condition, were less tolerant than family members at home.)

While returning to the woods was always in the back of my mind, I knew it would not happen in 2016. Casey inquired about a weekend stay at Cedar Lakes, but the thought of even attempting to mount a backpack was unthinkable. Even the feel of a shirt next to my skin was uncomfortable, and the idea of carrying a fifty-pound pack bordered on the absurd. The ever-present patches kept the pain partially in check, but I was never completely comfortable. The summer and fall passed without my engaging in any physical exercise at all. A trip into the woods was a non-starter, an idea that was instantly dead-on-arrival.

It was later in the year, as the leaves were beginning to turn, that I was tested for the potential presence of "bad bacteria," especially in locations that could create problems and cause pain. Although the initial read on the test was negative, a physician's assistant in my internist's office was suspicious of some of my symptoms. She placed me on a high-powered antibiotic for a couple weeks, with some nutritional supplements and general guidance. Miraculously, the pain began to dissipate, ratcheting down in small increments on a daily basis. I didn't make much fuss about it at first, as I'd experienced a couple other temporary reprieves over the past year. However, as day after day passed and I felt less and less discomfort, I quietly began building hope that this would be a final passage to a full recovery.

Weaning myself off the painkillers was another story. Thankfully, I am blessed with a non-addictive makeup, so I experienced no psychological need to continue the drugs now that the pain was almost non-existent. However, I learned quite quickly that you cannot simply go "cold turkey" from a high dosage to zero in one fell swoop, which is what I attempted (without my doctor's supervision). It was a very rough couple days, and I was thankfully rescued by my wife, who had done some research on the correct methods and timeline to safely remove these chemicals from the body. It was a process that would take almost a month, with the risk of seizures and other nasty consequences for those who proceed too aggressively.

Moving into the first days of 2017, I began writing this text in the present tense, as though it was a diary. The pain had completely vanished from my body for the first time in eighteen months, and I awakened each morning to that delightful realization over and over again as though it was a pleasantly reoccurring dream. To anyone who has never lived for a period of time (at least several months) with chronic acute pain, it is difficult to imagine how this phenomenon affects every phase of your life. You rearrange your physical environment to cope with the ordeal even as you alter your lifestyle to handle the pain and stress. Even relationships are strained, although in my case my wife and daughters remained the bedrock of my support. I am truly blessed in having such a wonderful family to stand behind me even when I am not at my best.

The only remnant of the nightmare that has been with me since 2015 is a little tightness across my chest, and even this appears to be fading in intensity as the months go by. I no longer need to take rest breaks throughout the day, and the occasional aspirin is the only pain medication I need.

So what lay ahead? The trails and forests of the West Canada Lakes still beckoned to me with unparalleled allure. Instead of attempting to build Seymourville, I had accepted the fact that my body was not what it used to be; carrying the tools and supplies required to construct such a place was no longer feasible or advisable. My only goal was to get myself back into the woods I loved and become comfortable once again in those surroundings. If I could get myself back to that point, if I could wind the clock back to my pre-2015 self, I would be more than satisfied.

Regardless of the outcome of my next excursion, I felt as though I had already won. The ordeal of the past year and a half had tested me as I'd never been tested, and somehow I made it through. They were the darkest days of my life, but now I was ready to move on.

Moving On—2017

—14—

The Pretext

Before diving into this final section of the book, I'd like to provide some backdrop, an explanation regarding what I was hoping to accomplish in this final extended voyage back into the West Canada Lakes region. This may be difficult because, in a way, I had no real goal in mind for 2017 other than just being in the woods again. I had abandoned my dream of carrying in a one hundred-pound pack and building a lean-to and miniature settlement. That was no longer within my realm of possibilities. But it really didn't matter anymore.

Ever since my earliest post-ranger excursions into the woods, I'd recorded the events of my hiking trips into Cedar Lakes and West Lake, along with my other shorter trips throughout the French Louie loop trails. I wasn't sure that I'd ever have enough to develop a follow-on book to the original trilogy of ranger stories, although many of my readers had encouraged me to do just that.

And so, with a possible fourth book in mind as a secondary goal, I packed up enough supplies to last me for two weeks in the woods. I figured on staying at lean-tos and meeting enough people to provide me with sufficient material to complete that goal. For, as funny as it sounds, camping in solitude makes for great memories, but only being with people can provide great stories. Whether sitting together around a roaring campfire and trading yarns or simply observing fellow lean-to dwellers as they do things in their own amusing ways, it is people that make the best stories, so my plan was to go where the people would be.

The rest of this book is a collection of the stories from my woods travels of the summer of 2017. It is a celebration that I was finally able to return to my favorite place on earth after beating the odds of a serious physical condition, not only once, but twice. For this fact alone I was very grateful, as I had spent many long months doubting my ability to ever return.

My two adventures of 2017 taught me a lot about myself, about my physical capabilities and limitations. I learned that I still had some great strengths remaining within me, but also some greater limitations. My second extended trip of the summer showed me that two friends can push each other to keep going even when the body says "No, I'm done." Meanwhile, those same two friends (presumably of sound mind) can also realize simultaneously that old age had finally overtaken desire, and that their days of extended hikes with heavy packs were now over. Nothing lasts forever, and I was glad that I was able to realize this fact by the end of that second trip and accept it gracefully.

With all this being said, this section of my book is about the two weeks I wandered about on my own in the French Louie loop of the West Canada Lakes area, mainly between Pillsbury Lake, Sampson Lake, and Whitney Lake. The last chapter describes the final four days I spent in an attempt to revert back to the lean-to to lean-to distance hiker of my younger years. And while parts of that voyage felt like a failure due to my physical limitations, I achieved my goal of gathering more stories to tell while perched around the campfire.

I wish that I could go on forever in this manner, spending my cherished time sharing lean-tos and tall tales in front of the glowing embers. But for me, this time is now passed. And so I pass along these few final stories and thoughts to the next generations with the hopes that they will treasure them as have I. Time, as the woods themselves are, is a true gift that needs to be utilized and valued without ever being taken for granted.

Please do this for me, and go in peace.

—15—

The Travelogue

Long before I heard the voices, I felt the footsteps. They were strong, determined footsteps that pounded down the trail toward the lean-to as though they were being delivered with intentional force. "I am here; I have arrived" they screamed, each step accompanied by a Richter-scale-inducing thud that was felt as much as heard.

With a few seconds, a grizzled and gnarled face appeared around the right front post of the lean-to. The gentleman had a lengthy beard that was streaked with white and ended in an unusual pointy shape, perhaps fashioned from the last few hours on the trail. He had inquisitive eyes that instantly scanned both me and the lean-to, sizing up the housing situation. I tried to break the ice before he had a chance to assume that the "No Vacancy" sign was already illuminated.

"Hi there," I chirped in my most friendly tone. "There's only me here if you folks are looking for a place to stay the night."

"Thanks" nodded the leader, sitting down on the front log while dismounting his pack. "We had planned on staying here, but we're probably going to set up our tents if we can find a primitive campsite within a short distance of the lean-to. I might end up staying in here with you though."

As he spoke, more members of the group arrived, including a young girl who appeared to be keeping up with the pace even though saddled with an adult-sized pack. Two other adults also made their way down the trail and into sight, both men in their forties who were bringing up the rear of the formation. They all appeared to be fit and outfitted with the latest gear.

After a brief conversation, I learned they were from Philadelphia, and that this was their first trip into the West Canada Lakes. "We just looked at a map of the Adirondack Park and headed for the place with the least towns and the most woods," one of the men explained. It was a bit of logic I'd heard over and over throughout my years in the woods.

I quickly learned that the three men were brothers (Tim, Eddie, and Mike) who enjoyed each other's company. Throughout the years they had hiked many of the trails in Pennsylvania that were closer to home, and now they were branching out into more distant destinations. The girl was eleven and the daughter of one of the hikers. She was enjoying her experience despite the quarter-sized blister that had formed on the sole of her foot.

"Tenderfoot!" cried Tim, the bearded leader, as he examined the source of her discomfort. "If you'd worn your hiking boots around town for a few days like I recommended, your feet wouldn't be feeling this hike at all."

"It wasn't the boot that gave me the blister," she replied. "It was getting my feet soaked in those huge puddles in the trail back there. My socks are soaked and that started the rubbing." And it was true; the trails were in very rough shape due to numerous days of wet weather that had filled the month of June, so avoiding the standing water along the way was next to impossible. Wet feet were just a part of life along the French Louie Trail.

I must admit, I felt a little sorry for the adolescent, as young as she was. We didn't see many youngsters inside the West Canadas, and I felt that she deserved some praise for even attempting the hike. It reminded me of my own daughter when, at the age of thirteen, she asked to accompany me on a complete loop of the French Louie Trail.

I quickly offered them a pair of scissors and some of my moleskin blister padding, which, as any hiker knows, is a fairly efficient way to cover up even severe blisters. They accepted, although seeming a bit hesitant to accept the bit of assistance.

"Are you sure you won't need it yourself?" asked one of the other adults.

"No, I don't believe I've ever had a blister in my adult life," I replied, a smile creasing my face. "My feet are like alligator leather. You'd need a surgeon's scalpel to get through the top three layers of callous."

As I opened the bag containing my first aid kit, Mike (the girl's father) gasped. "My God, you've got a lot of supplies in there!"

"Yes, I do. I'm prepared for just about anything. Do any of you have any cuts or open abrasions that need anti-bacterial cream? Does anyone have diarrhea? Heartburn?" I continued speaking as I pulled even more remedies and supplies from my kit. "Any contagious diseases, including typhoid, yellow fever, or malaria? Is anyone pregnant and need to deliver a baby this afternoon?"

By now, the entire group was laughing as each additional lotion, pill, or piece of surgical gauze came into view. And of course I was kidding the whole time. However, there was a certain degree of truth in what I was saying; I liked to be prepared for emergencies. And while I was not "on the hook" the same way I was when I lived here as a wilderness park ranger, I still liked to be able to provide assistance no matter what the infirmity.

As we spoke and became acquainted, I learned that not only was this a family of hikers, but they also enjoyed long-distance running and had completed numerous endurance races as a family around the Philadelphia area. That kind of activity would certainly keep everyone in shape for the summer hiking season.

Tim munched on an apple while the others unpacked, and I quickly deduced that he was the real deal of naturalists. He spoke at length about his holistic approach to being one with the universe. He raised free-range chickens, grew his own fruits and vegetables, and decried the evils of big corporations and crowded cities and their role in diminishing our quality of life. As he spoke, he paused from time to time to take moderate-sized bites from the piece of fruit, which he consumed in a completely random and non-discriminating manner. Most people eat around an apple in a pattern that avoids the core (and seeds), as well as the very top and bottom parts that contain the stem and bottom plug. Not Tim. He devoured the entire fruit from top to bottom, seemingly oblivious to its anatomy and inedible parts. I remained silent as he bemoaned the wickedness of modern living and trickle-down economics, not because of my interest in his political views but due to my amazement at his culinary preferences. As he concluded his monologue, he popped the last bit of apple skin into his mouth along with the entire stem and core. A few more crunches and the thing was gone. Amazing.

Another benefit of having Tim there was his ability to identify the birds that resided in the trees surrounding the lean-to. Tim knew them all. He quickly identified them from their songs, and then he matched them with the different berries and seeds that grew within sight of the shelter. He pointed out the songs of the white-throated sparrow, winter wren, rufous-sided towhee, Brewster's blackbird, robin, woods thrush, and (for good measure) great blue herons, loons, and seagulls. It was a treat getting this lesson in ornithology from an expert, as my own knowledge did not extend to that side of the fauna spectrum.

When it came to the various butterflies that fluttered across the site, I had the significant advantage, as I have retained much of my knowledge of insect taxonomy from my own years in graduate school. Even though I never completed my master's degree with its focus on entomology, I can still identify American butterflies and other insects better than most.

"What are those black and white butterflies that are all sitting together around that puddle?" asked Shanna, the young girl.

"Those are mourning cloaks," Tim replied, ready to launch into yet another lecture on the critters of the region.

"Actually, those are white admirals," I said, correcting the error.

Tim looked at me through narrowed eyes, his furrowed brow expressing doubt at my opinion. "Are you sure?" he said, obviously preferring his own identification.

"Yes," I said, fixing him with a steady gaze. "They do look a little bit alike, but the mourning cloak's stripe is yellow instead of white, and it extends around the very outside of the wings, unlike the white admiral's, which is inside the pattern of the wings. So that is my final answer, one hundred percent certain. But you will be happy to know that both these species are members of the family Nymphalidae, commonly known as the brush-footed butterflies."

I don't know whether it was my tone of voice or the certainty in my expression, but Tim seemed to accept my explanation without further question. I still sent him an email containing side-by-side photographs of white admirals and mourning cloaks when I returned from the trip. It seemed like the courteous thing to do.

As we spoke, the other two brothers took off to explore the immediate area, hoping to find some suitable tent sites within walking distance. I knew there were quite a few of them if you hiked a bit northwest of the lean-to. Some of these sites had obviously been used for many years, and the ground had been flattened into perfect spots to pitch a tent as well as start a fire, with well-established fire pits and cooking grills. However, the recent rains had evidently submerged most of these sites, or at least turned the ground into a muddy, semi-fluid mess that would have made a similar mess out of any tent bottom, and it wasn't long before the hikers returned to the shelter to discuss alternative sites.

"Hey, you don't mind if we pitch our tents next to the lean-to, do you?" asked Eddie. "It's a mess down there, and we'd be sleeping in at least an inch of water. These two spots next to the lean-to look fairly dry, and they've obviously been used before."

"No, of course not," I replied. "Anyway, it's not my lean-to, so it's certainly not my place to say yes or no. Please feel free to sleep wherever you want."

To me, it was rather comical that they didn't want to sleep in the lean-to, yet they were willing to spend the additional twenty minutes or so to erect a tent right next to that very same structure. Oh well, it wasn't my call, so whatever they wanted worked for me. By the time they set up their two tents, it was almost four o'clock, and the sun was casting longer shadows across the lake. I ventured down to the water's edge to filter a few quarts of water, enough to last me through the following day. By the time I returned to the lean-to, Mike and Shanna were sitting on the front log discussing the details of the next day's hike. They asked me a few questions about the walk from Pillsbury to the junction of the Northville-Placid Trail, which would be about six miles to the west.

In an attempt to make conversation, I asked Mike to tell me about where he had traveled over the past few years, whether his wandering had led him to anyplace more interesting than the West Canadas. Within ten minutes, I realized that it was a very bad decision.

"Well, since you asked, it's been an interesting time for my wife and me. We had to sell a property a couple years ago which resulted in us getting a check for about forty thousand dollars," Mike explained. "We weren't sure what to do with it, so we decided to take some time off from the corporate world and do some traveling."

"Oh, really," I countered. "Where did you go?" It was my second mistake in the conversation, and it opened the floodgates. Mike was now convinced that I desired to hear the details... all the details. And that is what I got.

"Well, first of all, we did some calculations on places we wanted to see and the amount of money it would take to get around to all the countries," he explained. "We figured that if we really budgeted our money, we could get it to last almost two years, especially if we could spend time with friends we had living in some of our destinations. So we just got started."

I was shocked to hear just how long they planned to travel, and I must admit that I admired their ability to pack up and hit the road on such a spontaneous basis. But without children in the house, they had very little to tie them down.

"So we started the trip by flying over to Turkey, where we landed at Istanbul. The flight itself was amazing, as it took over thirty hours including stops, and at the end it dropped us off in an entirely new civilization and culture. Amazing!"

I nodded that it undoubtedly was; I'd never been to Istanbul, and I actually found myself wanting to hear more about the adventure.

"So, we started by touring the area around the regional cities and taking a boat tour through the Bosporus Strait and past the small towns that line its shores. Then, we headed into the interior of the country, passing through the city of Ankara, which is another fairly major metropolis. From there, we continued on southward until we arrived at Antalya on the Mediterranean Sea. That was amazing, as the culture is so different from ours. We wandered through ancient streets and dined in some of the native restaurants. It was so far off the beaten path; once again, simply amazing! We then continued up the western shoreline, taking about two weeks to travel through the towns of Bodrum, Izmir, and Bergama, until we arrived back at the Sea of Marmara. That's the body of water through which the Greeks sailed to reach the Black Sea."

I was enthralled at the very thought of sailing through the Bosporus Straits and seeing the ancient minarets on the shoreline.

I had never been that far north in Turkish waters, although I had been to Antalya in my Navy days. "I hope you took a lot of photographs on your trip," I said. "That must have been incredible."

"Yes, it was. And that was only the first stop. From Turkey, we flew in to Chennai, India, and started a south-to-north sight-seeing visit to take in as much of the countryside as possible. We wanted to see it all."

"India is another country I've never visited," I replied, still amazed at the length of this trip. "Did you spend much time there?"

"Oh yes," Mike said, his eyes alight with the memories. "We traveled mostly by rail through Hyderabad, Mumbai, Indur, and on up into New Delhi, where we stayed with a local family and helped them with their tourist business. There is a lot of industry in that city, and unemployment is only around 5 percent. The rest of the country is over 30 percent, so New Delhi is actually a very advanced and prosperous city. We loved staying there. We even took a cooking class in the local school."

By now, I must admit that I was ready for a little peace and quiet, but I felt as though I had to be polite and toss in a question. "So was India the end of your trip?"

"Oh, my goodness, no! From New Delhi, we continued across the border into Nepal, where we stayed at a religious retreat in Kathmandu for a couple weeks. We then motored over to Biratnagar, which is the economic hub of eastern Nepal. We actually both worked for a week in one of the local tea plantations, which was hard work but really interesting."

"Sounds fascinating," I said, growing increasingly weary of the monologue. "So was *that* the end of your tour?"

"Not even close!" chuckled Mike, making it sound as though he was just getting started. "From there, we traveled into Tibet, and then we flew across into South Korea, landing at Seoul, which was a real eye-opener. South Korea is a really advanced country, and Seoul is more industrial than many cities in the U.S. So from there, we traveled by rail once again across the country to a town called Yangyang on the east coast, then north with a tour group because we wanted to see the DMZ between North and South Korea. What a sight! You can almost feel the tension about to explode between those two countries. The North just looks so primitive, and the military is just about all they've got going for them."

I had never heard of Yangyang and had begun to lose interest, so I simply nodded my head as the story continued.

"Next, we went back to Seoul and then caught a flight to Ho Chi Minh City in Vietnam. My father had been in the Vietnam War in the late 1960s, and we wanted to see the area and meet some of the people. I am so glad we did that, as it really put things into perspective for us. We met up with my friend, Trinh, from my days at Temple University. He had already offered to put us up for as long as we wanted to stay, so we accepted the offer and used that as a home base while we traveled around the country. We got to see a lot of the rice farmers working the patties in the Mekong delta throughout the harvest season, which was pretty cool. It's amazing to think that eighteen million people live in that region, and 80 percent of them are involved in rice farming."

"Amazing," I echoed. My eyes may have been completely closed by then, but I don't think Mike noticed. This description had already gone on longer than I had expected, and I was getting increasingly tired of the seemingly endless list of countries and cities he'd visited. I was, however, amazed that he could remember them all and impressed by his boundless enthusiasm.

As Mike continued with his recital, Eddie was setting up one of their tents and unpacking his pack. He and Shanna then began moving their sleeping bags and other items into the tent. Shanna arranged her bag on top of a large ground cloth, and then situated the rest of her gear along one side of the tent to make room for her father's equipment. Tim was also busy with tasks, which included blowing up a thick pad which would rest beneath his sleeping bag on the lean-to floor.

Only Mike seemed oblivious to the preparations being made for the coming dusk.

"So after staying with Trinh and his family for about six weeks, we moved on up the coast and rented a room in a fishing village in Ha Long Bay, not too far from Hanoi. The scenery was amazing, with incredibly steep rock formations coming all the way down to the waterline. You ought to see my pictures! We both tried working with local fishermen along the coast, casting lines and hauling nets to catch things like grouper and squid. It didn't pay much, but we made what we had to in order to survive without digging into our finances at all. It was hard work, but we learned a lot about the culture of the Vietnamese people in the northern part of the country."

"Hmm," I said, trying to limit my participation in this monologue to simple grunts and expressionless shrugs. I just didn't want to encourage him anymore.

I was able to retreat from the discussion on a temporary basis when the rest of the group decided it was time for dinner. To me, this meant simply boiling water using my new butane stove. However, I quickly gleaned that my new friends had something far more ambitious in mind. As Eddie lit a fire using the wood I'd collected, Shanna retrieved a moderately sized parcel wrapped in tin foil from her father's backpack.

"We always enjoy a bit of real food on our first night in the woods," he said, unwrapping the package and revealing a large pile of plump sausages. "Once we get a good bed of coals going, these babies should cook up pretty fast." They proceeded to build the height of the fire and lay out an old cooking grate over the rock fire pit. Looking at the fire, I would have to agree that the food would cook quickly. Actually, it looked pretty darn tasty.

"So by then, we decided that we wanted to venture off the mainland and see some of the islands in the Pacific we'd been reading about," resumed Mike. He obviously felt as though the travelogue needed more explanation, and launched into further discourse on the island nation of Papua, New Guinea.

"You wouldn't believe how the people of New Guinea work the farms and grow their own foods for consumption," he went on. "We stayed for a couple weeks on a working sweet potato farm. They've been growing crops like this for over seven thousand years."

"Amazing," I said, providing yet another one-word reply. As I did, I thought I saw Tim shoot a sideways glance at his brother, perhaps indicating that enough was enough. But maybe it was my imagination. Regardless, it was completely missed by Mike, who relentlessly pressed on.

Within a short period of time, they were dining on some deliciously scented sausage on rolls, topped with an attractive mix of onions and peppers. I was envious, as I was left to consume a totally tasteless meal of freeze-dried rice and beans. For all I know, it could have been cardboard and Styrofoam; it was that bad. And all the while, Mike droned on. By now, the trip had migrated down to New Zealand. Never in my sixty plus years had I been lectured on the merits of New Zealand's natural beauty, but for the next ten minutes that was the entire conversation.

I thought to myself, "Would someone please help me and change the subject?" I looked around the lean-to for a hyperspace button, knowing that no such thing existed either inside the West Canada Lakes or out. In a comical way, this was starting to remind me of the old dinner parties of the 1960s and 1970s, when people would venture over to a friend's house and, following the dinner, the host showed a three-hundred-slide presentation of their summer vacation. ("Best summer vacation ever!") Yes, it was getting that bad.

To escape, I announced that I was going to go out in search of firewood. It was at least partially true; they had burned through the stack of the good wood I'd collected over the past few days without contributing anything of their own. I really didn't mind, as long as they would pitch in and provide some help in that department. For some reason, the area appeared to be low on my favorite woods, which were maple and beech. Hopefully, with all of us scouring the area, we would be able to quickly restock our wood pile.

The search for firewood provided a suitable diversion, as everyone scattered in different directions to locate additional fuel. By backtracking to the trail, I was able to collect quite a pile of maple branches that were peeled and dry, all good signs of promising wood. However, the materials retrieved by the others were much less valuable. It was mostly a collection of large, soggy limbs from a yellow birch that had been rotting on the ground since last year, which meant that combustion of any kind was highly unlikely. These were accompanied by some dead spruce branches and pine logs that would pop and sputter if placed in a hot fire, but would not serve as a productive base for cooking (or any other purpose). Well, if nothing else, the topic of discussion was no longer a travelogue.

Shortly after the wood was stored and the supper dishes cleaned, two members of the Philly clan decided they were going for a quick, after-dinner dip in the lake. This one took me by surprise. The sun was starting to drop, which meant the mosquitoes were starting to rise—en mass. (Not that they ever really disappeared during the daylight hours, but the aggressive feeding hours commenced with the approach of twilight.)

I thought they may have been kidding until Mike and Eddie stripped down into swim suits and headed down the shoreline for a more convenient entry into the water. Then, with little fanfare, in they went. It took them surprisingly little time to reach a point about 150 yards from shore, which was about halfway out to a peninsula on the western end of the lake. Shortly thereafter, I heard a number of expletives, followed by the repeated expression of "ewww!"

"This is gross!" cried one of the men. "I'm getting out of

here," replied the other. It didn't sound like they were enjoying the experience.

Within about five minutes, the two reappeared hustling up the slope to the lean-to, both enveloped in a cloud of mosquitoes and biting insects. They did their best to fend them off by flailing T-shirts around their torsos, much the same as a horse would use its tail. But it was fruitless, and the entomological smorgasbord had begun. They both set unofficial records in dousing themselves with bug dope and replacing their original clothing.

"How was the swim?" I asked, observing their haste in dressing. "Was that as refreshing as you'd expected?"

"You've got to be kidding me" replied Eddie. "Have you ever gone swimming in this lake?"

"No, actually, I haven't."

"Well, don't bother trying. The entire bottom few feet of it is covered in a slimy, mucky mixture of rotting vegetation. It felt like we were wading through sludge. To tell you the truth, it was pretty darn creepy."

I had to laugh, as I know their intentions were to simply wash off after a day of perspiring their way along the trail. But I'd seen too much undesirable stuff happen to swimmers in this area. A few had emerged from the water with one or more leaches attached to their bodies. One claimed to have been chased by a snapping turtle, while yet another unlucky woman over at Cedar Lakes had stepped on a submerged broken bottle and required evacuation for medical attention. No thanks; I had long ago decided to remain a pedestrian and observe the aquatic fans from the shoreline.

By the time the sun dropped below the tree line at the end of the lake, Tim was feeding some new tinder onto the bed of coals in the fireplace and preparing to stoke up the flames for an evening fire. Eddie was helping Shanna place a new layer of moleskin on her blister, and Mike was approaching me to speak. I was dreading a return to his earlier topic.

"So as I was saying, New Zealand was wonderful, with some incredible waterfalls that we toured for several weeks. The waterfalls produce a mist that creates rainbows you wouldn't believe! We must have taken over one hundred pictures of rainbows alone!" (I have no doubt that had he carried those photos with him on his hike, he'd be showing them to me right now.)

"Sounds wonderful," I replied, employing my best boredom-induced monotone.

"Then, after spending about two months in New Zealand, we took a boat over to Australia and started a four-month tour of the entire country. Did you know that Australia is the only country in the world that is also a continent unto itself?"

"Uh, yes."

"Well, a lot of people don't know that, nor are they aware of just how large and diverse the place is," he continued, lost in the amazement of his own words. "Almost all of the Australian people live in a relatively small group of cities along the coastal regions, although there are native Aboriginals who inhabit the inner regions of the continent."

"You don't say."

I thought my responses must definitely have conveyed my desire for him to cease, although they apparently didn't have that effect. The next twenty minutes took us through a circuitous tour of Australia's major cities, followed by an excursion into the interior territory. He was particularly enthralled with a large rock that was located somewhere in the middle of the country, claiming it was the largest monolith in the world, or something like that. By this time, it wouldn't have mattered if it was a planet-sized block of blue cheese. I just didn't care.

During the briefest break in the conversation, Shanna asked me whether I had come face to face with any black bears in the area surrounding Pillsbury Lake. I explained that I had met a four-thousand-pound bear earlier in the week. (This is obviously fiction, as the largest black bear on record is probably less than seven hundred pounds, with most adults weighing in about half that number.) Even Shanna realized that this was a tall tale, as I'd told her the story of meeting a four-thousand-pound moose earlier in the day. I'd also bragged about the four-thousand-pound beaver I'd seen swimming along the lakeshore the same afternoon. I can't help it; I enjoy making up my own stories as I go. And the darker the night, the bigger I make the critters. It just goes with the territory.

In addition to my story about the various two-ton visitors to the lean-to, I told her about the smaller (and much quieter) Sasquatch variant, who loved visiting campers and rearranging the contents of their backpacks, removing items from pockets and replacing them in different compartments of the pack. This undoubtedly is why many hikers are unable to locate small items they've placed into their packs, such as flashlights, maps, silverware, and more. It is a baffling and most frustrating situation.

I was glad to note that the evening conversation around the campfire did not include any further descriptions of hikes in the wilds of Africa or fishing expeditions in the South China Sea. Instead, we were treated to a symphony of crickets, loons, and barred owls as they punctuated the night air with their respective calls. We all took turns recalling special times around campfires of the past, spinning yarns as so often happens at this time of night. Before long, we were all experiencing heavy eyelids and decided to call it an early night. Eddie, Mike, and Shanna headed for their tents, while Tim and I prepared to climb into our bags in the lean-to.

I'm a firm believer in the expression "those who live in glass houses should not throw stones." Accordingly, I should be the last person on the planet to make fun of another person's snoring. My own wife claims that I am in a category of my own, and she often wears headphones to bed to counter the effects of my bellowing. However, on this particular evening, I believe my commentary is justified.

Within ten minutes of lights-out, everyone except me appeared to have fallen fast asleep. Tim (my lean-to companion) was the first to start the snore-fest. It wasn't particularly bothersome, but it was quite audible, and it grew in both volume and regularity as Tim's breaths evolved into a rhythmic pattern of rumbles. No worries; I could live with that.

However, it wasn't long before his snorts were joined by an equally impressive series of staccato pulses from inside Eddie's tent. In, out, in, out, wheez, wooosh, wheez, whoosh. I was struck by the regular pattern of Eddie's respiration, matching that of his brother in the lean-to. However, what followed had me laughing to myself as I hunkered down in my sleeping bag. The two men soon settled into a stunning pattern of reciprocal snores. While Tim was inhaling, Eddie was exhaling, and vice versa, each with his own tones and rhythm. One, two, one, two, one, two. They remained in lockstep, their snores keeping time better than any precision metronome I'd ever heard. I lay there listening for some time, amazed at the absolute perfection of the pattern.

Thankfully, the rhythmic duo did not keep me awake for long, and I quickly dozed off. Unlike on many recent nights, I didn't awaken until the rays of the morning sun reached into the back of the lean-to. Still, one of my first waking thoughts was the concert of the previous evening.

My four companions did not waste time the following morning. It was a quick breakfast followed by a rapid and efficient take-down of the two tents. By the time their cell phones chimed at eight o'clock, they were filling their water bottles and adjusting the loads on their pack straps. It didn't take long.

Tim jotted down his email address for me because he wanted photographic proof that the butterflies he'd seen were truly white admirals instead of mourning cloaks. "No worries," I said, "I'd be happy to send you photos of the two species side-by-side. You should have them by the time you get back to Philly."

"That's a great idea!" added Mike, his face alight with joy. "Once you send Tim the photos, I can use your email address to send you pictures of our trip. You know, I never did get to tell you about the final six months, when we visited the Australian cities of Sydney and Brisbane before venturing into the central wilds of the country. It was incredible! I can't wait to fill you in!"

—16—

Follow the Leader

It's a funny thing about groups, but whether they want an officially designated leader or not, every group appears to have one. No matter how big or small, young or old, whenever a gathering of individuals gets together for a stated purpose, there is at least one individual who seems to take charge of the collective mass.

The same is true of assemblages in the woods. Whether dictated by the rules of some organization, level of knowledge, or force of personality, there is always an individual who assumes the role of top dog. And the interesting thing is that the role isn't always filled by the "alpha male" type, or the biggest or the baddest in the bunch. It is instead a phenomenon that cannot be defined, but one which has others looking to that person for leadership, sometimes for other-than-obvious reasons. It's just the way it is.

I've always been fascinated by the people who lead groups of hikers through the wilderness. They never seem to share a common denominator, although there are a few trends that tend to be repeated more commonly than not. Very often, if the group is a male-female couple, the male appears to be the leading character. I'm not saying this out of deference to my own gender, but rather as a casual observer of hundreds of couples encountered in the setting of the woods. Guys just assume that they know more about living in the woods and taking care of survival, whether they actually do or not. The truth (or fiction) behind this assumption may be legitimately questioned anytime, and I've personally met hundreds of female group leaders who are on par with any man in the woods. But in heterosexual couples (whether married or not), guys invariably want to be out in front.

I only met two couples on this recent stay in the woods, although many larger groups were mixed between the genders. Both of these duos were walking in single file, guy in front, heading in whatever direction he deemed appropriate. One of the couples had done some genuine off-trail adventuring, including a circuitous hike around Whitney Lake that led to their discovery of a boat. They used this vessel to travel out to an island where they discovered some stashes of fishing equipment and other gear that had been left there from years gone by.

"It's a really cool place that shows very few signs of recent use," reported the man, whose name I never did get. "We had a great time exploring the island as well as some old campsites, one of which we used as a base for the night."

While he spoke, his female companion smiled and nodded her head as she looked on with an interested expression, but she never said a word. She had obviously enjoyed the trip into the land around Whitney, but she let him do all the talking.

The only other couple I came across in those two weeks was a young pair who simply passed by the Pillsbury Lake lean-to en route to someplace else. They stopped only long enough to say hello and confirm that I was staying at that spot for at least one more night. The guy, once again out in front, simply turned around and said to his partner, "Maybe we'll head down to the waterfront and see if there are any nice tent sites down there." He never waited for her to answer him or even nod her head in agreement. He just took off and she followed. They didn't stay the night at any of the nearby tent sites, and I never saw either of them again. He had evidently decided to lead them off in a different direction, and she had followed.

As groups increase in size, their leadership tends to expand in diversity across genders and age (and other factors). While staying at one of the lean-tos on the French Louie loop this summer, a group of six or seven hikers appeared out of nowhere and gathered around the crumbling fireplace. They were part of a well-known hiking club in Utica that planned and conducted numerous Adirondack hiking trips every summer. I was not only familiar with the group, I had actually addressed them in the past and had enjoyed talking with their members, most of whom were seniors.

They had planned this trip for months and had come in for an expanded day hike through part of the West Canada Lakes. It was an in-and-out tour that permitted them the luxury of travelling with only day packs, which is a wonderful way to get to some of the closer lakes without undue stress on the back. Their leader was a fifty-ish woman who had obviously been designated by the club to serve as their guide and mentor. She was extremely friendly and very knowledgeable about the territory as well as about backpacking in general. As she spoke, the rest of the group turned an attentive ear in her direction. I found myself listening as well.

"The main route through this region is the Northville-Placid Trail, which was designed and cut out between 1922 and 1924. It runs the full 134 miles from Northville up to Lake Placid, although parts of it have been re-routed over time," she intoned to her followers. "But right now, we are on the French Louie Trail that was originated sometime in the years after 1870, when the early trappers and hunters used this route to access some of the inner lakes and camps."

Knowledge is power, or so the old saying goes. But in this case, this woman's experience and storehouse of information clearly justified her authoritative status with the group. This was in direct contrast to a group I encountered near the end of my stay inside the loop later that week. I was sitting on the front log of the Pillsbury Lake lean-to eating a small lunch when I heard a large group of youngsters approaching. It is always easy to identify the demographics of a group based solely on the sounds being produced by the assemblage. The best groups I've encountered were those who made little or no noise as they approached; they just appeared in near-silence and said hello. The worst (or largest or most rowdy, all of which are perhaps synonymous) could be heard approaching from hundreds of yards in the distance.

The group I am describing fit all of the characteristics of the latter. From the time my ears first detected their clamoring voices, I dreaded the mass that would soon be upon me. Voices, there were so many voices: high voices, low voices, boys' voices, girls' voices; laughter, shouting, whooping and hollering as I'd seldom ever witnessed this far into the woods. I ceased my munching and waited for the crowd to materialize.

The first two people to appear were a boy of about sixteen and a girl who was probably closer to twenty. "Oh, someone is already here," stated the boy in a disappointed tone. The girl remained silent, but cast a glance back up the trail. She looked as though she was getting ready to address the troops.

As I sat there, not saying anything but observing the young bodies as they piled into the clearing, the group grew in size until there must have been at least a dozen present.

"Wow, that's quite a group you've got there!" I said, directing my comment to the first two hikers.

"This is only the lead group," replied the female. "We've got another group of about six or seven who are trailing behind a ways."

Wow! Twenty people in one group? I wasn't going to say anything as I wasn't there in an official capacity, but I wondered if they realized there was a limit of ten people at any one lean-to or tent site without getting an official camping permit. There was a sign listing the rules back at the trailhead, but I guessed that this group hadn't bothered to read those rules or bother with the permit.

As much as I didn't feel like sharing my lean-to (or the woods in general) with so many young kids, I felt it my responsibility to offer them a place to sleep.

"These lean-tos sleep six," I explained, "and there are lots of tent sites in the area below this clearing. You could easily pitch tents, if you have them, and sleep everyone here overnight."

"No, that's OK," replied the girl in a commanding voice. "We're from a YMCA camp south of here, and our rules say that if someone is already camped at a spot, we can't stay there. It's just the way we operate." She spoke in a very firm tone, as though she was used to being out in front. I noticed with interest that her arms were adorned with numerous tattoos, which added even more to her tough image. She looked as though she wouldn't take much in the way of backtalk or monkey business from any of her followers.

Following her explanation to me about their regulations, the girl turned around to address her cohorts.

"OK, EVERYONE LISTEN. WE'RE NOT GOING TO STAY HERE TONIGHT. WE'RE GOING ON TO THE NEXT LEAN-TO, WHICH IS ABOUT TWO OR THREE MILES DOWN THE TRAIL. DOES ANYONE HAVE ANY QUESTIONS?"

Yikes! There are several leadership techniques that can be used to gain the respect of a group, and intimidation is definitely one of them. (Not that it is the best or most preferred, but it is certainly a method.) There was no doubt in my mind that this leader fit into this category, and the rest of the youngsters present seemed to accept her in that role. My guess was that the remainder of the YMCA party that was lagging behind represented the youngest and more "tenderfoot" members of the group. However, I also guessed that, even at a distance of a half mile, they too must have clearly heard their leader's words. She had no need for a bullhorn or loudspeaker. Her commanding voice had that feature already built in as standard equipment.

On a side note, there was some unvoiced grumbling as this massive group did an about-face to return to the trail. One particularly goofy-faced boy turned to me with an unhappy expression and asked me, "What are you doing here?"

I found the question to be so odd that I simply looked at him and said, "Camping. Living."

He was about to give voice once again when the female leader grabbed him by his shirtsleeve and virtually propelled him up the trail. "All right, let's get moving. We're not staying here, and I'm in no mood to hear anything about it."

Uh... goodbye!

There are other groups who come close to being leaderless, but these are usually older folks who are all highly experienced and have been together for many years. The group of seniors with whom I stayed that same week fit this mold. No one would tell anyone else what to do, and the decisions all seemed to be reached via consensus. This is perhaps my favorite form of organization, although these days I hike either alone or with one other person. Sure, I could easily lead a group of less-experienced folks into the woods and be the leader. But after twenty-seven years of service as a senior naval officer, I'll admit that I'm tired of always being in charge. I just want to get there, collect firewood, and gaze into the embers at night. That's enough for me, and I'm too old a dog to want to learn new tricks.

On my final day in the woods of my two-week stay, I encountered the leader of the YMCA camp once again. She was out at the trailhead of the Pillsbury Mountain Trail, standing by her camp's van while talking to someone. They were alone, with no sign of her other campers anywhere in sight.

"Looks like you lost a few of your members along the way," I said as I hoisted my backpack into the trunk of my vehicle.

"No, we just got back to the parking lot about a half day earlier than expected," she replied, once again in that loud, commanding voice. "So the kids camped at the bottom of the hill last night, next to the Miami River, and then climbed Pillsbury Mountain this morning. Believe it or not, they still had energy to burn, so I decided to let them go for it."

"Wow, I remember having energy like that," I said wistfully. "It was back in the days when I worked in here, and I could run up two or three of these mountains every day."

"These kids are all between the ages of thirteen and seventeen and they're all pretty spirited individuals. And since we've got a two-hour drive to get back home, I figured I'd let them get tired out before we got started."

I smiled at her strategy, which I imagined would probably work. If nothing else, I'm sure her mere presence and authoritative tone could handle anyone who became overly boisterous along the return route.

"Are you expecting them back soon?" I asked, looking up the mountain towards the summit, which was about two miles distant.

"They've been gone for about four hours, so yes, they should be back any time now."

With that, she cocked an ear toward the trail leading into the woods and announced, "I think I hear the first ones coming now."

"OK, YOU PEOPLE, LET'S GET A MOVE ON. THE BUS IS LEAVING IN TEN MINUTES, AND ANYONE NOT ONBOARD BY THEN WILL HAVE A LONG WALK HOME!"

I have no doubt that anyone on Pillsbury Mountain, from the bottom of the trail to the top of the fire tower, would have clearly heard her words. Possibly on the next mountain as well.

—17—

Whoosh!

I've always said that truth is stranger than fiction—and I'd have a very hard time making up some of the characters I've met in the woods. Not that they were all strange, or smart, or boring, or different, but when you take the time to sit back and observe people and their habits, you'll discover we all have our eccentricities, and that is what makes life interesting.

Case in point: Meeting Alex and Matt at the Pillsbury Lake lean-to was quite the experience. They were both amazingly straight-laced, all-American kids who possessed cartoon-like tendencies. I had the pleasure of meeting this dynamic duo not only once that week, but twice. The first time was in the middle of an afternoon rain shower, when not many people were busy moving between lean-tos; most folks will stay put on rainy days if their schedules permit. Even though they've come to the deepest forests of the Adirondacks to be near nature, they prefer not to get wet if they can avoid it.

The rain was falling at a moderate rate when I first heard the sound of distant voices. From the faintness of the conversation, I figured the speakers were over one hundred yards up the path leading to the French Louie Trail. So I was quite surprised when, within a matter of five or ten seconds, they appeared around the front corner of the lean-to. It was so quick that I was certain there must be others following farther back on the trail. However, the two gentlemen assured me they were traveling alone and had seen no one else over the course of the past hour.

They stopped in for a quick break and decided to eat lunch underneath the roof of the shelter. They introduced themselves as Alex and Matt, a pair of Adirondack enthusiasts from my part of the state.

"I'm a student at Rochester Institute of Technology," explained Alex, "born and raised in Batavia. My friend here, Matt, is a high school senior at Honeoye Falls. I wanted him to see the West Canada Lakes territory, so we're going to visit Cedar Lakes tonight via the shortcut."

"The shortcut?" I repeated. "What's the shortcut? Are you talking about cutting through to Pillsbury Bay from the Whitney Lake Trail?"

"That's the plan," nodded Alex, evidently well-versed in the geography of the area. "Then we're planning on spending the night at the Third Lake lean-to on Cedars."

Hmm, now this was getting interesting. Most people who have never visited the West Canadas don't even know about the Whitney Lake Trail, and even if they've heard of it, couldn't find it if they tried. It is an old path that hasn't been maintained since the 1970s, although most halfway decent woodsmen and women (and all the local fishermen) could follow it once they come across its starting point.

I looked at the pair in wonder, and then asked the obvious question: "OK, so let's say you make it to the Whitney Lake Trail and from there to the back of Pillsbury Bay on Cedar Lakes. What then? I'm sure you know there's no trail from Pillsbury Bay to Third Lake. And that will be a tough bushwhack, even if you know where you're going."

In response, Alex held up his wrist to display a strapped-on device that resembled a large wristwatch, only bigger.

"GPS. It gets me where I need to go, and I'm pretty good at navigating with it. I've used it all over the Adirondacks, and so far it's worked well here."

I looked at him with more than a bit of skepticism. "Are you serious?" I asked him. "Have you ever been back in that area? It's pretty dense and not easy to cut through even if you know your direction. It'll take you a lot longer than you think. Personally, I think it would be much shorter to just backtrack to the Old Military Road, then take that to Cedars and walk down along the lake. Someone like you could probably do that in about five hours."

"More like three," Alex replied, without a trace of humor or smugness in his voice. He was being serious.

"Three hours to get to the Third Lake lean-to? No way!" I exclaimed. "You'd have to be flying low and not touching the ground!"

"Well, it took us less than an hour to get here from the Pillsbury Mountain trailhead, so we're averaging almost four miles an hour."

I gasped when Alex told me they'd made Pillsbury Lake in under an hour. It's only about three and a half miles, but the first mile and a half is straight up hill, climbing the bulk of Blue Ridge to get to the junction of the French Louie Trail. That was incredible time, time that I may have been able to match at the peak of my condition as a ranger, but certainly not now.

As we spoke, Alex and Matt consumed their sandwiches at light speed. Seriously, it seemed as though they were unwrapping them and taking the last bite simultaneously. I wondered whether they lived their entire lives at that frenetic pace.

"So regardless of how we get there, our plan is to spend a night and then double back and stay here at Pillsbury the following night," Alex explained. "Then we'll drive up to the High Peaks and get in a few climbs before we head back home."

"Oh, really," I replied. "When do you have to be back in Rochester?"

"On Monday," Alex said. "I've got to work, and Matt has to be back to finish packing for another trip."

I had to laugh, as it was already Thursday, which meant they were going to buzz through the West Canadas, then drive up to the High Peaks and do their climbing, then return back home—all within three days. That would have been a full week for me, and I wondered if Alex drove the Thruway as fast as he motored along the wilderness trails. It was mind-boggling.

Once the pair finished lunch and re-mounted their packs, it was a matter of seconds before they were ready to hit the trail. They promised they'd be back to Pillsbury lean-to the following evening for their final night in the area, and I looked forward to seeing them again. They were two nice, young men with bright futures and the highest of ambitions, and I certainly wouldn't mind sharing the lean-to with them. Then, with a quick goodbye, they took off along the path leading up the hill to rejoin the French Louie Trail. And I do mean "took off." With a little effort, I could envision the cartoon dust clouds left in their wake as they zoomed up the incline at a jogging pace. I watched them go, but only for a second, as they were quickly lost in the plumage of the summer vegetation.

Whoosh! And then they were gone.

True to their word, the pair showed up again late in the afternoon of the following day. I asked about their transit through the thick, coniferous-choked thicket between Pillsbury Bay and Third Cedar Lake.

"We decided not to try that," said Alex. "We did make it to the end of the Whitney Lake Trail, though, and also backtracked to the spot where it looks like a lean-to used to be on Whitney Lake. Then, after some more poking around, we decided to head over to Sampson Lake for the night."

"That's a nice spot," I countered. "And it's less than an hour from Whitney, so you probably got there fairly early in the day."

Both Matt and Alex looked at me with confused expressions.

"An hour?" inquired Alex. "It took us all of about ten minutes to go over the hill from Whitney to Sampson. What would take an hour to go from one to the other?"

Once again, I had to smile at their progress motoring from point to point. To make it from lake-to-lake in ten minutes was physically possible, as the two bodies of water were separated by little more than a half mile of fairly open woods. But there was no trail, and the hills were steep. However, if anyone could make it in ten minutes, it would be them.

I had been alone in the lean-to, so Alex and Matt had plenty of space to spread out their gear and sleeping bags, which took them all of about eleven seconds. I envied anyone who could get down and back up from the lean-to floor without their knees and other joints sounding a cacophony of pops and assorted grating noises.

As they arranged their equipment, I asked Alex more about his schooling at RIT.

"I'm in an engineering program that is supposed to take five years, but I'll be graduating in four," he said. "RIT is a really good engineering school, and I'll be able to put my education to immediate use."

Somehow it didn't surprise me that he was on an accelerated path to an early graduation. But I winced at the thought of paying for all those RIT credits in a condensed period of time. I had completed my own master's degree from RIT back in 1993, and I knew how much it cost way back then. It was prohibitive, and I'm sure the expenses had probably doubled in the past twenty-five years.

"So how are you going to pay for all that?" I asked. "Are you getting loans for the entire degree program?"

"No, I only paid for the first couple years," he replied. "I'm in a Navy ROTC program, so the Navy is picking up the cost for my final two years. All I have to do is put in six years as a naval officer after I graduate and it's all paid."

"You're kidding!" I exclaimed. "I'm a retired Navy captain; I put twenty-seven years into that canoe club! So please, if you have any questions on Navy careers, feel free to ask."

Alex was quite pleased to hear about that, and he soon began peppering me with queries about the differences between Navy aviation versus surface (ship driving) career paths. I truly enjoyed the conversation, as I pride myself on my accomplishments as a captain as well as my background working with junior officers in their own career development. When I had first joined the Navy, I was certain it would be for four years only. Never would I have imagined that my stay would span over three decades and put me in positions of responsibility I could have only dreamed of as a ranger.

The more we spoke, the more I learned about both of these individuals. Matt was an honor student in a high school near my home. He was an Eagle Scout and excelled in just about everything. I couldn't believe that he not only kept himself perfectly neat and clean in the woods, but even the part in his hair was perfectly maintained. I myself haven't owned a comb or hair brush in close to fifty years, and I wouldn't know what to do with them if I did.

Matt's experience in the Boy Scouts became obvious as he volunteered to arrange the firewood for the night's blaze. He carefully lined up a perfectly symmetrical box pattern, using overlapping wood of matching lengths and thickness with just the right amount of starting material inside. It didn't resemble my own method, which relied on a teepee of interlocking branches, but I could tell that he'd done it before and had probably taught it to hundreds of newer scouts as well.

Meanwhile, Alex quickly went about making preparations for their meal. He and I started our stoves at the same time, and I wasn't surprised that he had his water boiling a full minute before mine, even though my stove was brand new. Nothing about these two happened in normal speed. Everything was done quickly.

Once we'd finished our meals, Alex and Matt decided to go down to the lake and refill their canteens. I had done that myself a few hours before. I had a very good filter pump which was made to rapidly pump "both ways" (when moving the lever both up and down), so it took me only five or ten minutes to fill my gallon jug. I knew these two would take longer. I knew it.

Once again I was proven wrong. Within sixty seconds of disappearing down the earthen bank to the shoreline, they were returning with full canteens. This I knew was impossible. There isn't a filter on earth that could pump water that fast. It defied logic. And yet the canteens were filled to the top with water.

"Don't tell me you already filtered two quarts of water," I stated. "You were only down there for about a minute!"

"Nope, we didn't filter anything," Alex replied. "We simply filled the canteens."

"You aren't going to drink it like that, right out of the lake, are you?" I asked with concern. "You know you'll end up getting sick from the *Giardia* in the water."

"Of course," replied Alex as they marched past me and retrieved a pair of strange-looking devices from their packs. "We just use a different system for doing the purification."

I remained silent as the two boys removed a tube-like apparatus from each of the two cases. Upon pressing a small button, the tubes illuminated, which sent a cascade of bluish-purple light across the lean-to. They each inserted one of the contraptions, which I then recognized as a UV (ultraviolet) light, into their respective canteens. The stirring lasted for only fifteen or twenty seconds, and they were done.

"That's all it takes?" I asked incredulously.

"That's all" replied Alex. "The UV light doesn't kill the bacteria immediately, but it does alter them genetically so they cannot reproduce, and thus, they can't hurt you. They end up dying a little later. Overall, it's been proven to eliminate 99.99 percent of all bacteria and microorganisms from the water, and it weighs a lot less than a water filter."

I was rather ambivalent about the whole idea of waving a

blue flashlight around in my own drinking water and calling it safe. The whole thing smacked of witchcraft to me, and I was half waiting for the two to commence a chant while performing a dance around the illuminated water bottles. However, I have read that this method is perfectly safe, although it cannot remove chemicals like chlorine or heavy metals from the water.

My only experience with the UV treatment method had been while deployed to South America while on active duty with the Navy. We were visiting Rio de Janeiro, Brazil, and I had splurged to pay for a room in one of the fancier hotels in town. A group of us played about five sets of tennis that night over a period of three hours, and I sweated out at least a half-gallon of water. When I returned to my room, I noticed a sign next to the bathroom sink that announced "UV treatment used on all hotel water for your convenience." This was great, since everyone knew that Rio had some of the worst water in the world. But I trusted the message regarding the water treatment, which had also been filtered with a back-up system to "kill any remaining bacteria in the water." No worries; they used two systems to eliminate all living organisms. I would be fine.

Our ship got underway to leave Rio the next day, and I don't think I've ever felt worse in my life. My intestines ached as though they'd been run over by a cement truck, and I was doubled over in pain. Additionally, I was due to stand watch on the bridge of the ship, which is tough to do if confined to the small area around a toilet seat. I will spare my readers the details of the next twenty-four hours, but it was not something I'd wish on anyone. Suffice it to say that Montezuma did get his revenge.

Armed with this remembrance from my Navy days, I remained highly skeptical of the UV light waved around in the canteen, and I remained faithful to my own filtration pump. I do hope it worked for Alex and Matt, though, because I wouldn't wish what I experienced on anyone.

The evening passed quite peacefully, and Matt's prepared fire stack lit incredibly quickly. (No surprise there.) We sat around the fire talking about the Navy and college and other academic pursuits. I was impressed that Matt had already completed Calculus Level 1 in high school and was preparing for a degree program in engineering as well.

"I dated a math major when I was a freshman in college," I told Alex. "She used to show me these books of math problems that had triple integrals to solve. Yikes! I don't think I could ever get my head wrapped around that no matter how hard I studied. To me they will always be patterns of squiggly lines on a page."

Alex chuckled as I spoke. "I actually enjoy those problems. They're not as hard as you think, and you certainly need to be able to do more than that to get through an engineering degree."

As he spoke, Matt nodded his head in concurrence. "You're kidding," I thought to myself. "This kid is still in high school and he can do third year calculus?" I suddenly felt more inadequate than I had all afternoon. I guess some people are just smarter than others.

We also talked a lot about hiking in various parts of the Adirondacks, as Alex had been exploring the different wilderness areas for several years already. At one point he spoke of climbing Mount Marcy, the tallest peak in the state, and getting back down by a particular time. I did some quick math and then, after subtracting his time on the summit, I decided to challenge his claim.

"Now hold on one minute," I started. "You're trying to tell me that you climbed Marcy from Heart Lake, and you made it round trip in three hours?"

"Well, it was actually closer to three and a half, but yes."

"No way!" I screamed. "No one can climb Marcy from Heart Lake and make it down in three and a half hours. That's a sixteen-mile hike with three thousand feet of vertical ascent!"

"Well, I guess I will admit that we jogged a good part of the way down. It would have taken longer had we walked the entire route."

Personally, I don't care if he had traveled using a flying carpet—

the times he was quoting were straight out of a cartoon episode. But I know that I did trust him, and he had already achieved some impressive trekking times while visiting our West Canada Lakes, so who was I to dispute his claims?

"So what are your plans for tomorrow?" I asked them. "Just heading out of the woods and heading north?"

"Yeah, we're going to head up to Upper Works and then into Flowed Lands just to check out the views and stay overnight, maybe do a couple short climbs."

"And you're doing all that in one day?" I asked, no longer really surprised at the haste of their voyage.

"Yeah; it'll take a couple hours to drive up there, and then maybe an hour to hike in from the parking lot at Upper Works."

This time, I didn't even begin to challenge his assertion. If they said they could hike to Flowed Lands from Upper Works in an hour, then I believed them. The imaginary cartoon dust cloud following them up the trail just became one shade darker. Whoosh!

As we made preparations to call it a day, Matt set an alarm to awaken them at five. It was an early start, but they had a lot of ground to travel the next day, so I could understand the selected departure hour.

I too am an early riser these days, although I wasn't at the time I lived in the woods as a ranger. But age changes many things, and I am often up several times during the middle of the night. Accordingly, I found myself wide awake at four-thirty and decided it would be a good time to get up and start a small morning fire.

I had a picturesque blaze going and was already heating water for a cup of tea when I heard the electronic tones of Matt's alarm sounding off in the lean-to. Unlike most folks, who turn off the alarm and then return to the pillow for a few additional minutes of snooze time, both Alex and Matt sprang from their sleeping bags as though launched on springs. I'd never seen anything like it.

They dressed so quickly that, for all I know, they may have slept in their hiking clothes, although I doubt it. (To anyone who uses the expression "He puts his pants on one leg at a time, just like everyone else," I have an example of an exception to that statement!) Once dressed, they performed a synchronized packing act that had their sleeping bags stuffed into their backpacks within two minutes of the alarm. If Guinness World Records had a category for speed-packing, I'm sure they'd have broken it without competition.

Breakfast was some kind of a granola bar or two, as they obviously didn't want to stop to cook a morning meal. It was zoom, zoom, zoom, and then finish packing. To this day, I'd still swear that it's impossible to get up, dressed, packed, eat breakfast, clean up your garbage, and hit the trail in less than thirty minutes. But I know it can be done because I saw it occur that morning.

Before they left, I jotted down my name and email address to give to Alex, in case he wanted to contact me with any questions about the Navy and his upcoming commissioning as a junior officer. We then shook hands one final time and off they went. Once again, at light speed.

Time of alarm: 5:00 AM. Time of departure: 5:26 AM.

Not even in my youth.

—18—

Visions from the Past

Although I have made a lot of friends through my writing, it's very seldom that I am recognized by anyone outside of my own hometown. So imagine my surprise when I was greeted with open admiration by a group of hikers arriving at the Pillsbury Lake lean-to.

"Are you Larry?" asked the first gentleman to step around the corner of the lean-to. "We saw your name at the trailhead register booth and hoped we'd run into you. I've read all three of your books about your experiences as a ranger back here. You also came and gave our Adirondack Mountain Club chapter a talk a few years ago. We really enjoyed it."

I was immediately impressed by this gentleman who seemed to remember more of my own book series than me. He was an elderly fellow, at least seventy years of age, who was accompanied by three other hikers of senior status. When they saw my information in the register booth, including the fourteen-day duration of my trip, they figured they'd cross paths with me sometime during their own three-day visit.

"We noticed your sign-in said you were going to Cedar Lakes first, so we figured that maybe you'd be back around this way sometime in the next few days," explained Mel, who introduced himself as a local from the town of Cold Brook. His compatriots were announced as Glenn, Jean, and Eleanor. Jean was from Ithaca and the other two were from North Carolina. From what I could tell, none of the newcomers were married; they were just close friends who traveled as couples. They were all friendly, amicable people with a lot of experience in the woods. Especially Mel.

"I remember my first trip into this area; it was sometime in the middle of 1953," he said, recalling his memories of that very different era. "We stopped into the caretaker's cabin on West Lake and met Floyd, the ranger on duty who lived at the station. He had a revolver sitting on the table while we spoke, and I must admit it made me a little bit nervous."

For once, I had met someone in the interior woods who was older than I was. His first trip was two years before I was born, so I quickly did the math and realized that he was my senior by at least fifteen or twenty years.

As if he'd read my mind, Mel chuckled and said, "I'll be seventy-nine in a couple months. I reckon you don't run into too many people here older than that."

"No, I think you're right," I replied. "It's fantastic that you can still make it back here with that size pack." And I truly meant what I'd said. They all looked in better shape than I following their march in from the Pillsbury trailhead. To add to my astonishment, Glenn announced that he was seventy-eight, although he could have passed for someone in his mid-sixties. Thin, lean, and tough, he looked as though he would be hiking well into his 80s.

The two men also joked about their choice of hiking partners. It turned out that Eleanor was not only a physician, but also a specialist in emergency care. "We believe in being fully prepared for anything," Glenn said, "so we made sure to bring along our own medical staff in case something happened along the trail."

I noticed that neither Mel nor Glenn mentioned the ages of their female companions, and neither Jean nor Eleanor volunteered that information. They just said they were "younger" and left it at that. I followed the rules of good etiquette and did not pursue the matter any further.

The foursome pulled out their lunches to eat while sitting on the front of the lean-to. Their plan was to move along to the Sampson Lake lean-to for the night, then head up into the middle West Canadas somewhere along the Northville-Placid Trail the following night. They would then stop over at the Pillsbury Lake lean-to on the last night of their trip before returning to their car for the ride out. It was an ambitious itinerary for a group of older hikers, although they were all in good condition and obviously used to the rigors of the trail. I made a mental note to try to be back at Pillsbury myself on the third night, as I enjoyed their company and wanted to learn more about Mel's early days in the region.

As they removed the wrapping from their lunches, I became somewhat envious of their midday repast. It consisted of chicken salad wraps accompanied by various fresh fruits. The wraps looked positively delectable, with a moist, meaty interior sheathed in the rolled casing. The fruits consisted of peeled oranges and a Tupperware container of gorgeous cherries. Cherries are my favorite fruit, and I was almost drooling as they passed around the container for sharing.

The four of them quickly consumed their meals and then asked me if I minded them disposing of the cherry pits in the fireplace.

"No, I don't think that would upset anything," I replied. I couldn't imagine even the most sensitive of bears' noses detecting the small remnants left behind to be consumed by the evening fire.

Shortly after eating, they re-mounted their packs and said their farewells. They were good people, and I looked forward to seeing them again for further conversation.

True to my intentions, I did end up back at the Pillsbury Lake lean-to following some perambulations that took me to Sampson Lake and then across to Whitney. There are so many beautiful places to visit and camp back there that you really don't have to intersect the busier Northville-Placid Trail for enjoyable locations. They are all good sites, and they can all accommodate several groups of campers if people are willing to spread out and get away from the lean-tos. Only a tent is required in these alternate sites.

I returned to Pillsbury Lake following two days of tent camping and found the Pillsbury Lean-to empty with nary a camper in sight. The day was overcast with intermittent rain, which did not stop the chipmunks from scampering about looking for additional handouts from my container of GORP. I also noticed that they were scurrying about the unburnt logs in the fireplace retrieving residual cherry pits left over from the group of seniors. Very little food of any sort goes to waste in the deep woods, and they were scavenging everything that was considered to be refuse by the humans. They were efficient cleaners.

It was mid-afternoon by the time Mel, Glenn, Jean, and Eleanor came tromping down the trail, now familiar faces in a familiar site. They had made it through almost their entire planned route, although they did report some difficulties further to the west.

"We made it as far as the lean-to on West Canada Creek, which is where we planned on camping for the night," Mel explained. "There were a couple of younger folks, a man and a woman, who had spread themselves out in the shelter. We wanted to stay there, and we asked their permission to share the lean-to. But the man said that it would be kind of crowded, while the woman refused to even make eye contact with us."

"Ugh, that's crazy," I replied. "All these lean-tos are large enough to sleep six people easily, and you can fit eight in an emergency. What's wrong with people these days?"

"Well, we didn't want to impose if we weren't welcome. So we started setting up our tarp at a nice spot near the lean-to while Glenn ran ahead to see if the South Lake lean-to was available. But there were people staying there too, and since it was starting to rain again we just decided to stay under the tarp last night."

"Did the young couple speak to you folks once you started setting up the tarp?" I asked.

"Yes, as a matter of fact they did appear to start feeling rather guilty, and they finally came over to offer space in the lean-to. But by then we already had the tarp up and our sleeping bags unpacked, so we just stayed there. Actually, it was kind of comfortable.

As we spoke, I detected some sideways glances from Mel at the mosquito netting which I had set up in tent fashion inside the lean-to. It literally took up half the width of the lean-to, and they probably wondered whether I was going to provide a repeat performance of the selfish couple of yesterday. I decided to immediately set that concern to rest.

"I hope you're sharing the lean-to with me," I remarked quickly. "I've got the netting up, but I can easily move it much closer to the right side of the floor." As I spoke, I was already up and removing the anchor points to compress my sleeping space.

"Of course, we'd love to join you," the four of them chimed in simultaneously.

"But I do have to warn you," I continued. "If you stay here you'll have to put up with two things. First of all, I snore. Secondly, I have the world's largest supply of bad jokes, and I'm not very good at keeping them to myself. So you'll have to tolerate a little of each."

Eleanor got the biggest laugh out of this. "That's OK," she said. "Glenn snores too, so we're used to that. And I'm sure both of these guys will be writing down your jokes to reuse at some other time, so it will be a very useful stay."

It was still mid-afternoon, so Mel and Glenn began telling stories from their hiking past as they took turns unpacking for the evening. I found Mel's recollections to be fascinating because he had so many years of experience on the very trails I'd patrolled while stationed here. He recalled vividly his time in the West Canadas, including being flown in back in the days when Herbie Helms operated his seaplane business.

"I remember going into his office and asking about getting flown back into Whitney Lake," he intoned wistfully. "I was a young man back then, and he looked to be about eighty. So once we agreed on a price and a takeoff time, he shocked me by informing me that it would be his *father* who would pilot the flight! I had no idea how old his father might be, but I guessed that he had been behind the controls since airplanes first took to the skies. If nothing else, he certainly must have had a lot of experience."

I agreed that he had, as I'd heard the legendary stories of the famous seaplane pilot passed down from generation to generation, including tales of night landings on the lakes to evacuate sick or injured campers.

"You know, it was the land trades between the State and the large paper companies that really ended the plane landings back here," Mel said. "After that, those guys could still give sightseeing rides over the area, but it ended the remote camping business. I've met a lot of the old-timers who still resent that exchange because it means they can no longer come back here with all their supplies and other stuff. Most of them are too old to backpack in, so they can no longer visit the lakes they fished as youths."

"Yes, but it's a mixed bag," I countered. "All of these lakes have numerous garbage dumps, some of which are fairly sizeable and will never be removed. You can tell just by poking around the contents of those dumps that the stuff was flown in, not packed in—things like stoves, heavy pots and pans, coffee percolators, and more, all left behind. And gradually, those dumps are disappearing beneath the yearly deposits of leaves and other fallen vegetation, soon to be permanently hidden from sight."

"Oh, I know," Mel agreed, nodding his head vigorously. "That's why I never minded them banning the seaplanes from landing. There's too much garbage back here left in too many dumps."

I had been working here during the last few years of the seaplane business. All of the other lakes were already off-limits except for Whitney, due to its status as a privately-held body of water. This was in contrast to the Cedar lakes, West Lake, Pillsbury, Sampson, and the other lakes which were part of the designated wilderness region, where no motorized vehicles of any type were permitted.

As a side note, I'm still amused when I think back to the 1970s, when anything with a motor was supposedly outlawed from going beyond the steel barriers at Perkins Clearing. Some of the old log camps still existed back here, however, and most of the owners had possession of the keys that opened that gate. I still recall one occasion when I was quite ill with a fever but still hiking into the woods following my two-day weekend. As I climbed Blue Ridge under full pack, I was overtaken by a pickup truck (driver will remain unnamed) and offered a ride to the stream crossing at Grassy Brook. As I mentioned, I was quite ill and not thinking clearly, and I quickly accepted the ride up the remainder of the ridge, thus saving me a mile of steep hiking and significant effort. It never crossed my mind until later in the week to ask the driver how he got there.

But I digress; none of those camps still stand today, and only the smallest vestigial remains can be spotted in some locations, if you know where to look. Jean pointed out one such object that was placed next to the outer rocks of the lean-to fireplace.

"That's the front plate of the wood-burning stove that was over in the Lawrence's camp," I stated. "That was a beautiful structure, built with heavy hardwood timbers and well-chinked for four-season use. Someone must have brought the stove plate over here to keep the fire covered during rainy nights. It's a good idea, but it probably weighs a ton."

The mention of fire got Mel and Glenn thinking about their

own evening blaze, and they decided to take a scavenging trip around the area to round up some wood. Even though I had accumulated quite the stack already, I pulled myself up from my prone position and laced up my boots. I enjoyed the task of gathering wood, as it permitted me to explore the area in places where others seldom go.

Within fifteen minutes we had all returned to the lean-to, each carrying our own respective loads of downed limbs. In my case it was more of the smaller branches from beneath mature maple and beech trees, those being my favorite to feed the flames due to their degree of seasoning after falling from the tree. Mel and Glenn arrived at about the same time, each carrying logs of impressive girth. I believe there were three of them, each about five feet long and at least eight inches in diameter. I had never in my life collected timber approaching that mass, and I waited to see just how they planned to reduce it to a usable size for the fireplace.

Jean was the first to burst out giggling as she watched the two men manhandling the logs. While I used my knee to snap my branches into twelve-inch lengths, Mel and Glenn rigged an improvised workhorse using the spruce log as a crossbar. Jean's mirth increased in volume and intensity as they pulled the other timbers over the top of the crossbar and prepared to commence sawing.

It was at this point that Mel revealed another laudable trait in his personality—that of creative inventor. He carefully removed a long, thin parcel of wooden blocks that were fastened together and had sharp metal teeth along one side. He unfolded these and reassembled them into a shape resembling a bow saw, which he tensioned by turning a small wooden block attached to the frame. The blade became quite taut as the bow saw took form, and my amazement grew with each additional step in the assembly.

Despite my readiness to declare Mel as the supreme Renaissance man, Jean continued to giggle, and her laughter was joined by Eleanor's own glee. Apparently it was contagious, as the two women continued to spur each other on. For the life of me I failed to see the humor in the activity, and I thought it rather odd that they would poke fun at their companions without sharing in the effort. But this was none of my business, so I kept my thoughts to myself as the sawing began.

For reasons unknown, Glenn quickly pronounced the wooden handmade saw unusable. He borrowed my new, all-metal saw, which quickly cut its way through the wood until they had a stack of uniform-length pieces. They then stacked individual lengths on top of a larger log and attacked them with the ax in order to split them into firewood. Once again, Jean and Eleanor were in full fettle, laughing with each hack of the blade. And once again I could not understand the merriment, as the men's wood-chopping skills were quite good. This continued for about fifteen minutes until the last of the logs was split into perfect chunks of firewood. And even though at least one of the logs was a bit waterlogged with little promise of igniting and rendering heat, I was still impressed by the job they'd done. It was a fine showing by these two almost-members of the octogenarian club.

As the dinner hour approached, all of us retrieved our cooking equipment and foodstuffs for the coming meal. Once again, a pair of surprises awaited me as we prepared our freeze-dried culinary delights. I was soon to receive a lesson in the two extremes of just how good and bad a dehydrated meal could be.

The foursome of seniors had done some research into preparing their own version of the space-aged meals. Their supper consisted of potatoes that had been cooked with lentils, chopped spinach, and a wonderful mixture of herbs and spices. As they mixed the dried packets with boiling water, plumes of aromatic steam arose from the mixture until the air was thick with the aroma. Even from across the campsite I could detect the fragrance of the oregano, onion, and cumin seed, which had combined with the other ingredients to form a wonderfully scented casserole dish fit for serving in the best restaurant. The combination was tantalizing, and I looked forward to my own meal with much anticipation.

Rather than purchase all my meals from the major makers of freeze-dried foods, I decided to go with the recommendation of a camper I'd met several years earlier. He had told me about a start-up firm run by a retired professional chef who designed the recipes as well as perfected the technique of dehydrating and packaging the product. I figured I couldn't go wrong, since *everything* tastes better in the woods anyway. (This is an odd phenomenon; even the pickiest of eaters in the civilized world would devour their own hiking boots in the woods if they were seasoned properly.)

The package I selected for the night was called "Italian Farmhouse Pasta." (I have altered the name and omitted the identity of the brand to protect the guilty.) It contained beef, pasta, white beans, tomatoes, and cheese, among other ingredients. With lots of good stuff like that, how could it possibly fail to satisfy? Right?

The first thing I noticed after I added the water to the mixture was that the pasta was not cooking or evening softening. Instead, it remained as a cohesive collection of hardened pieces firmly stuck to one another. I waited the obligatory fifteen minutes, then five more, followed by five more. As I waited, the chunks of beef floated to the top while the cheese congealed and stuck to the sides of the container. The crushed tomatoes were almost invisible except for a few hardened, red strands that seemed to be attracted to the floating beef bits.

After waiting for double the listed time, I ventured a taste of the mixture, hoping that it tasted better then it looked. My first bite was an interesting taste sensation, as the crunchy pasta pieces lodged themselves in and around my molars. The hot water had done little to cook or rehydrate the bow-tie forms, which crackled between my teeth with each chew. To label them as "al dente" would be an understatement. They were raw, and not improving with time.

For a few minutes, I considered walking this pot of petrified stew up to the French Louie Trail and leaving it out for the local bears. Then my more pragmatic side took over and negated that thought. After all, the bears in the West Canada Lakes had done nothing to justify such abuse: they had never bothered me or my food. I certainly didn't want to be the cause of them losing their teeth while attempting to consume the mess. My final consideration was actually quite comical; I considered the possibility of these bears visiting our lean-to that night as they carried the bowls of stew back to our fireplace uneaten. It was that bad.

After discarding the contents of the freeze-dried meal into the flames of the campfire, I grabbed a couple handfuls of GORP and a freeze-dried ice cream sandwich. These snacks did the trick, after which I decided that I was no longer hungry and called it a night. (The ice cream sandwiches are actually quite good, for those who have never tried them.) My days of ordering from this particular trail-food distributor were over, never to be repeated.

"By the way, I met your replacement last year," said Mel as he washed out his drinking cup. "I think her name was Leah, and she's been back here for at least a couple years."

"Yes, I know," I replied. "I've heard good things about her. The last several people they've had in that job have been called Assistant Rangers; my official title was Wilderness Park Ranger. I believe they have more responsibilities than we ever did."

In truth, the people who perform those duties do indeed have a much greater workload than did we. In addition to public education and public relations (which were 90 percent of our jobs), they also help out much more with land management functions, and they are asked to become familiar with areas that we never visited in the 1970s. I became friends with one of these individuals, whose first name was Brendan, and he had explained their expanded responsibilities.

One of his first assignments was to circumnavigate every lake in the West Canada Lakes Wilderness, which would have been a major undertaking for anyone. Some of these lakes, while only a couple miles long, have a shoreline that is in excess of fifteen miles, much of which is bordered by extremely dense thickets of conifers and undergrowth. But what better way to learn the territory? Brendan has told me of several rusted-out automobile hulks he located while conducting these patrols, as well as a number of illegally constructed camps.

We all sat around the campfire that night, watching the flames dance. True to my prognostication, some of Glenn's logs burned while others simply refused to catch. The wood that came from the spruce log sputtered and popped for close to an hour, while spitting out embers from the sap that burned within. I never liked using softwoods in a fire for just that reason, but I didn't say anything about it to the group.

As we watched, the stories flew and laughter prevailed. It was fun to listen as each member of the group poked fun at the others.

"Hey, do you remember the time Mel took us down the backside of Pillsbury Mountain as a shortcut to get to the lean-to here?" asked Jean.

"No way," I said, interrupting the story. "No one comes down this side of Pillsbury as a shortcut. Most people would get lost!"

"Oh, yeah. And we didn't have GPS either, just a map and a compass," Jean replied.

"And then, halfway down the mountain, Mel dropped the compass," added Eleanor. "So we were all crawling around on our hands and knees in some really thick bushes trying to find the thing. And somehow we did, which was lucky because otherwise we'd probably still be stuck in there."

"Yes, but if you recall, my guiding skills brought us out on the French Louie Trail within about a hundred yards of the lean-to," boasted Mel.

"OK, OK, I agree. You got lucky," said Jean. All four of them were chuckling over their recollections of that episode. It was fun to see four people who had done so much together and still enjoyed each other's company.

As we sat around the lean-to watching the sun go down, Mel and Glenn boiled some water for tea. As Jean placed the teabags into their cups, Mel retrieved a plastic flask from his pack and plied it over the steaming tea cups.

"Care for a little brandy, Larry?" he asked.

I had to smile to myself over that one. As much weight as these folks had to carry, they still made certain to leave enough space for the brandy flask. Some things never changed, and brandy flasks (or other after-dinner drinks) always seemed to make it into the woods, even with the most senior hikers.

Whether necessary or not, the brandy must have warmed them all up before climbing into their sleeping bags because they all appeared to stay warm once the sun went down. The temperatures can dip quite low on the lakes in the West Canadas region, even in July. And Pillsbury Lake has always seemed to feel colder than the rest. I still don't know the cause of this phenomenon; perhaps the cool air rolls down the side of Pillsbury Mountain and flows over the land around the lake? It's just a theory, but I have no other explanation for the coldness of the nighttime air at that location.

The following morning, as they packed their gear and prepared to leave, Mel and Glenn asked me about the extremely wet conditions on the trail.

"Doesn't anyone do any trail work back here?" asked Mel. "It seems like in the past, they used to have trail crews who put in boards over the standing water and cleared out the blowdown. It doesn't seem like any of that's being done anymore."

"You're right," I replied. "There simply is no money available in the State's budget to keep a trail crew going for a season. That's why the Adirondack Mountain Club has been raising funds for areas like the High Peaks and other popular hiking trails. If they don't do it, it just doesn't get done." It's sad, but that's a fact of life in remote areas such as the West Canada Lakes, especially once you get off the Northville-Placid Trail. Lack of use equals lack of funding.

Before departing, Mel drew me a map of the roads leading to his farm in Cold Brook where he made his own maple syrup. I wanted to stop by and purchase some. My entire family loves maple syrup—and I might as well give him the business. While I watched him draw the map, I quietly added syrup production to the already-lengthy list of his accomplishments. He had been a dairy farmer, an educator, an inventor, a skilled woodsman, and lots more. I wished that I could someday match his record of endurance and achievements.

I try to take away a little something from almost everyone I meet, something I can learn or emulate that will make me a better person. In the case of my four new friends, it was easy. If you want to go into the woods, then simply go. Don't let a minor detail like age stop you until you are physically unable to do so. But I will also try to remember to mimic them in one additional way. Once I attain the same age as Mel and Glenn, I'll try to bring along my own doctor.

New Technology & Updates in Hiking

It's been close to forty years since I first headed into the West Canada Lakes wearing the drab green uniform with the DEC shoulder patch. That's a long time, especially in an age when technology is moving along at light speed, with new materials and products being introduced faster than we ever dreamed possible. The rapid-fire appearance of new gear is slightly reminiscent of days when the pack basket was replaced by the first external-frame backpacks. The old-timers would never accept such advances, regardless of their superiority over the primitive (but aesthetically pleasing) antiques of the past.

This is the way I feel today as I observe the modern-day updates incorporated into the most recent selection of hiking gear. Canteens? Forget about it. They are now engineered into the "camelback" designs of the latest backpacks. Hikers of the modern era no longer need to remove a water bottle from the waist belt on their pack. They simply squeeze a clip on a tube that is attached to their backpacks and sip whenever they want. They don't need to stop, and they never need to mess around with a bottle cap. It's all part of a single integrated unit. Simple. Easy. Convenient.

Great improvements have also been made in the area of

cooking and camp stoves. My white-gas stove that self-destruct-
ed on my previous excursion had lasted for about four decades,
but there is no doubt that its time had come. Bringing that
ancient brass stove into the woods meant filling a pair of metal
gas containers with liquid fuel and hoping that the rubber gas-
kets on top were still intact. All told, the package weighed in at
around four pounds, which is more than twice as heavy as the
newer butane models.

In addition to the weight issue with the old stoves, they could
also be a major pain to light, even in warm weather. I had to perform numerous acts of manual dexterity to unscrew the top of
the stove from the bottom in order to feed the control key
through the correct aperture to adjust the flame. Likewise, I had
to replace the regular top of the fuel bottle with the piece containing the pouring spout, hoping all the while that I didn't drop
it or spill the highly-flammable gas over myself and my belongings. It was even a bit tricky when all of that went perfectly, as
lighting the fuel in the priming ring of the stove was always a bit
touchy. I'd strike a flame on the lighter I carried for starting
fires, and then hold it up to the stove until the fuel ignited with
a "whoosh." I never actually set myself ablaze while performing
this act, but it was a concern every time I needed to use the
cranky old stove.

Now that I'd been forced into the modern era, I was amazed
at just how easy life could be. My friend Casey had recommended
a butane-fueled stove from JetBoil, which is what I purchased.
After a quick five-minute demonstration by the clerk in Eastern
Mountain Sports, I was an instant expert. OK, so there really isn't
much to it; even a total klutz could do it. Just assemble the
parts, screw on the fuel tank, and press the ignition button. And
presto! The stove becomes an instant blowtorch that can have a
two-cup pot of water boiling faster than you can say "There's a
moose in your tent!"

The only knock I've ever heard against the butane stoves is

from rangers who claim that the empty butane tanks become lit-ter, as many hikers do not want to carry them out of the woods. Personally, I do not consider that a valid concern. First, I was amazed at the fact that I used the same fuel canister for two weeks this summer, cooking every meal without running out of butane. So it isn't as though the hikers have a pile of empty tanks on their hands. They can all be used again and again, which means they seldom become "trash" to be discarded. Besides, I have never once seen a discarded butane tank in the woods. Ever. (And I've seen a lot of bizarre stuff left behind, including a skimpy pink, lace negligee that somehow made it onto a clothes-line behind the South Lake lean-to!)

Improvements have even been made in mosquito netting, which I know must puzzle some of my readers. I have always ridiculed the idea of carrying netting of any sort into the woods, as biting insects are just part of life when camping in the West Canadas. However, with old age comes the need for "creature comforts," and one of those is preventing the loss of several pints of blood to the mosquitoes, black flies, deerflies, horse-flies, and no-see-ums that forever pester hikers in the woods.

I've never minded the buzzing and swatting activity during the daylight hours. It's at night when things really become a nui-sance. Especially after a long day on the trail, when you're tired and your body aches and you just want to drift off to sleep. You're almost there when suddenly, out of the darkness comes the first "bzzzzzzzz," which starts off as a distant drone and then grows louder as the little bugger paints a target on your exposed skin. As you wave impatiently in the general direction, hoping to at least swat it aside, more and more of its friends join in the attack. You are soon overcome by a fleet of kamikaze insects all thinking the same thought: Dinner!

To try to overcome this problem, I purchased a simple bit of mosquito netting prior to my 2015 voyage into the woods. The package came with illustrated instructions on how to set it up. It looked childishly easy, and I (like a complete idiot) believed it would be. However, once I arrived at the Cedar Lakes lean-to and tried setting up the kit, I quickly realized that I'd been duped. I could find none of the spots referenced in the instructions, which left me unable to "Attach A to B," and "Fold tab C into the cleft behind loop F," or "Tuck flap J into pocket K and snap it closed." As I worked, my silent curses became audible, until I finally gave up and stuffed the entire mess back into its original bag. It had cost me only $9.99 and I quickly realized that you get what you pay for. Every mosquito in the entire region surrounding Cedar Lakes was probably in hysterics, and I could see why.

Because of this failure, I had sworn to never again purchase mosquito netting for any outing, ever. But as my 2017 trip grew near, I began doing some research and learned that there were some "new and improved" products that were rated quite highly. I read all the reviews, including the problems that some campers had with the set-up process, and I felt that I could handle this, especially if I carried some simple materials to correct the documented issues. So, with some misgivings, I spent forty dollars and ordered the latest and greatest in mosquito netting.

And by golly it worked! This new product was wide enough to allow me to comfortably get my sleeping bag and all my nightly necessities inside without being cramped. To give myself vertical room, I screwed the upper loop into a cross-log in the top of the lean-to, and then spread the bottom out around my sleeping pad. I climbed in to test its integrity, and yes, I could hear the drone of the mosquitoes and the buzz of the black flies, but on the other side of the netting. Hooray! It was so efficient that I actually took a daytime nap, just to celebrate the victory. (And for anyone who might be feeling sorry for the hungry mosquitoes, please don't. I had already made hundreds of donations to their piecing proboscises that caused me to itch for weeks after returning from my excursion.)

The topic of warding off insects and other biting critters has become even more important with the appearance of Lyme disease and other tick-borne ailments. In my days of living in the woods as a ranger, this wasn't even a thought. Lyme disease? What was that? Perhaps someone with a serious addiction to green citrus fruit? However, in the last twenty years it has become a major concern and has spawned an entire new industry.

Items used to prevent ticks from biting or for removing ticks that have already latched onto one's body are available in every major camping and outdoors store. Some of these are more general in nature, such as the lotions and potions that claim to repel ticks, mosquitoes, and other biting insects. Others are targeted specifically at ticks and make bold claims about "preventing 80 percent of ticks from ever attaching." (Gee, that's great considering the fact that it only takes one tick bite to transmit the disease.) They are also diverse in their willingness to use strong and toxic chemicals as ingredients. Some make claims about being 100 percent natural, with compounds such as tea tree oil and other organic compounds. Others go the complete opposite direction and brag about being straight DEET, a chemical that has proven effective but also "not for direct application on exposed skin." There must be a good compromise in there somewhere, although I'm not sure what that is.

A completely separate category of apparatus is also available for hikers who discover that a tick has already attached itself to their skin, or worse yet, begun to burrow its head down into the skin. The danger here is that removing the body can leave the head attached, thus passing along Lyme disease even after the majority of the tick is gone. Many stores sell pairs of fine-tipped forceps for performing this operation, which would appear to do the trick. An even more lightweight device is a flat metal plate (like a razor blade) with a small hole that narrows into a groove of finer and finer proportions. From reading the direction, I have deduced that the body of the tick is inserted into the hold and then the card is slid backwards until the groove removes the entire animal in a single piece. It seems a bit complicated to me, but if it works, it works. All this being said, I have never seen a tick in the West Canada Lakes area, although I know they must be present.

Water filters are another requirement these days, although I know I've discussed them before. Still, in the 1970s no one bothered with them because no one needed them. You just dipped your canteen into the nearest flowing water and drank what you got. *Giardia lambia* did not exist back then, so it was not a concern. I had personally filled my canteen from West Canada Creek right as it flowed out of Mud Lake. I'd rather not discuss the contents of Mud Lake, but to anyone who has hiked there and observed the quantity and diversity of wildlife living in and around its shoreline, you will know what I mean. I'm sure I ingested millions of bacteria of questionable nature, but none of that ever harmed me.

You can't do that anymore. Drinking water directly out of the lake will probably confine you to an outhouse for a week or more. (And spending more than five minutes in a well-used Adirondack outhouse is already excessive!) So while I never considered carrying a filter in my ranger days, it is safe to say that anyone born after 1980 has never ventured into the woods without one.

To combat this danger, a plethora of camping gear companies have developed a mind-numbing number of products, each with their own claims and bragging rights. Some remove particles of finer dimensions. Others offer varying settings for cleaner versus murkier waters. Still others boast of two-way action, allowing quicker filtering by working on both sides of the reciprocal stroke.

Personally, I go for the "safe versus sorry" strategy and use a filter that removes everything but the water itself as it pumps the fluid into a large storage jug. I'm sure I paid two or three times what I needed to pay, but it sure beats sitting on the throne for days on end waiting to get rid of all those little *Giardia* critters. (And who carries that much toilet paper anyway? OK, too much information.) Regardless, the device I selected has worked every time I've used it, never clogging or choking, so I'm happy with the results.

I can also tell that I'm getting old by the flashlight I carry. Yes, it is small and lightweight, and uses only tiny AAA batteries. I carry two, in case one breaks or is lost. But the key word here is "carry." No one carries a flashlight any more. Everyone (and I mean everyone) under age thirty uses a headlamp. These little bulbs, which are surrounded by a conical reflector to direct the beam, are attached to an elastic band and worn on the head. This permits hand-free operation and is particularly handy if someone wants to hike at night and not have to bother holding a traditional flashlight. It actually makes sense because you never have to aim the headlamp; it is always shining in the same direction as you are looking. I still don't own one of these devices, but I think I will purchase one before my next hike.

Another piece of camping equipment that has evolved significantly over the recent decades is the sleeping pad, that rolled-out piece of insulation that goes beneath your sleeping bag on the lean-to or tent floor. I've always found this bit of gear to perform dual functions. Sure, it provides an additional layer of insulation beneath your bag to prevent the cold ground from seeping through to your body. However, as any senior citizen knows, lean-to floors (or hard-packed earth with a few rocks tossed in for good measure) don't get any softer with age. I know I'm much more sensitive to the bumps and lumps than I was in my earlier days, so anything that will soften these annoyances is a welcome addition to my pack.

I've tried a number of different sleeping pads in my time, but they were all pretty much variations on the same theme—basic, foam pads that are rolled up (or folded up) and used as is, with no assembly required. However, these have all become passé, and the new trend is toward the inflatable, air-cushion pads.

Constructed of a more rubber-like material, they are inflated and then sealed shut before being put to use. From what I hear, they are favored by a majority of today's hikers, and some even operate as a self-inflating unit. I'm still not sure how that works, but I've seen it done so I know it's possible. Others, though, require about five minutes of setup time, with the user blowing into a small nozzle as the pad slowly unfurls and its compartments fill with air. It's a process that can leave some people with a purple face from all the blowing, but they appear to be content with the trade-off.

I've debated the pros and cons of foam versus air with many of the new blow-up users, and there appears to be no clear-cut winner. I can vouch for the fact that my pad is lighter in weight than any rubber inflatable model, but others argue that fact as well. Still, I must admit that I've been tempted to prank one of my air-padded hiking buddies by reaching over in the middle of the night and pulling the plug. The very thought of listening to the hissing of a rubber sleeping pad as it deflates, while simultaneously watching the unsuspecting sleeper sink down to the floor, is enough to have me in stitches.

The entire wardrobe worn by modern hikers has also taken huge strides into the space age. Even back in the 1970s we knew to avoid cotton; wool and polyesters were the way to go. This was one of the points we really pushed while educating the public about being in the woods. However, fleece had not yet been invented. A fleece jacket will maintain its bulk and dry more quickly than wool when it gets wet. It is also much lighter than wool and equally warm, and as a result, fleece has almost completely replaced wool in most weather conditions.

Over the last ten to twenty years, we have seen the introduction of numerous advanced fabrics, such as the thin microfiber undergarments that wick moisture away from the skin while providing superb insulation. They weigh almost nothing and can be layered beneath fleece and other outer layers to provide protection in almost any weather. By using these materials to replace my old insulated long johns, I've found I can carry more clothing while using less space in my pack. Once again, technology has made hiking easier and more comfortable.

Electronic devices have also found their way into the hiking world. On more than one occasion this year, I have run into trekkers who were wearing GPS devices on their wrists, allowing them to venture into areas that were previously out of bounds for the weekend hiker. As I've mentioned in the past, very few individuals venture far off the trail, which means that only about .001 percent of the territory in the West Canada Lakes is ever utilized, or even seen. Of the vast 165,000 acres in the territory, only a thin ribbon of trail ever feels the weight of a hiker's boot. GPS has changed everything, and people are visiting isolated lakes and ponds that haven't been seen in years. It isn't uncommon to hear "We're going in to Twin Lakes," or "We thought we'd try the fishing up at Northrup Lake." This is a great thing, as long as they are not alone and are very familiar with how to use the GPS device.

I have a confession to make here: I too have been smitten with the technology bug. But I do have an excuse—it wasn't my idea. When I decided to return to the woods, my family made me promise to bring along a satellite phone, which I did. I had plans of going off-trail, and since I was alone and already a senior, it did make sense. Unlike normal cell phones, which are blocked by mountains and completely useless when not near a cell tower, satellite phones will work from anywhere. I used this phone to call out about three times on my most recent excursion, which provided peace of mind on the home front. I had no way of recharging the device while in the woods, however, so I had to leave it turned off except when making my calls. But if someone really needed to be accessible, there are solar-powered chargers which would do the trick given a couple hours of direct sunlight. (Then again, if you really needed to be reachable on a continuous basis, what's the point of being there in the first place?)

I am pleased to report that I have yet to see a laptop or tablet PC make it into the woods, nor should they. Perhaps it's none of my business, but I am of the opinion that folks should finish their office work before ever venturing into the woods. PowerPoint presentations and Excel spreadsheets have their uses, but not in wilderness regions surrounded by majestic trees and murmuring steams. Granted, most tablets can take nice photographs, but so do cell phones. Besides, I have yet to see a single lean-to with a USB charging port. (Heck—most of them don't even have Wi-Fi!)

High-tech tents and sleeping bags? I suppose the companies that produce these commodities will be the first to boast of new concepts in lightweight materials and improved baffling, et cetera. But not a lot has changed outwardly in these staples of camping. Tents have continued to add features such as lightweight composite poles and improved venting and entry points. Likewise, sleeping bags make better use of lightweight fill (if not down). But most of these materials have been in use for many years. I still believe that the greatest improvements to tents in the past half century are the advent of the outer fly and shock-corded, lightweight poles. Better yet, I'd pay a premium for a truly high-quality tent that erected itself when removed from the bag. They do make some models that spring open with no assistance, but these appear to be more gimmicks than top-of-the-line gear. But my opinion is still open for adjustment on that matter.

One change that I'm happy to see is in the area of footwear. I'm not talking about the latest advances in Vibram soles or Gortex uppers. That stuff has been around for years, and while the names have been updated, most of what people wear on the trails has remained constant for the past ten or twenty years. What is most noticeable is what folks do when they kick off their boots upon reaching their daily destination.

I must admit I felt rather daft last trip when I packed my fleece-lined leather moccasins. They added a full pound that I did not need to carry, and they used a significant amount of space in my pack that I could ill-afford to spare. Yet the thought of encasing my sore, aching feet in a velvety-soft layer of fleece at day's end was more than I could resist. I decided to forego this luxury on this year's trip only because my pack was already excessively heavy.

For younger folks, the newest trend going is Crocs, which I have never worn. Roughly half of all hikers who shared my accommodations this year wore these lightweight, open-air sandals around the shelter. Their weight, according to what I've read, varies between eleven ounces and one pound, which makes them a viable option for packing. I also came in contact with at least one pair of "flip-flops" this summer, which weigh almost nothing but offer very little in the way of protection for the feet and toes, even in the relatively clear area directly surrounding the lean-to or tent. I've also seen people wearing water shoes, which also weigh almost nothing, although they cost much more than the ubiquitous flip-flops. Personally, I think I will stick to the same pair of fleece-lined moccasins. For the few extra ounces, that's one trade-off that these old bones will gladly accept.

Finally, one other great product I saw for the first time this year (although it may not be new) is a little device called the Pocket Bellows. It is an incredibly handy bit of gear that weighs almost nothing and takes up no space in the backpack. It is literally a tube the diameter of a drinking straw that folds up like a telescope into a length of about three-and-a-half inches. When fully extended, however, it measures about twenty inches in length, and can be used to blast air into the base of a flame with high velocity and pinpoint accuracy to get a campfire started. Now, young people can easily get down on their knees and blow into the fireplace until the desired result is achieved. However, for those of us who are no longer young, the Pocket Bellows can accomplish the same result without the bends and bumps. This is one device I am definitely acquiring for my own use.

In summary, so much has changed in the world of hiking and camping gear that I'm sure my own pack looks like a museum piece to most youngsters. But the same could be said for the generation that came before me. I still remember a number of old-timers who wouldn't be caught dead with anything but a pack basket. John Remias, the caretaker at West Lake (and my "woods dad") enjoyed poking fun at most of my equipment, including my two canteens. After all, those were the pre-*Giardia* days when all you needed was a cup to dip into the nearest stream. The times can sometimes dictate our actions, and this is certainly true with our choices on survival gear.

Still, I'm amazed that, despite the advent of all this light-weight equipment, our packs still weigh so much going into the woods. How is that possible? If the pack itself weighs four pounds, the tent (with poles and tent stakes) weighs five pounds, clothes weigh two pounds, and a sleeping bag weighs three pounds, where does the other half ton come from? The truth of the matter is that we also load ourselves down with pack covers, rain gear, first aid kits, flashlights, and way too many pounds of "almost weightless" dehydrated food. Throw in the additional tonnage of stoves, cook pots, silverware, and filtering gear, and you start to get an idea of how the scales get tipped. I once wrote down a line-by-line, complete listing of everything that was in my backpack, and the accounting came out to over two hundred items. It can get rather daunting.

Someday, they may find a way to make everything so high tech that the pack will weigh almost nothing, with contents that shrink to a small percentage of today's volume. Someday, we may not even need all those pockets that line the outside of our packs, or the compressible stuff sacks that squeeze sleeping bags down to the size of a softball. I must admit that I wouldn't know what to do with the extra space. Maybe I'd bring along my lap-top. OK, maybe not.

—20—

Three New Friends

It was a frightful situation; I was sitting on the front of the Pillsbury lean-to, minding my own business and munching on some cashews and peanuts, when the head of a *Tamias striatus* came into view. It had seen me, and it had seen my food. In other words, it was too late. Slowly, the hungry animal came closer, then closer yet. Its eyes were laser-focused on my every movement, and that movement might be my last.

I considered attempting to run, but I knew that the creature was much faster than me. I could climb upon the roof of the lean-to, but I recognized with certainty that it could use its claws to reach the roof even faster than I. Even if I could climb trees, it could shimmy up trunks at five times my speed. There was no way out.

Even as I sat there, frozen in place, it continued to stalk my physical being until it was a mere eighteen inches from my position. The look on its ravenous face told the whole story; it wanted food, and it wanted it immediately. As if to confirm its expression, it stood up on its hind legs and drew itself to its full height directly in front of me.

There was nothing I could do, so I submitted and tossed the chipmunk a couple of nuts and a banana chip. It quickly scurried from piece to piece and stuffed the tasty bits into the pouches lining its mouth. Then, after giving me an expression as if to say, "I'll be back," it was gone.

Almost all lean-tos in the Adirondacks have at least one resident family of chipmunks, and Pillsbury Lake is no exception. Other shelters in the region have many more, and I recall at least one trip to Beaver Pond lean-to on Cedar Lakes when I donated my entire supply of GORP to the cute little rodents. This is OK, because truth be told, I enjoy giving them snacks and always carry at least double what I need so that I'll have extra to feed them. (I'm sure that most rangers do not appreciate campers sustaining them in such a manner, but I enjoy it.)

Anyway, the part about seeing this fellow's head appear around the corner of the lean-to did really happen, although not in quite as dramatic fashion as I originally stated. I had only recently arrived at the empty shelter on the edge of Pillsbury Lake and was enjoying a quick snack when the small, slender chipmunk appeared on the base log that jutted out from the front right corner of the lean-to.

I didn't do anything at first; I just continued to grind the big cashew between my back teeth while he cast an appraising stare in my direction. I wasn't going to show my hand too easily, so I continued to ignore him as I tipped a few more samples from the GORP bottle into my hand. I then quietly unpacked my ground cloth and bottom sleeping pad onto the lean-to floor.

After a few minutes of observing my actions, punctuated by some rapid trips back into the vegetation (presumably to its nest), the striped critter appeared to overcome its initial shyness and bounded between the fireplace and my feet, only about three feet away. I responded by tossing it a couple nuts, a raisin, and a sesame-stick snack. This must have been a sign to the rodent, who fearlessly approached my feet and retrieved the pieces before scampering away. A quick look back in my direction appeared to signal his sentiments, as if to say "Now we're getting somewhere!"

The fact that the small, furry critter disappeared for some time shouldn't have surprised me. Chipmunks are notorious burrowers and can dig complicated mazes of interconnected tunnels that reach thirty feet in length and extend down to three feet beneath the surface. The architecture of these subterranean dwellings is often complex, with separate branches and chambers for storing food, sleeping, giving birth, and raising their young, and even for their form of pseudo-hibernating. There are often other tunnels beneath the living quarters for the purpose of drainage; it amazes me that they know how to construct this so intuitively. The openings to their tunnels are almost always next to or beneath some other form of protection, such as the thick growth of shrubbery that has blossomed in front of the stone fireplace at Pillsbury Lake. I could not begin to guess where the entrance might be, but I'm sure that the occupant has no problem finding the front door.

I used the next twenty minutes to complete the rest of my unpacking, all the while conscious that my new friend was watching me from his position perched on top of a fallen tree trunk across the campsite. Since he was most definitely a chipmunk, and he looked like a "Chip," that is what I decided to call him. I already mentioned that he was small and slender, but up close I noticed that he was even smaller than most chipmunks I'd observed in the past. Perhaps it was a juvenile. I tried calling him by his new name, but he either did not yet recognize it or didn't approve of it, as he failed to respond to my summons.

Even though eastern chipmunks build chambers in their burrows for the sole purpose of winter sleep, these rodents never enter true hibernation. Instead, they enter a torpid state where the body temperature drops considerably and their heartbeat can fall from 350 beats per minute all the way down to 4. However, they accumulate little or no fat prior to the start of the winter season, and they awaken once every few days to feed and defecate. During these interludes of wakening, their bodies and heartbeats return to normal just long enough to conduct their natural functions. They then return to their deep sleep, which will last (on average) from late October through April. Failure to accumulate enough stored food in its den to last until spring would spell trouble for any individual.

It's always interesting to note what happens when only one person is in residence in a lean-to at any given time. Of course there is wood that needs to be collected, tinder that must be gathered, lean-to floors that want sweeping, and water to be collected and purified. But what happens after that? In my case, I've usually occupied myself with a good book, or (in recent years) worked on materials for new manuscripts. But once all that has been completed, what then?

On this trip, I spent a lot of time talking to Chip and enjoying his travels about the site. He amused me by appearing through cracks and crevices in the walls of the fireplace, where he would freeze and deliberate about whether I was still friendly. After reaching his conclusion, he'd jump down into the bottom of the fire pit, often threading his way through the charred remainders of those logs that had failed to burn completely. I wondered on several occasions just how he was able to determine that the ashes contained no burning embers that might scorch his feet. But however he did it, he seemed to recognize when the fireplace had recently been in use and avoided it accordingly.

Chip also had a habit of approaching me from different angles, perhaps to confuse a potential predator. After all, there are a great many animals in the area that consider the chipmunk to be a food source. Owls and hawks swoop in from above and snatch these animals off the ground. Many land mammals, including the fox, coyote, pine marten, fisher, raccoon, and even bobcat have been observed poaching chipmunks. Because they are so small and lacking in defensive properties, they must remain vigilant at all times or risk becoming a meal for one of these forest predators.

The next place I discovered Chip was sitting upright on one of the protruding base logs that runs from the rear to the front of the lean-to. He wasn't doing anything, just sitting in a stationary position watching me. I opened the GORP canister one more time and selected a few more cashews and a dried, sweetened "pineapple plug." (Pineapple plugs are the small circles of fruit cut from the center of each pineapple ring. They are sort of like the donut holes of the fruit world.)

Chip was quick to snag the cashews, as nuts are part and parcel of their normal diet. And while no cashews grow natively in the Adirondacks, there are enough different kinds of nuts and seeds for them to instinctively collect anything of the sort. However, the pineapple plug was something entirely new, and Chip began a thorough inspection of the morsel before attempting to transport it to his burrow. After sniffing the bit of dried fruit on the ground, he picked it up using his two front paws and turned it over several times, as if to say "Well, it's not my brand, but maybe I'll take it home anyway and give it a try."

Chipmunks actually enjoy a very diverse diet in the Adirondacks and other forested regions. Their favorite food is the beechnut, which is available in abundant quantities in our area due to the composition of the forest flora. In years when the beechnut crop is limited, these foragers have been observed climbing beech trees and using their sharp teeth to detach clusters of the nuts from the branches. Then they scamper back down the tree and harvest what they have cropped from the canopy, carrying great quantities back to their homes in their expandable mouth pouches. It's an efficient system that works for them, assuming that they don't have to compete with the larger mammals (i.e., the black bear) for the fallen nuts.

On this particular afternoon, Chip suddenly ran into stiff competition from a critter much smaller than a bear, another member of its own species. He was sitting on the compacted soil in front of the lean-to when I detected a movement coming from the wood stacked next to the fireplace. It was another chipmunk, much larger than Chip, who was staring across the clearing at the pineapple chunk. Chip had almost managed to stuff the oversized bit of fruit into his mouth when this intruder leaped. He flew with incredible speed off the woodpile and across the site, making a beeline for Chip. Chip didn't wait around for the newcomer to arrive. He took off at light speed for the shrubs, where (presumably) the entrance to his burrow would provide safety.

He didn't quite make it.

I am not familiar with the habits and defense mechanisms that protect chipmunks when competing with animals of their own clan. I only know what I can observe, and on this particular afternoon Chip was running away from his larger compatriot so fast that he either missed or did not see the opening to his own tunnel. (Or perhaps he didn't want to lead his pursuer right to his front door?)

What followed was both comical and astounding, as the two camouflaged rodents zigged and zagged about the scene with incredible velocity. How they could follow one another with such speed and agility and turn on such short notice was nothing short of phenomenal. The scurrying was accompanied by some frantic chirps, most likely some form of antiphonal vilification between the two participants. Finally, the motion and noise ceased and all was quiet once again. I'm sure that Chip made it back to his burrow, as I heard no further indications of the pursuit.

The larger chipmunk who had been the apparent aggressor returned to the fireplace and regarded me in a questioning manner. "You gave the little guy a bite to eat; how about me?" He continued to stare, much like his competitor had, while I went once again to the large Tupperware container for another sample. Instead of hopping away after two or three pieces, he stuffed his mouth with at least a dozen nuts and raisins before retreating to his own abode.

Beechnuts are far from the single source of the chipmunk's natural diet. They enjoy devouring berries, maple tree seeds, tubers, and certain fungi. They have also been observed consuming invertebrates and small vertebrates, even preying on some newly hatched birds. This appears to be rare, however, and most of their diet tends to be restricted to seeds and nuts.

Since I had named the smaller of the two "Chip," this larger animal was a natural for the appellation "Munk." They seldom appeared at the same time, especially if I was feeding one or the other. Chip seemed to know his place in the pecking order and would scurry off at the first sight of his nemesis. Munk would seldom give chase unless he knew that Chip was actively receiving pieces of my GORP supply, in which case it was no-holds-barred pursuit.

I was always amazed at just how much these fellows could hold in their pouches if they weren't escaping from an immediate threat. Munk was capable of transporting especially large hauls; he could stash at least ten to fifteen nuts in his mouth at any one time. Academic research on this topic discloses that a mature chipmunk can carry up to thirty-two beech nuts in its pouches at a single time, an astounding number. There were times when Munk's head seemed to double in size from the accumulated haul protruding from both sides of his face.

Within a day or two, I noticed with some alarm that my supply of GORP had dwindled to less than half its original size. Since I had consumed very little of it myself, I could only imagine the accumulation that had taken place inside the storerooms of their respective burrows. I did, however, come up with a rather comical way of making them break off an existing visit if I thought they had already received their fill: I would toss a banana chip their way. That created a problem for the chipmunks because, unlike smaller and more compact nuts, their oblong shape takes up a lot of room in the critter's mouth, and they are not compressible. After just one of these tidbits, both Chip and Munk usually hopped off to store the bounty in their subterranean warehouse.

I was surprised at the level of familiarity I was able to achieve with these two companions. Even though my stay at Pillsbury was interrupted by a break in the middle when I ventured over to Whitney and Sampson lakes, the two immediately recognized me when I returned and resumed the same level of cordiality. Chip especially seemed to accept me as a friend, as he began sitting between my two feet while he consumed a particularly tasty cashew. There were even a couple surprising visits when he hopped up on top of my hiking boot while he snacked. I can't be certain that he knew my foot was inside, but nevertheless he remained perched there while he dined. It was quite the experience.

Chip and Munk were in constant sight while I was alone at Pillsbury, but they remained completely elusive when others were in residence. My egotistical side reasoned that my furry new friends preferred my solo company to that of other campers in the area. The more logical explanation was that the amount of noise and commotion was greater with three or four folks in the vicinity than it was with a single individual. Regardless, whether it was two, three, or four additional guests in the lean-to, the chipmunks were more-or-less invisible in their presence. (There was one time during the week when a single other camper stayed in the lean-to with me. However, since he was accompanied by a rather "barkative" dog, Chip and Munk remained hidden in their respective lairs.)

After I had been at the lake for about six or seven nights, I noticed something different in the approach of one of my friends. He appeared to be coming from a new angle, far to the left of the lean-to and across a new approach log. I'd become so accustomed to these two fellows that anything out of the ordinary really stood out. As the wandering chipmunk drew near, he disappeared from view for a few moments before reappearing on the left side of the lean-to. It was then that I realized he was different in appearance than my two established co-residents. Instead of being thin and slender like Chip, or meaty and broad-bodied like Munk, he was about average, neither husky nor thin. He also had a cleft in his tail, almost as though it had been bitten or broken on one side so that it bent to the left at a slight angle. A bit of hair was missing on the opposite side of the tail from the bend.

I instantly recognized that this newcomer was making its initial visit to the lean-to, perhaps as part of a scouting trip to seek out new food sources. It wouldn't be unusual for an individual animal to stray a significant distance from its burrow. Eastern chipmunks can occupy a territory of up to one acre, which translates to a square that is 208 feet on each side. Forest zoologists have determined that the territories of several chipmunks can overlap, sometimes resulting in a much more dense population center. Adult males can wander significantly farther when seeking to mate or when food sources are restricted.

Chipmunks also display a number of burrowing habits that are reminiscent of Adirondack French Louie and his multitude of shelters throughout the territory. E.A. Spears (Utica *Observer-Dispatch*) once noted that "French Louie had as many homes as a Newport millionaire only they were log cabins, bark shacks, and lean-tos." Like Louie, chipmunks have a single main burrow that is the focus of their daily lives, but they can construct much simpler, shorter tunnels that give them protection when they travel some distance from their primary home. They also adopt tunnels made by other animals when they discover them uninhabited in the woods, much in the way that Louie would take over an abandoned shanty or utilize a hollowed-out log. Similar to the old hermit of West Lake, chipmunks were opportunistic in their habits and mannerisms.

Because the third chipmunk first made its appearance from the left side of the lean-to and his tail was crooked to the left, I promptly named him "Lefty." He was just as attracted to my supply of cashews, peanuts, raisins, sesame seeds, and pineapple plugs as the others, but he didn't appear to have any conflicts with Munk as he collected my offerings. Munk seemed intent only on chasing Chip whenever he saw the little fellow begging for

GORP at the lean-to. Perhaps he was unfamiliar with Lefty's fighting skills, or Munk was a male and Lefty was a female he desired to ask out on a date. (OK, probably not.) But for whatever reason, Lefty continued to make infrequent, sporadic appearances, perhaps once or twice a day, and then disappear from whence he came.

By the end of my stay at Pillsbury Lake, I was extremely well-acquainted with all three of these critters and could tell them apart at a distance of at least twenty feet. (Considering that my vision is no longer that keen, making any such determination is a mark of extreme familiarity.) Over the last few days of my visit, Chip became especially accustomed to my presence and would strut along the front log of the lean-to until his nose almost touched my knee. At such times, I could feed him by placing a cashew almost directly into his front paws, although I intentionally avoided making contact. When in such a position, or when he chose to sit directly on top of my boot-clad foot, I think he felt protected from the onrushes of Munk. With a small amount of imagination, I could picture him staring back at the larger animal as if to say "Go ahead; let's see you take on my big brother. I dare you!"

By the time I departed Pillsbury on my final hike back to the trailhead, my entire quart container of GORP had been emptied. I had personally consumed very little of this stash, which means that my three friends must have accumulated massive troves in their underground dens. I knew I would miss them, and they (especially Chip) would certainly miss me. More than his two companions, Chip had managed to overcome his fear of me and learned to trust my movements and intentions. The appearance of my hand meant the offering of something edible rather than a physical threat. And to a lesser degree, that level of friendship and trust grew into a common bond among all four of us.

So when I think back on the many friendships I established during this voyage into the woods, I can definitely describe my favorites in one quick description: "The ones with the stripes."

—21—

The Biker-Hiker (or Hiker-Biker)

I've seen a lot of strange things in the woods in the course of my wandering, some more bizarre than others. The simple appearance of a lone hiker arriving at seven-thirty at night, while not highly unusual, is a bit out of the ordinary, as most folks tend to pull into a lean-to in the middle hours of the afternoon.

But not Levi.

I was standing on the side of the Pillsbury Lake lean-to, sorting out the best pieces of tinder from my woodpile when I got my first glimpse of Levi and his companion dog. Right from the get-go, it was an odd scene, and I paused momentarily to confirm that my eyes were not playing tricks on me. However, since my second glance was consistent with the first, I assumed they were telling me the truth.

The man who approached me, canine by his side, was a tall fellow with long, curly black hair, who appeared to be in his late thirties. (I later learned that was incorrect.) But what so surprised me about his appearance was his clothing, which bore no resemblance to that of any hiker I'd ever seen this far into the woods. He wore none of the traditional hiker's garb—no Gore-Tex hiking boots; no ventilated, space-age shirts or lightweight, polyester cargo pants. As a matter of fact, the only item he had on his body that would identify him as a backpacker was the backpack itself. The rest was right out of an advertisement for Harley Davidson. The leather jacket was embroidered with some form of biker design, and the boots were designed for someone who spent more time on the highway than on the hiking trail.

Levi wasn't shy. He strode right up to introduce himself as he was throwing his backpack into the lean-to. This too was a bit unusual; most folks ask if they can share a lean-to before they move in. But no matter, as I would have offered him space anyway. It was just different, that's all.

"This is Ezekiel," Levi said as he hoisted the small, mixed-breed pooch into the crook of his arm. "He comes with me everywhere I go, don't you, Zeke?" Zeke answered by shaking his entire body right along with his tail. I couldn't tell what breeds were mixed together in that fluffy ball of fur. But whatever the combination, they must all have been recognized for their proliferation of long, curly hair, as Zeke resembled an overgrown dust mop. He was a sight, and I wondered how he managed on the hot days of mid-summer. (As a matter of fact, the shape of Zeke's fur resembled Levi's hair style in almost every regard, and I wondered whether they shared the same stylist.)

As we exchanged our first greetings, the dog—now back on his own four legs—was already displaying his frenetic personality and abundance of energy, as many smaller breeds do. He commenced a series of circuitous sprints that took him around and around the two of us at an amazing rate of speed. He alternated that with an occasional lap of the lean-to, all with a randomness that neglected all reason or regularity. Amazing, I thought to myself. This small pooch had just walked several miles of uphill-downhill terrain while keeping pace with his much-larger master. Every one of Levi's strides must have required about five from Zeke. Regardless, he showed no ill effects from the journey in and gave no indication that he was ready for a rest.

Levi wasted no time getting unpacked and arranging a quick

meal for himself and Zeke. Since he had been through the town of Speculator only three hours earlier, he opted to bring along an oversized submarine sandwich instead of prepackaged trail food. I must admit I envied his selection as he unwrapped the roast beef and vegetable creation on the front of the lean-to.

"So where are you coming from today from that gets you into the woods so late in the day?" I asked.

"We live in New York City, over in the Bronx," Levi replied, while sampling his first bite of the sandwich. "I left work a little early today so we could get an early start and get in here before dark."

"Wow, you must have taken off quite early," I countered. "It's at least 250 miles from here down to the city. That's at least four to five hours away."

"No, it took about two-and-a-half hours, including the ride up to the trailhead parking lot" he said in a matter-of-fact tone.

"What!?" I looked at him with eyes wide-open, waiting for him to smile and admit he was joking. It never happened.

"Yeah, we left home at around two this afternoon, and it took a little while to get through the city traffic and over the bridges," he explained. "But then, once we got clear of all that, we averaged about one hundred miles an hour the whole rest of the way up here. Even when we hit a little rush hour traffic on the Thruway, I used my bike to move between lanes and pass it by. Honestly, it took no time at all!"

I really had no reply that was worth making, so I remained silent and set about my own activities. One hundred miles an hour? All too often I have seen motorcyclists traveling at extreme rates of speed, although most of the drivers I've observed tend to mind the speed limit and other rules of safe driving. I closed my eyes at the thought of this man's passage that day and how one pothole or unavoidable obstacle could have spelled doom for the man-and-dog duo. But it wasn't my place to say anything, so I changed the topic.

"You don't sound like a New Yorker to me," I said. "I go down there several times a year to visit my daughter, and you don't have any of the typical accents."

"You're right about that," Levi replied. "I was born and raised out in Colorado, which is where I gained my love for the great outdoors. Most people in New York don't even think about getting out of the city and into the woods. They're kind of crazy down there."

"So how did you find out about this area and decide to come all the way up here?"

"I've got a good book that lists all the best parks and areas like this within three hundred miles of the city," he said. "I've been using my weekends and vacations over the past few years to visit as many of them as I can. That's one thing this country does well; it has nice parks. As far as I'm concerned, the rest of the country could easily be replaced."

I shot a sideways glance at my lean-to companion to see if he was joking. Once again, he wasn't, and it wasn't long before a few other signs of discontent began to creep into his conversation. He was evidently displeased with the entire American form of government and business, declaring that the American "Evil Empire" would most likely be gone within twenty years. I suddenly wished that I was alone rather than in the company of this rebellious-minded individual. I was only able to move him off the topic of politics by switching the conversation to more personal matters.

Levi surprised me by stating that he was fifty-two years of age. "You're kidding," I exclaimed. "I would have guessed you were in your late thirties."

"No, I've got about a decade and a half on that," he said, smiling at my misguided estimate. "I probably look younger because I try not to let stress bother me. Plus, I don't have all the worries and tensions of a wife and kids to aggravate me. It's just me and Ezekiel, so I can do whatever I want, whenever I want."

"So you just do everything by yourself? You don't date, or

have someone you can hike with and do stuff together?" It was more of a personal question than I normally ask, but Levi didn't seem like the kind of person who would mind the query.

"No, that kind of thing has never worked out for me," he explained as he continued to devour his sub. "I tried doing some Internet dating for a while, but I lost patience with it. I don't understand women these days, even the older, more mature women you can meet online. It seems like they all have a tiny, pinhole-sized set of requirements that make for the perfect man. And if you don't meet all the specifications on their checklist, they aren't interested. I just don't want to go there. I'd rather remain single."

Once again, I remained silent as I tallied up my observations of the newcomer. He was a fifty-two-year-old, anti-government radical who rode his motorcycle at one hundred miles per hour and lived in a small city apartment with a hyperactive mutt. I could easily understand the reticence of potential female suitors when it came to responding to his advances.

Speaking of Zeke, he had ceased his sprints around the shelter and was now sitting at attention, mouth open while he panted, awaiting bites from the hoagie that Levi was tossing his way. From his diminutive stature, I guessed that he probably didn't need much to satisfy his hunger pangs, but he never showed a decline in enthusiasm as he pounced on each morsel. Levi was quite generous in the portions he shared with the little mongrel considering their comparative size. Overall, I'd guesstimate that Zeke ended up with about a quarter of the sub.

As we prepared for the night, Levi appeared to crawl into his sleeping bag complete with all his biker attire except the leather jacket. Unlike many of the canines I've seen in the woods over the years, Zeke wanted no part of sleeping on the lean-to floor. Nope, it was right into the sleeping bag with his pet human, where he curled up in a ball next to Levi's head. Levi pulled the top corner of the sleeping bag over both their heads and they were done for the night.

Because of my advancing age, I tend to be an early riser, and the following morning was no exception. The sun was just beginning to rise when I wriggled my way to the front of the lean-to and fired up some hot water for tea. Zeke quickly scurried out from the sleeping bag to investigate the source of the commotion. Naturally, once two of us were up and about, Levi also chose to rise and join us to watch the sun come up.

I was sitting on the front log of the shelter observing the pink and orange hues as they tried their best to burn through the morning haze. This was always one of my favorite times of day, and I preferred silence above all else as I marveled at nature's kaleidoscope of colors dancing over the lake. Conversation at that hour is something I could do without, much less political monologues on the evils of our government and society.

"Have you ever read anything by John Perkins?" Levi asked nonchalantly, as if the author cited wrote a cooking column in the local paper.

"No, can't say that I have," I replied, my eyes still focused on the expanding rainbow of colors reflected in the mist. For crying out loud, I hadn't even had my first morning cup of tea!

"He wrote some amazing stuff," Levi continued. "He explains how our government is in cahoots with the big corporations to fleece developing countries around the world out of their money and resources. It's how the rich get richer and the poor lose whatever assets they might have. It's sad, but so true."

"Hmm, I've never heard of him." (Nor did I really want to, but I decided to leave that unsaid.)

"Another favorite of mine is Jerold Mander," Levi went on. "He argues convincingly that capitalism is wrong—wrong for our country and wrong for the world. It's just another way of ensuring that the people with all the money just keep accumulating more, and those without money don't even have the resources to fight the system. It's all part of the plan of the elites to keep us down."

By this time I had given up on having a few minutes in peace to finish watching the sunrise. And as much as I know it's impossible, I could swear that I detected an apologetic look from Zeke, as if to say, "Hey, he's only my human. I can't control what he says any more than you can!"

For the second time in as many days, I fervently wished that someone with whom I shared a lean-to would just stop talking. At least I had the satisfaction of seeing him packing his gear to start his trek out of the woods. I had heard all the talk I cared to hear regarding how the United States was the "bad guy." I decided not to mention that I had served twenty-seven years as an officer in the United States Navy and usually voted Republican. No sense rocking the boat even more.

Eventually, Levi realized that I was not responding to his remarks on social realignment and wealth re-distribution and finally fell silent. As he continued to pack, Zeke stepped off to the side of the lean-to and vacated his bowels on the ground of the best tent site in the area. I looked at Levi with an expectant expression, as if to say, "Are you going to clean that up?" Nope, it never happened. Evidently his concern for the environment and looking out for others didn't extend so far as cleaning up after his own dog.

After another few minutes of silence, I began feeling a bit guilty about ignoring his attempts at conversation, even if they were outside of my areas of interest, so I reinitiated dialogue with a couple harmless questions about his visit.

"So tell me, how is it having to drive all those hours to get up here and then hike another few hours to get into the woods, all for a short twelve hours spent at a lean-to? Is all that worth it to you?"

Levi sat back down and faced the lake, casting an appraising eye out over the water. He took a while to answer my question, as though he needed to think carefully as he selected his words.

"Oh yes, every minute of the time and effort it takes to get to places like this is well worth it to me," he said slowly. As he spoke, the mists swirled over the lake, and the first breezes of the morning churned up little ripples on the water's surface. "It injects just enough peace and beauty into my life."

"I know exactly how you feel," I murmured. "I get the exact same thought every time I watch a scene like this."

Levi seemed to be lost in thought as he gazed at the water. "I want to remember this moment exactly as it is. I want to be able to see this in my mind forever."

Those were the last words I heard Levi speak before he departed on his race back to the madness of his city life. But I decided right then and there that he wasn't such a bad guy after all.

—22—

The Final Descent

This chapter is written as a close to several things that are near and dear to me. Not only does it serve as the terminal chapter of this book, but it may also mark the end of my days as an awestruck voyager into the deeper forests of the Adirondacks. The events described within the travels of this week include not only the comical and serene, but also the discomforts and occasional agony of someone who has become an old man in a young man's pastime. The years of our lives with which we are blessed can be productive and rewarding, but they do not make the load of the backpack any lighter nor the mileage of the trail any shorter. At some point in time, every individual comes up against that trek that is just a mile too long, or the mountain that is but a thousand feet too high. For me, that time has arrived, as the pain of the voyage has now overcome the reward for completing the adventure. This is the story of my last week on the trails; my final descent.

Day 1—Thursday:

I'm still not sure why I agreed to do this final trek into the woods this fall. After all, I'd made a fairly complete recovery from a complex medical issue just nine months earlier and had already completed a two-week's stay inside the French Louie loop of the West Canada Lakes Wilderness earlier this summer. I really didn't have anything left to prove to myself. I was almost sixty-two years old, and I'd passed over most of the miles of trails I'd traversed when I was less than half my current age. So what the heck was I thinking?

Yet something had been nagging at me for the past couple years that told me I needed to go one more time. Instead of merely going in "one day's worth," I needed to travel through the heartland of Louis' hermitage. As the hiker I'd met a few years earlier said to me after passing through the clearing that once held Louis' main camp, "These are sacred grounds." Deep down inside, I knew he was right.

My proposal for a four-day loop through those revered lands was met by whoops of approval by my hiking buddy, Casey. Casey was born a mere eight days after me, so we are of identical age. Yet he has preserved himself much better through rigorous exercise and a training regime of martial arts. He is always the first one to suggest a backpacking excursion to the backwoods of the Adirondacks, whereas I have been the reluctant one who has spent more time on the recliner with television remote in hand. But I did want to do this. Rather badly.

Our trip-planning conference (which every wilderness trek requires) was held at Sticky Lips Bar-B-Que, as is mandated by Adirondack code. No, there really isn't a set of codes and statutes for planning a hiking adventure. But if there was, a BBQ joint is as good as any place for getting one's soul ready for the voyage. Plus, it's pretty hard finding a rack of ribs that will travel well inside a backpack, so you might as well have it before you hit the trail.

I had one goal in mind above all else as we laid out our itinerary for this trip, and that was to reduce weight! The packs I had carried into the woods on my previous two excursions had been ridiculous, both in excess of eighty pounds. Granted, they had been necessary to support extended stays of up to fourteen days, but I had to find a way to drastically decrease that payload or I knew I wouldn't be able to make the shortest of distances between our nightly stays.

Unfortunately, neither of us owned a true lightweight two-man tent, so we each would carry in our own one-person shelters. I had serious misgivings about the necessity of this, as I had spent significant time in the woods after Labor Day and I knew that the lean-tos would be vacant or underutilized. But I relented and packed my ultra-light tent anyway, comforted in the thought that I could still use it as a pillow. (But who needs a three-and-a-half-pound pillow, right?)

We decided on a "divide and conquer" strategy that would eliminate duplication of all other essential equipment and supplies. After much deliberation, not to mention the tasty half-racks of BBQ ribs, we decided that we could save weight on stoves, water filters, and cooking equipment. I would bring along my new butane stove, while Casey would pack in his new water filter. This is gear that we both owned, but decided not to duplicate inside our packs. One of each would work.

Or so we thought.

I was still embarrassed with myself for holding on to my old Svea white-gas stove model for as long as I had, keeping it until it failed on the job. The brass frame of the ancient stove's wind shield alone weighed as much as my new JetBoil, and that's not even considering the full internal gas tank and additional sixteen-ounce refueling canister. It was excessive, but I've never been the first one to jump at new ideas, so I had carried it all in good spirits.

The water filter wasn't a big deal as they really don't weigh that much. Casey would bring along his new model, which replaced a ceramic filter with a newer substance. He tried it once at home before packing it, but he also suggested that I bring mine along "just in case." I ignored that request, as I had already donned my horse blinders to prevent me from considering anything but the lightest available option. This probably wasn't smart, but I was ready to consider anything that would lighten the load.

While packing for this trip, which would be my first hiking (versus camping) excursion in several years, I took a number of additional weight-lessening precautions that fall outside of my normal set of preparations. For example, I removed all but one small flashlight from my pack, whereas I normally have at least one backup. I carried just three small AAA batteries, in case I ran out of the first set, but no more. I'd just have to conserve the use of my flashlight or pay the price in darkness.

Other duplicates were removed as well. No spare pieces of silverware rode in my pockets. Only one small knife blade would make the trip. Fleece replaced heavier materials, superfluous emergency gear was pared down, and toothpaste tubes were replaced with smaller and mostly-empty backups. By the time I had finished my preps, I was excited to note that the overall weight of my pack was down to about thirty-eight pounds, and I could hoist it above my head with one arm. I was pleased.

Casey had similarly labored over the weight-reduction process and had pared his own down to about thirty-five pounds. His pack was significantly smaller in dimensions than mine, his being an internal frame construction with newer and more modern features. He also took the additional time to wrap the contents of each pocket and compartment in plastic, in case a hard rain caught us out before we could place our pack covers over our backpacks. It made sense, although I never went to those extremes of protection.

We had a brief discussion the day before departing for our hike. Casey had business that would take him later into the evening than anticipated, and we would get a later start the next day than we would have preferred. Because of that, we didn't arrive at the trailhead until a bit after noon, so our start on the trail was pushed back until about twelve-thirty. We decided to make our first day's destination Pillsbury Lake instead of Cedar Lakes for that reason. It took less time and we'd be more certain of getting space in the lean-to at Pillsbury.

We were impressed to see that the Old Military Road leading from Sled Harbor up to the parking lot at the base of Pillsbury Mountain was in better shape than in prior years. This route, which is gravel over sand and rock, can be treacherous during wet seasons when runoff can be voluminous and erosive. Heavy downpours can create ravines within the roadbed and expose large boulders that will tear the exhaust systems off vehicles with insufficient ground clearance. Our transport on this day was a passenger van with a long body and an alarmingly low frame. However, it was the best we had, and it somehow made the grade along the incline to the trailhead with nary a rub on its bottom side.

It was surprising to see that we were the only car in the trail-head parking lot at noon on Thursday afternoon. We knew that the level of traffic on the trails always falls dramatically once Labor Day passes, but this was unusual. Perhaps the light rain that had begun to fall also contributed to the lack of visitors at the parking area. We just hoped this translated into an equally desolate scene at the area lean-tos, at least until we hit the Northville-Placid Trail junction in another day.

One other detail I had considered, which was a "pack or not-pack" question regarding bringing my camera into the woods, finally settled itself in the parking lot. I owned a tiny, ultra-light version of a popular camera that took much better photos than my cell phone. But I quickly opted to leave the camera behind in the truck rather than tote it around in a pocket for the next four days. It would be just one more thing to lug, one more thing that could break or give me headaches. My cell phone was fully charged and in airplane mode, so the camera on that device would have to capture any images I wanted to bring home with me. Less is better; less is wonderful. Leave the camera behind!

The climb up the steep parts of Blue Ridge seemed to fly by in comparison to the past few visits. My pack seemed feather light compared to the way it felt on those previous trips, when I found myself laboring after the first half mile and stopping to catch my breath every one- to two-hundred paces. I was grinning from ear to ear each time I crested the next hill along the way, and at one point I almost suggested trying to do the first couple days' hiking in one marathon shot. Little did I realize that feeling would not last, that age and mileage would catch up to me sooner than I expected. But for the time being I was doing fine.

We made it to the Pillsbury Lake lean-to in two hours, which may be slow for many younger hikers but was fine for us. I could tell just by feeling the air as we descended the hill to the lean-to that it was unoccupied. The air and silence and the absence of wood smoke all serve as indicators regarding the occupancy status of a shelter. I don't know what else is involved, but I can discriminate between a filled lean-to and an empty one long before glimpsing the interior of the structure. Perhaps it's just a sixth sense, but it's there.

By the way, it's always interesting to hear a new arrival heralding their approach with loud calls of "Hello... hello?" There is some merit to this form of salutation, as it alerts any dogs that might be in residence with their masters that other humans are about to appear. Canines can become somewhat territorial over the space around their lean-to, and the sudden appearance of another person or persons can trigger aggressive behaviors, so I do not begrudge the newcomers their "hellos."

As expected, the lean-to at Pillsbury was empty, and we quickly dumped our packs and set up housekeeping inside. This involves only the spreading of the sleeping pad and bag across the floor boards and the arrangement of a few personal belongings on the various shelves and hooks, yet it establishes residence. I've always tried to do this in a way that left large parts of the lean-to completely devoid of gear, as if to signify that we're here but space is still available for others. Anyone who has ever slept in a lean-to before either gets this or they don't. It depends on how neighborly you happen to be.

After setting down my belongings, I extracted the bag of GORP from my food canister and selectively pulled out some cashews and sesame sticks, which I thought would serve nicely as an afternoon pick-me-up. I was perched on the front log of the shelter, munching on snacks, when suddenly one of my friends from a few weeks earlier appeared. Or perhaps I should say appeared-and-disappeared because as soon as he was there he was gone. Which one it was I could not say. He popped his head up from beneath the lean-to and gave a startled leap before bounding across the grass and into his burrow. I was slightly saddened by the rapid retreat, as my ego goaded me into believing that they might remember me. (Or at least remember the pounds of GORP I fed them earlier in the summer.) Evidently they didn't, and it was a clear-cut case of "What have you done for me lately?" It would be the only time I'd catch a glimpse of any of them during this brief overnight stay.

After a short break and about thirty minutes of shut-eye, we decided to tackle our afternoon chores, which included gathering wood and filtering water. Here we parted ways, as Casey headed down to the waterfront while I ascended the hill back to the main trail. Unfortunately, the area surrounding the Pillsbury Lake lean-to is filled with various conifers, along with white and yellow birch trees. None of these shed limbs that are of much use in a camp blaze, although the "paper" from the base of the white birch does make excellent fire starter. It took me a good thirty minutes before I was able to return with a semi-impressive haul of lumber.

As I dumped my pile of timber on the ground in front of the shelter, I was surprised to find that Casey was still absent from the site. Pumping water with a new device is normally a quick task, even if filtering four to six quarts, which is more than we needed at the time. New pumps advertise rates of up to a quart per minute, and Casey's pump was brand new. I wondered what was causing the holdup.

I was even more puzzled after the passage of an additional fifteen minutes, which is how long it took me to rest and then break up the firewood into fireplace-sized pieces. I stacked the wood inside the lean-to based upon size and age, with a separate stack for kindling and birch paper "starter" material.

Forty-five minutes gone by, and still no sign of Casey.

I was on the verge of sending out the Saint Bernards when I glimpsed my companion heading back to the lean-to. He did not look happy.

"We have a serious problem," he intoned, his eyes cast downward. "This pump started out working just fine, but went downhill in a hurry. I got a blister started on my finger from pumping this thing non-stop for a half hour and all I'm getting now is a slow trickle down the side of the bottle. It's just no good."

"Is it possible that the input or output tube is plugged with a pebble or piece of vegetation?" I suggested.

"It's only got one tube, and that's the inflow side. The output nozzle screws right onto the top of the water bottle, so I know it can't be that."

"Well, if it worked at first but then slowed down, at least we know that it can function," I offered. "Maybe the water is so dirty that it clogged the filter on the first bottle. Perhaps you need to disassemble the filter piece and clean it off."

I knew Casey was almost certainly sharing my thoughts that it was highly unlikely the filter would clog so quickly, regardless of the water quality. However, since I had neglected to bring along my own pump, which I knew did work in this lake, we had no other choice. Our only alternative besides boiling water would be to turn around and head out of the woods, which neither of us desired. So disassembling the apparatus became the focus for the next hour.

I was actually quite impressed with the speed with which Casey was able to remove the enclosed components of the pump and clear the various sediments off the filter. The buildup was significant, and we quickly realized that the pump had indeed been rendered useless by the accumulation of materials around the micro-pores. After a quick series of maneuvers to put the device back together, Casey scored an instant victory at the waterline, collecting several quarts of water in short order. We were back in business.

The next few hours were quite pleasurable as we prepared our dinners and arranged the wood so we could start our evening blaze with the application of a single match. A campfire is one of the tasks that form the centerpiece of life at a lean-to, and it's something I refuse to forgo unless experiencing the most severe of circumstances.

After finishing a sumptuous dinner of freeze-dried lasagna (some degree of sarcasm has been applied to this description), we settled back to watch the sun migrate down towards the end of the lake while painting the skies a rosy shade of pinkish-orange. For about the third time in an hour, Casey turned his head and cocked an ear, thinking that he'd heard voices from the top of the hill. However, this time it wasn't his imagination, and a pair of younger backpackers strode into view in front of the lean-to.

"Hi! Mind if you have some company tonight?" The speaker was a tall fellow with dark hair and an untrimmed moustache who introduced himself as Gordon. "The suspicious-looking guy following me here is Spencer, and we're hoping that we can share the place with you until we get going in the morning."

"Of course you can," I declared in a welcoming voice. "I enjoy having company. My friend here has already heard all my old jokes so I'm looking for a new audience to bore!"

Casey rolled his eyes and agreed. "Yes, you will hear them all. I can guarantee you that."

It turned out the men had once lived near one another and been friends in Buffalo. Spencer had moved south, into the concrete jungle of Brooklyn, while Gordon remained in upstate New York. They still managed to get together every year to hike and climb. That's one more thing I've noticed about friends; they come and go, often losing touch with one another over the years, but friends who hike and camp together tend to be more perennial than most. Perhaps this is because there aren't a lot of people who enjoy the real deep woods experience enough to actually go through with it on an annual basis, so those who do have learned to stick together.

Despite our offer to share the lean-to, the two newcomers decided to set up their tent for the night. The forecast had called for sporadic rain throughout the next twenty-four hours, so I didn't want them to have to use their tent unless they truly wanted to do so. Packing up a wet and muddy tent in the morning is not only a messy job, but it also adds at least an extra pound to your backpack. I know; I've been there.

Once Gordon and Spencer decided to sleep in their tent, they set about the task of actually erecting the thing, which was a bit of a comedy act in its own right. While it was a quality tent manufactured by a recognized name, they had never actually attempted a trial setup prior to entering the woods. It was brand new, just out of the bag, and I could swear that at one point I saw the sales receipt slip flutter to the ground in the early evening breeze.

Setting up a modern-era tent is an art, and I'm sure there is a tried-and-true method that works on 95 percent of all models. However, I have yet to find that procedure listed anywhere, nor had Gordon and Spencer, so they had to resort to reading the "stick figure" illustrations on the tag attached to the bag, which was where things began to deteriorate. It was filled with all the typical lines, including "attach poles A, B, and D to the Y connector piece at the end of pole C, then thread through sleeve 2 until able to pull the O-ring over the grommet on pole F. Repeat for poles C, E, and G using the other Y connector and O-ring 2, and adjust if necessary." Somehow, the easy setup advertised on the outside stuff sack had fallen by the wayside, and the two struggled for some time with their purchase. They had almost completed their task when one of them discovered that the bottom pins were color-coded, and they had the entire contraption arranged backwards!

I had long since tired of observing the performance, so I finalized my own sleeping arrangements by placing my tent (which was still packed in its bag) by the head of my sleeping bag and then wrapping it in my heavy fleece jacket. This always made for a comfortable pillow, as the fleece material provide sufficient loft to mask the stiffness of the tent poles inside. I was soon changed and zipped into the downy comfort of my sleeping bag. The hike into the woods had made me drowsy, and I noticed that the conversation around me was sounding more distant as I quickly drifted off to sleep.

I freely admit that I have always been a creature of habit, and I am prone to repeating my own routines for almost everything, from ordering at a restaurant to placing items on my nightstand. This habitual reiteration of actions even extends to the positioning of gear I arrange next to my head when I fall asleep in a lean-to. I want my flashlight, my watch, and my canteen within easy reach in case I awaken during the middle of the night. I also like to have the top of my walking stick within reach, as it is no longer easy for me to rise from the floor of the shelter without something to use for leverage.

One thing that I do *not* keep handy is a package of facial tissue. I seldom catch colds or need tissue for anything; the toilet paper I keep in my backpack is what I use should the need ever arise. So when I awakened in the middle of the night with a very runny nose, I was quite surprised. I hadn't felt anything the previous evening, not even a sneeze to indicate an oncoming bug. Yet my nose was definitely running. A lot.

Uh, oh.

I turned on my pocket flashlight to locate my roll of toilet paper and instantly noticed something discomforting. Everything was red. My hand, my fleece, even the floor of the lean-to was stained the bright red color of blood. At least I knew I didn't have a cold, but that made me feel no better. I put my head back and tried pinching my nostrils together, but the blood was still flowing. I did eventually get it stopped, but I must have looked rather ghoulish by the time it was all over.

Sure enough, I awakened the following morning to a ghastly sight. As I pulled myself up to get dressed, I gasped at the appearance of my head rest. The mustard-yellow-colored fleece looked like an article from a murder scene. It was covered with large patches of blood, which was now drying onto the garment in rusty red swaths. Additionally, there was blood on my hands, arms, and face, and further splashes appeared on the floorboards of the lean-to, adding even more gaudiness to the picture.

Casey was somewhat amused by the crime-like scene to which he awoke. We had been kidding the night before about the likelihood of fighting off a grizzly bear bare-handed, so that's how he explained the mess. "Wow, he must have been a big one!" he exclaimed. "I'm surprised I didn't hear the two of you wrestling over there, especially since he must have smacked you pretty hard for you to lose all that blood."

"How do you know it's not the grizzly's blood?" I replied, playing along with the game. "I got him pretty good too, you know."

Once I got myself cleaned up and removed the blood from my nose and cheeks, we decided to hit the trail as quickly as possible. Gordon and Spencer were just stirring inside their tent as we were putting our gear in our backpacks and munching on breakfast food. For me, breakfast on the trail has always been a bit of a conundrum. There just isn't much that I like to eat in the morning, and I've long since tired of those few items I can tolerate. The standard breakfast bars produced by the health food companies all taste about the same, and there is only so much oatmeal I can swallow in a lifetime. I forced myself to consume a protein bar and a few handfuls of GORP as I watched Casey open his food canister.

"Care for a bite of sausage or cheese?" he asked as he opened the zipped plastic bag.

I peeked inside at the combined mixture and instantly caught a whiff of the stuff. Real food!

"Oh my gosh, yes!" I replied enthusiastically. "I'll help you lighten your load a bit!"

I took only a chunk of the summer sausage, which tasted like the brand I'd carried when I lived on the trails for months at a time. It was wonderful. It reminded me that "man cannot live by freeze-dried food alone," and I silently cursed myself for not bringing along something similar.

We were ready to mount our backpacks on our shoulders when Gordon and Spencer emerged from their tent, slightly bleary-eyed but awake nonetheless. We had a short conversation about what they would see on the trail to West Lake. They were doing the same loop as us, but they were under some time constraints and so had to make good time in order to be out of the woods early on Sunday. We assured them that we were old and slow, which meant they would probably pass us on the trail even if they left an hour after us. It's a fact of life; you slow down when you get older.

"If we do get there first, we'll save room in the West Lake Lean-to #1," we assured them. "It's the best spot in the area, and there's plenty of room."

"We'll probably take you up on that," agreed Gordon, nodding enthusiastically. "We've enjoyed listening to your stories and advice, and we could pick up even more by sharing a lean-to."

And then it was time to be on the trail. So far, we were doing well and feeling fairly good, although I had probably lost a pint of blood to the nosebleed during the night. But not to worry; in my time as a ranger I had probably lost more than that to the mosquitoes on any given day. I was still feeling fine.

Day 1 was gone, three days to go.

Day 2—Friday:

By the time we started our trek away from the Pillsbury Lake lean-to, it was already well after nine. It was much later than I'd wanted to depart, as we were certain we'd have a tough time getting the lean-to we wanted at West Lake. Even though it was now after Labor Day, when school starts and vacations end, the southern lean-to on West Lake was still the most coveted shelter in the epicenter of the West Canada Lakes, and it is seldom unoccupied. We also knew that the trail would be very, very wet, with some portions submerged under as much as half a foot of water, which meant the going would be very slow.

After climbing the small rise to the height of land where we picked up the French Louie Trail, we turned right and resumed our hike west. Within a few hundred yards, we descended into the muck that has become a fact of life on this route. Back in the 1970s, when this was part of my regular patrol, this trail was still a roughly-formed dirt road, with dual ruts where the tires of large pickup trucks used to haul the Lawrences in to their camp. But in the years following, the beavers took over the territory and dammed up the various creeks and tributaries of those lowlands, causing widespread flooding which crept up over the trail roads. Beavers are persistent animals that are not easily dissuaded from their native instincts.

The first mile of trail was quite wet, although there was no place where we actually went in over our boots. By picking our way along and balancing carefully on some rotting corduroy and planking we were able to maintain our course without any undue soakings.

Even though it was supposed to rain sporadically throughout the day, I had forgone donning my rain jacket. The last thing I wanted to do was become soaked in my own sweat, which was guaranteed if I covered myself in a long-sleeved garment that didn't breathe. I did, however, decide to put my pack cover over my oversized Kelty frame pack, which would keep my gear dry in case of a downpour.

The official distance between two lakes or lean-tos in the woods can be a very deceptive figure. A dry trail that has relatively few geographic topo lines (meaning it is fairly flat) can fly by, even for "seasoned" hikers who require a bit more time than in earlier days. However, a flat, dry trail is pure fiction in the West Canada Lakes region. Sure, we don't have four-thousand-foot peaks to climb, nor do we have spindly ladders and platforms that guide us tenuously over large boulders on the edge of a mountain lake. But the truth of the matter is we are *always* going up or down something, and the trails often degrade into a morass of quicksand-like material that will grab onto your boot and suck you down into the muck quicker than you can say "Northville-Lake Placid." It is that bad.

Once we rounded the end of Pillsbury Lake and commenced the uphill, I knew we were within two miles of Sampson Lake, although the trail (or part of it) had been re-routed since my time as a park ranger. The wide track of the old road I'd used continued straight ahead, while the narrower detour path slowly diverged to the right. I was happy they changed that, as the old road was extremely wet and sloppy. However, the new trail had already developed its own sinkholes and boggy areas to the point where the low-lying stretches of the reroute were as bad as the original road.

The further into the trek we progressed, the worse it got. As always, hikers tend to go around muddy patches rather than through them, and this area was no different. In places, the "trail" was twenty feet wide, as people created ever-wider walk-arounds into the woods in order to preserve their dry feet. (Casey called these circuitous routes "cut-throughs.") There were some spots where the trail appeared waterlogged even where it made no sense, such as on the side of a steep slope where the excess fluid should have drained downhill to the left or right. Regardless, it was everywhere, and it added mileage and sapped our energy levels as we plodded along through the thick ooze.

After finally gaining the elevation I thought we needed to reach the turn-off to the Sampson Lake lean-to, we trekked on past "the car." This rusted-out relic from the early days of the last century has been a landmark for hikers for years. In truth, it is really just a large cart with thin rubber wheels and a body for carrying cargo or passengers. It doesn't appear to have ever contained a transmission of any type, so I'm not sure how it moved through the woods. But however it came to be, it is one of the few reliable mileage markers on the Whitney Lake side of the trail.

I knew it was a bad sign that I was already tired by the time we reached the steep downhill turnoff to the Sampson Lake lean-to. We took a short break there, even though we'd only come a few miles since breakfast, because with all the sidestepping and detouring around mud puddles, it was probably more like four or five. (This is not really the case, but it certainly felt that way.) Still, I was not used to being out of breath on short uphill climbs.

Once we passed Sampson, we had about another three miles to hit the junction of the Northville-Placid Trail. It was all up-and-down (isn't it always?), and our speed varied based on the grade of the inclines. But the route seemed to be a lot drier than the first few miles, and we gratefully accepted those precious yards where the footing was solid. It made things so much easier and less strenuous.

Somewhere within the last mile before the French Louie Trail intersects the Northville-Placid Trail, there is a steep downhill stretch where you come off the ridge that encircles Sampson Lake. We had barely left Sampson when Casey chirped up from behind.

"I think we're on our final descent now," he said, alluding to the fact that we were almost to West Canada Creek.

I turned around while still walking and gave him an incredulous stare. "You're crazy," I replied. "We have three miles from Sampson to the creek, and we've barely covered a half mile."

"Well, I think we've come a lot farther than that," he said encouragingly. "After all, we're moving a lot faster now that the trail is dry."

I chose not to reply to that comment as I knew that we were still far from the bridge that would cross West Canada Creek and lead us to our final mile of hiking for the day. I was surprised that our two young friends from the previous evening had not yet passed us. I was certain they'd be making better time than we were, and it was already several hours that we'd been hiking. Surly they couldn't be far behind.

Uphill and downhill, then uphill and downhill. More mud, more water, followed by more hills. In the distance we heard the low rumbling of thunder, although we had yet to feel a single raindrop all day.

"This must be the final descent," Casey called out for at least the fourth time that day. We were strolling down a mildly-sloping decline that I knew was not the hill in question.

"Nope. Not this one," I said, eying the woods around me. "We're not close to the creek yet. I know we've got at least a mile to a mile-and-a-half left."

Keep putting one foot in front of the other. Left, right, left, right. We climbed another hill, punctuated with another rest stop and drink of water. Then another downhill.

"This must be the final descent," came the now-familiar refrain. I answered the declaration with pure silence. It no longer required a reply.

Shortly after this statement, the trail bent around to the left a bit and we could hear something that sounded too good to be true—the musical tinkling of water flowing over rocks. It was a strong and steady flow, like a genuine creek rather than the runoff from a small pool or bog.

West Canada Creek!

"See, I told you we were on the final descent," Casey said, smiling at the sound as we rounded the corner of pathway merging with the Lake Placid Trail. "You should have believed me, but you didn't."

"That's because you said the same thing every time the trail dropped a few feet down a hill."

"Yeah, but this time I really meant it," he countered. "Anyway, let's get across the bridge and take a break up in the lean-to."

It sounded like a great idea to me, and I quickly bounded up the impressive crushed rock stairs and onto the new bridge. This structure was replaced a few years ago after the winter ice pushed the old bridge downstream. The wide, wooden planking and handsome construction was such a welcome change from the previous years when hikers were left to ford the river without any assistance. There were no rocks for them to use that could possibly keep a body out of the swiftly flowing current. Someone had strung a rope across the span to use as a temporary hold so that hikers would not get swept off their feet. But the water was waist deep in any regard, and there was no way around it.

After stopping to take a few "selfies" of our expedition crossing the West Canada Creek Bridge, we mounted the sharp incline that dropped us off at the lean-to. (Note to self; the word "selfie" did not exist when I worked as a ranger!) We now had just over one mile to go to reach our destination at West Lake. But the time was already after one-thirty, and we both wanted to stop for a breather at our current location. I was becoming more doubtful by the minute that we'd gain the squatters rights once we reached West Lake.

The lean-to at West Canada Creek is one of the big, old-style shelters that can probably sleep seven people across the back row. Someone had dropped an enormous log across the back of the fireplace. Sawed and split, it could have provided several face cords of firewood. I couldn't see how anyone had possibly moved this giant piece of lumber without the aid of a large fork-lift vehicle, so perhaps it had fallen on its own.

"Do you hear more thunder in the distance?" Casey asked, turning his head towards the trail leading north.

"Maybe a little," I replied, turning in the same direction. "Then again, you've got a much better ear than me, so you'd probably know long before I do if there's a storm moving in."

What I said was the whole truth. Casey is a musical composer by trade and well-known for being the consummate professional in his area. I take bass guitar lessons from an instructor who has played a number of performances with Casey. He describes Casey as having "the ears of an elephant; he hears *everything*." So if my hiking partner said that he heard thunder, I believed him. Thankfully, though, there was still no rain and we were almost there.

Following a short break and multiple handfuls of cashews, pineapple rings, and M&Ms, we hit the trail once again, this time with an eye cast upward into the darkening skies. We had covered about two hundred yards of trail when Casey declared, "I hear wind."

"That's not wind," I replied. "That's rain hitting the tops of the trees, and plenty of it. Let's get moving!"

And move we did. I was surprised at the pace we could attain after feeling so drained just a few minutes earlier. We hadn't bothered putting on rain gear, although my pack was still protected by the large waterproof cover. The heavy canopy of trees overhead was catching most of the water without allowing too much through, which is characteristic of the first ten minutes or so of any downpour in the woods. It's like a natural umbrella that will absorb the rain for a short period of time. (The downside of this, of course, is that when it stops raining, the leaves will still drip to the ground for ten to fifteen minutes. You can literally get soaked long after the sun has reappeared overhead.)

The nice thing about the stretch of trail from West Canada Creek to the West Lake Lean-to #1 is that there is a break at the halfway point. Only six-tenths of a mile north of the creek lean-to is South Lake, which has its own shelter on the east end. It used to be one of my favorite spots in the entire region, with a rare, white-sand beach which made for excellent sunning. Additionally, the bottom was entirely made of sand, so there were no leaches in the lake and you could wade out hundreds of yards from shore. It was great for swimming and getting away from the mosquitoes. I loved the place and stayed there often.

But not today.

First of all, it's been close to twenty years since the beavers moved in and dammed up the outlet from South Lake. This raised the lake level by several feet and completely wiped out the sandy beach. Gone. Additionally, as we scurried down the path leading away from the main hiking trail and into the lean-to, we noticed that the opening in the bushes in front of us created a wind tunnel that seemed to scour the back of the shelter. We were protected from the rain that was still falling, but we were chilled by the drafts that were sweeping down the full length of South Lake and into our faces. It felt like the air temperature had dropped at least ten degrees in the last few minutes. Any fleeting thoughts we harbored about spending the night at South Lake quickly vanished, and we hit the trail one last time.

Battle override. It's a naval term I learned while serving onboard various ships. The term is used when a situation or circumstance forces you to continue using a piece of equipment even when it is worn or broken. Battle override is not considered wise, but sometime it is necessary in an emergency, when that piece of gear simply has to be used or the ship is in deep trouble. That's the way my feet felt by this time. They were aching, my feet and legs were soaked, and I just wanted to get there. Battle override. Put one foot in front of the other and move on.

Six tenths of a mile is not long, but it certainly felt it to me. We finally crested the final ridge and began dropping down into view of West Lake.

"This must be the final descent," Casey called out one last time. This time I could agree with him.

As we strolled down the final slope, something rather embarrassing took place. Casey began making a left turn down a side trail that he claimed led to the lean-to. I heartily disagreed.

"No, the lean-to trail is right next to the old caretaker's cabin," I countered. "It's still ahead of us about a hundred yards."

"I don't think so, but you can go ahead and check that out," he stated firmly. "I'm staying right here."

By the time he finished his proclamation, I had already turned around and was stepping out towards the *real* trail to the lean-to. I never got there. Within about one-hundred-fifty yards, I emerged into the clearing that had once been home to the West Canada Lakes caretaker's cabin, and French Louie's cabin before that.

I had gone too far, and with egg on my face I turned around and retraced my steps to where Casey was patiently waiting. Old age plays tricks on both the body and the mind.

We were about to proceed down the last few yards to the lean-to when suddenly another person appeared on the trail. It was a young woman clad in red hiking apparel who was apparently on her own. She stepped up to us and we began conversing about the trail. She had come up from Spruce Lake that morning and was going all the way to Lake Placid; a true "thru-hiker."

"I think I'm going on to Cedar Lakes this afternoon before making camp," she said with a smile. Her whole persona appeared to be brimming with energy, despite the dirt and the rain and the muck. "I planned this out to make about ten to twelve miles a day, and it looks like a nice walk over to the lean-to on the west end of Cedars."

I looked at her in admiration, as it was already mid-afternoon, and she'd have another four miles to go to reach the lean-to.

"You'll have a tough time finding the place," I explained. "The trail to the lean-to is under some water, and the local fishermen do their best to hide the trail as they like to keep that lean-to for themselves."

"That's OK," she chimed in again. "If I have to, I can either pitch my tent or else continue on to the other lean-tos further on. I'm having fun walking through this beautiful scenery. I can't believe how gorgeous it all is!"

And so she departed for Cedar Lakes, leaving me behind to wonder where all that energy had gone in me; why couldn't I still go all those miles without feeling like my legs were made of cast iron? Perhaps it was the result of the passage of forty years since my tenure back here? Regardless, it was a bit of a jolt, and I watched her walk away with envy. I also learned the following day that the location of the third Cedar Lake lean-to is no longer a mystery. Some beautiful work by the Adirondack Mountain Club has re-routed the trail and re-marked the path in such a way that anyone can now find and use this remote lean-to. It's still not a fan favorite for some hikers because it is a good quarter mile (or more) off the Northville-Placid Trail. But it is beautiful, remote, and usually available for those who desire the additional solitude.

By the time I heaved my body and pack down to the lean-to, Casey was already unpacking and getting his gear stowed for the evening. We were both surprised to find that the lean-to was empty, despite our late arrival. We figured on seeing Gordon and Spencer, so we made sure to leave plenty of space open for their arrival.

To say that I was "spent" would have been the understatement of the day. Again I wondered at why a hike of six or seven miles with a pack should wear me down to exhaustion. It's true that I probably wasn't drinking enough water along the trail, which may have led to some minor dehydration, but not enough to feel the way I was feeling. My shirt was sticking to my back, not as much from the rain as from my own sweat. I felt much more fatigued than after our initial day's hike in, and my eyes were playing tricks on me as well. I was seeing the water stains on my hiking pants seemingly appear darker and lighter as I stared at them. Not a good thing to witness when you have two more days of hiking to get out of the woods.

Casey decided to filter some water immediately after we arrived. I felt too tired to collect firewood right away, so I wandered around in back of the lean-to and marveled at the changes. The land back there had been so filled with small trees and shrubs in the 1980s that it was almost impossible to walk in a straight line. It was possible back then to cut from the caretaker's front yard through to the back of the lean-to, but you had to be willing to push through the dense vegetation surrounding the lean-to. Today, that situation is completely reversed. The grassy lawn that my friend and "woods father" John Remias had so carefully kept mowed and trimmed was now completely overgrown with maturing trees, making it impossible to see the lake from the spot where his cabin once stood. But now the ground leading up to that thicket is wide-open, resembling a campground picnic area. This has been caused, no doubt, by campers hacking down trees in an attempt to gain easy access to firewood. It was a sad sight, and I quickly returned to the front of the lean-to.

I can't honestly say I remember much of what was said or done over the next few hours, other than preparing supper and getting ready for an early sleep. I was exhausted and wanted no part of any physical activity. As the sun dropped lower at the end of the lake, we agreed that we'd forego the normal campfire rather than spend time collecting wood. Gordon and Spencer never showed up, although the woman we spoke to on the trail mentioned that she ran into a couple of young men at the West Canada Creek lean-to. Perhaps they had arrived in the rain and simply decided to spend the night down there.

As we prepared to turn in for the night, I mentioned something to Casey about my physical well-being (or lack thereof).

"I don't like admitting this," I murmured in a subdued tone, "but this trip just hasn't been fun. Not so far. I am totally drained of energy, and the trail has been such a mess. I'm just hoping I can make it these next two days."

"I know what you mean," Casey agreed while nodding his head. "To tell you the truth, when you had that nosebleed last night and said you couldn't get it to stop, I would have been perfectly happy to stay at Pillsbury Lake for a couple more nights and then just call it a weekend."

"I would have as well; I just didn't know that *you* felt that way too. Anyway, we're all the way in here now, so we might as well go ahead to Cedar Lakes tomorrow and complete the loop. It will feel good after we're done, even if this is the last time I make it back here."

As much as I ached, I knew I'd be happy after we were out of the woods. I'd wanted to pass through the West Lake sites and see French Louie's fireplace at least one more time.

The sun had now dropped below the horizon causing the temperature to plummet. Without a campfire there was little reason to stay up, so we completed our nightly preps and climbed into our sleeping bags.

The skies blackened, the winds blew, and the loons sang.

Day 2 was gone, two days to go.

Day 3—Saturday:

The following morning dawned with a cloud-filled sky, and we wondered whether we heard rain in the distance. I knew I wasn't looking forward to walking in a downpour, although my pants were already damp from the previous day.

I desperately wanted to hit the trail by eight, as I wanted to arrive in time to camp in the Beaver Pond lean-to on Cedar Lakes. This is another very popular spot, and anyone left hiking the Northville-Placid Trail would probably try to end up there for the night. Additionally, it would be Saturday night, which meant that some folks may have come in from Perkins Clearing just for the weekend. I knew we had to make tracks.

I finished packing my gear at least ten minutes before Casey, so I told him that I'd wait for him up in the clearing. I really wanted to get up there in time to take some photographs of French Louie's fireplace and stroll around the ruins of the old caretaker's cabin. As I've mentioned numerous times throughout my writings, this was perhaps my favorite spot in the entire region, especially when John lived there and maintained the area's trails. His wife Barb was also in residence from time to time, and we spent a lot of time talking and laughing about the things we saw every day. They were good times.

Just the act of getting to the fireplace was now a bit of a task. The field has become quite overgrown, making it necessary to wade through wet vegetation that is now shoulder high. The foundation from the caretaker's cabin is becoming overrun with weeds and shrubs as well, although most of the brick wall base is still evident.

The fireplace itself, which was built by Louie in 1913, is in sad repair. I have always said that I believe the State should declare it an official historic site, with a restoration project and a plaque or other marker to explain its significance to the public. But this will probably never happen due to the remoteness of the location and the unfamiliarity of French Louie's name to most of the citizens of New York State.

I stood on the rocks that had been part of John's front porch, staring at the remains of the fireplace and shaking my head. The mantel piece that he sledded in from the southern shore of the lake has long since cracked in half and fallen into the bottom of the fire pit. Many other rocks that had formed the side walls have likewise crumbled to the ground, victims of the harsh winters and decades upon decades of wind, weather, and water. Nothing man made lasts forever back here, not even Louie's fireplace. I find myself becoming overly reflective whenever I visit this spot, and today was no exception.

As much as I wanted to hit the trail for the trek over to Cedar Lakes, I was pleased to see that Casey was not hot on my heels as I moseyed through the ruins of the cabin. I wanted some time to take photographs, and also to just stand at that point and look around one last time. I strode across the stones that comprised the front porch, which still stood pretty much intact from the 1970s. The left wall of the cabin was still evident in the straight line of brick that ran back towards the rear of the house. That wall would have served as the backdrop for John's fireplace, as well as the wood burning stove that heated the room on chilly autumn nights.

Moving to the other side of the foundation, I found the inner and outer walls that formed the storage room. This was where John kept the tools and equipment that he didn't bring inside the house proper. And further back, in the rear right corner of the foundation, I could almost still see the refrigerator and spot where his dining table had sat. I had joined John and Barb for several meals around that table, and the memories of those times made me smile.

Having a few minutes to stop and reflect was wonderful. But I soon noticed that the "few minutes" had lengthened to five, ten, then twenty minutes. It was getting later and later and still no sign of Casey. So much for my idea of getting an early start. Finally, after I'd spent about twenty-five minutes pacing, Casey emerged from the opening in the woods and walked into the clearing. He had a rather embarrassed expression on his face, and I waited for the explanation.

"You're not going to believe what I just did" was all he said.

"I might have some ideas, but go ahead and tell me."

"I just walked out from the lean-to and turned the wrong way on the Placid Trail," he confessed. "I spent about ten minutes hiking back towards South Lake before I realized where I was."

"Oh my God, that's about opposite of what I did yesterday when I walked right past the lean-to trail."

"Yeah, I know," he grinned. "I think you're right; we're getting old and feeble-minded."

It was after nine by the time we signed the register and actually got moving on the trail to Cedar Lakes. The problem was, "getting moving" was a relative expression. The trail was so mucky and filled with deep, water-filled depressions that it slowed us to a crawl. The entire area behind the West Lake caretaker's headquarters had been flooded by beavers years ago, and the direct path across the marshy area was simply un-navigable. This caused the State to re-route the short and straight two hundred yards of trail by creating a half mile of soggy, muddy, tree-root-filled obstacle course that would leave any hiker cursing under his or her breath. It was a mess, and we were soon questioning our own sanity for being there in the first place.

There were a few places where we knew we had to cross small streams, and we were pleased to see that the first one had been routed over the top of a strong beaver dam. It was a solid structure with sturdy branches and limbs that had been woven into a secure crossing. For once I found myself thanking these industrious animals for building one of their trademark creations in such a convenient spot.

The next crossing, however, which was the outlet of West Lake into Mud Lake, was not nearly as easy. I arrived at the flow about a dozen paces ahead of Casey, and I surveyed the scene skeptically. It was maybe twenty feet wide and perhaps three feet deep. There was no bridge, and the only stones protruding through the water's surface were large, angular boulders that were situated about four feet apart.

Once upon a time, this would have been a cakewalk. I remember my earlier days when I lived at the fire tower cabin up on Pillsbury Mountain. I could fly down that incline in about twenty minutes, leaping from stone to stone without stopping to balance. Catching myself on any given stone was child's play to me then, and I simply thought that I would possess those balancing skills forever.

Unfortunately, a lot of things deteriorate with age, and balance is one of them. I mentally plotted my path across the stream by detailing every step of the way, including which foot would land on which rock. I thought I could do this, and I resolved to take my time and move deliberately with the aid of my trusty walking stick.

"Do you want to take one of my poles to use in your other hand?" Casey offered from behind. "You could use it to get to the other side and then toss it back to me."

"No thanks, I think I've got this," I replied, already moving across to boulder number one.

Some of the rocks were far enough apart that a small amount of leaping was required. I knew I could make the leaps, but it was steadying myself on the next boulder and rebalancing that would give me the trouble.

I didn't want to stop and overthink this thing. Just keep going; step-step-leap-step, move forward and keep going. But carefully!

I was on the second-to-last boulder, beyond the hard parts and reaching for the other shore when I heard the commotion behind me.

KERSPLOOOOSH!!!

There are different sounds achieved by various objects hitting the surface of water. For example, a canteen dropped into the water might make a small splash. A hiker taking a misstep and landing a boot into the creek would produce more of a "ker-plunk." The sound issued from behind my back resembled neither of those. It was a full-scale, all-encompassing tsunami, the kind that could only result from a total "belly-flopper" submersion of the entire body. I knew in a heartbeat what had transpired.

I leaped across to the other side, landing on solid gravel, and immediately turned to see the predicament in which Casey had landed. As expected, he had not quite completed one of the mid-stream leaps and had fallen backwards into the rushing water, completely submerged. To his credit, he landed with poles down and instantly used his arm strength and the planted spikes on the poles to catapult himself back into a standing position. As he did so, rivulets of water streamed off his arms, elbows, legs, and various parts of his backpack. The whole scene reminded me in no small way of the photographs I'd seen of a breaching whale that has its tail poised in the air before diving, with water similarly cascading off its tail fins. It all appeared to happen in slow motion, and I was likewise rooted in place, mouth open but with no words to speak.

For the life of me, I could not figure out what the heck to say. "I'm so sorry that happened," was the best I could salvage on the spur of the moment. "Are you OK?"

"Yeah, but I can't believe that just happened," Casey sputtered, water still flowing off every part of his body. "I tried to jump from one rock to the next, but I just didn't fully commit. I needed to push off with everything I had and I just didn't get enough into it."

"How bad is it?" I asked, hoping he didn't completely submerge.

"I went all the way in. I'm totally soaked from head to foot."

"How about your pack?" I asked hopefully. "Do you think the water got into your sleeping bag and your clothes?"

"I don't know," he replied with a concerned expression. "I'll just hope for the best, but I really won't know until I unpack at Cedar Lakes. The only saving grace may be that everything in my pack is wrapped in plastic, so hopefully that kept the water out for those few seconds I was in the water."

We didn't say too much after that, although I knew we were both plenty worried. The temperatures over the past few nights had made it down into the thirties, and tonight was supposed to be even cooler. A wet sleeping bag and wet clothes could make for trouble, unless we could make a fire and dry some things out.

If nothing else, Casey could use some of my spare clothes, but that would be the worst case scenario.

We continued slogging on through the muck and mess that is the Mud Lake detour trail, with thick vegetation on either side of the trail making it impossible to venture around the goop to drier ground. My hiking boots looked like little more than mud-covered stumps at the end of each leg, with the fluid oozing out of the top with each step. Casey's boots were making a squelching sound each time he lifted a foot and put it down again, testament to the submersion he'd endured just a few minutes earlier.

Thankfully, it wasn't much longer before we passed the end of the detour trail and regained the original Northville-Placid Trail. From there, the route gained a little altitude and became a bit drier.

"I want to stop and change into dry pants, assuming that my clothes are still dry," Casey announced. "Plus, this will give me a peek to see how much water got inside my pack."

"OK, you go ahead. I'll just stroll up ahead for a few hundred yards and get the next uphill out of the way."

Casey unharnessed his pack and started loosening the straps while I moved ahead slowly through the green shade of the deciduous woods. The sun had finally broken through the clouded sky, casting rays of bright sunshine against the lush vegetation that proliferates around the Mud Lake shoreline. I have always felt that the view across Mud Lake was one of the wilder scenes in the region, and I enjoyed the experience in its entirety. Even though much of the shoreline has changed, and the great blue heron nests I used to watch with such fascination are no longer visible, it is still a wonderful spot to stop and ponder the wilderness that is the Adirondacks.

I suppose I would have stood there transfixed in my wonder for a week had Casey not come hiking up the trail, in better spirits than a short while ago. He obviously felt better and had good news to share.

"Not only do I feel about ten times better in dry pants, but the clothes in my pack appear to be dry as well," he reported. "I'm so glad I had that stuff protected inside plastic. It saved my pack for sure."

"How about your sleeping bag?" I asked. "Is that dry too?"

"That's tough to say. It's in a different compartment all the way at the bottom of my pack. If anything, it would have gone deeper into the water than my clothes. But it's wrapped pretty well, so I think I'm probably OK." With that said, we both breathed a sigh of relief. It could have been worse.

The rather sad thing is that I've interviewed a number of people about that stream crossing, and no one else appeared to be particularly challenged by the footing. Thirty years ago, it probably wouldn't have bothered Casey and me either. But lots of things change, including strength, endurance, and to a large degree, balance. It just ain't what it used to be.

From there on, the trail remained drier than over the past two days, and we were able to make better time, although the steeper uphill stretches still taxed me to the limit. But we established and maintained a good pace while passing Cat Lake and then King's Pond, leaving each of them behind us as we motored on towards Cedar Lakes.

Within another hour, we began feeling good again, confident that we had left all our misfortunes behind us. Casey was dry, the sun was shining, and we were able to make better time due to the relative dryness of the trail. Things were looking up... for the moment.

Fast-forward about fifteen minutes.

"Oh, no. Nooo! You've got to be kidding me!"

Casey was thirty feet ahead of me on the trail, and he was picking up his right foot and inspecting something invisible from my vantage point.

"What's the matter?" I called up to him. "Did you hurt yourself?"

"No, but you wouldn't believe what happened to my boot!"

I moved ahead until I was standing right next to him, which is when I witnessed the subject of his consternation. The entire rubber heel from his right hiking boot was hanging off at a right angle, pointing directly down at the ground. It looked like it could separate and fall off at any time, and he didn't know how thick or strong the layer was that constituted the remainder of the heel construction. If he lost the rubber heel, would he be able to hike the rest of the way out using whatever was left of the boot? It wasn't a pretty thought, and he quickly decided to stop for some repairs.

"I'm going to try to put this heel back on with duct tape," he said while inspecting the soul of the boot. "I'm glad I've got some with me or this could have been a lot worse."

"You're kidding me! You've got duct tape?" I asked incredulously. "I've never in my life considered packing a roll of duct tape in my backpack."

"See? You never know what you're going to need," he replied with a smile. "Duct tape can fix just about anything."

For the second time in as many hours, Casey found a convenient log on which to sit and then proceeded to work on his footwear. He carefully wound the tape around and around the separated heel, binding it as best as possible until it looked as though it might hold. Then we set off once again, looking all the more ragtag, but still in good spirits.

By the time we reached Cedars, I was ready to show Casey the worn out, submerged path that led to the third Cedar Lake lean-to. I had been telling people all week long about how much of a mess this was; how the path was unmarked and you had to walk through a foot of water to find the final few hundred yards that led to the lean-to. The fishermen had always chopped down the sign, which is what I expected to find. However, once again I was shocked at just how wrong I had been.

"Cedar Lakes Lean-to #3" the large sign boldly proclaimed in bright yellow letters, the placard nailed straight and tight to the tree. The trail, which had obviously been rerouted since my last visit, was dry and beautiful. I had made a series of recommendations to the Adirondack Mountain Club several years earlier on possible detours, and I wondered whether they had used any of my thoughts in cutting through this new route. Regardless, it was gorgeous, and I marveled at their handiwork.

Even more than at the sight of the lean-to trail, we were both elated because it meant that we had arrived at the west end of Cedar Lakes. Only two more miles to get to the Beaver Pond lean-to. We could have stayed at the Lean-to #3, but it would have added those additional miles onto our final day, and I wasn't sure I had that in me.

Proceeding further along the trail, we met a pair of hikers who had just come in for the weekend and were doing the loop, but in the opposite direction.

"You'll have fun going out to Perkins Clearing," they informed us. "The trail is dry and in really good condition. But that crazy bridge going over Grassy Brook is a real adventure. We had to turn sideways and reach up to grab the handrail, then sidestep one foot at a time to get to the other side."

I was very familiar with this bridge, which had been in the same sad state of repair for many years. After returning from our trip, I traded correspondence with a fellow hiker who called it "the Funhouse Bridge." It was that bad. But that would come the following morning. For now, we still had a couple more miles to make before reaching our destination for the day.

Even though the ascent of Cobble Hill is only about 250 feet, it still felt as though it went on forever. The forest was magnificent, and I found myself recognizing some of the more significant landmarks along the way, which was encouraging. But more than anything, I just wanted to get there. Once again, I was "spent," and Casey wanted to see the condition of his sleeping bag following the drenching back at Mud Lake.

It was with no small amount of satisfaction that we finally

rounded the top of the Cobble Hill Ridge and started the decline toward Beaver Pond. Still too far away to see the water, I barely contained my smile as we strode forward, entering the final half mile of our day's trek.

"This must be the final descent," Casey said, now from the lead position. (He had taken the lead after falling in the water.)

"Oh shut up" I said, laughing harder than the comment merited. "You don't have a clue where we are, do you?" We had both made inaccurate assumptions about our location throughout the week, so I was in no position to make a snide remark.

It turned out we were both correct in our assumptions. The short spur trail to the Beaver Pond lean-to soon appeared on our right, and we scooted up the steep incline that would lead us to the final hundred yards. We were there!

Once again, we were the first ones to arrive at the empty lean-to, which seemed like an enormous stroke of good luck. I had debated leaving my tent at home and had almost done just that before a last-minute change of mind. I had lived in these woods for years, sleeping in the lean-tos at every opportunity, and only once had I been forced to sleep on the ground due to overcrowding. The chances were strongly in my favor.

As we removed our packs, I know we were showing a lot more energy than on the previous day. Casey immediately tore into his pack to check on his sleeping bag. The news was all good. The plastic layer surrounding his sleeping bag had kept the water at bay, and the entire bag was dry. Everything was OK.

Meanwhile, I found that I wasn't as drained as I'd felt back at West Lake. Perhaps I was regaining a bit of my "trail legs," although I certainly hadn't done any special training other than these past three days in the woods. I was even up for heading out to collect firewood without an extended break, although I did wait for Casey to return from pumping a few quarts of water.

Within an hour, we had all the water we could use, as well as a healthy pile of semi-dry firewood. Unlike what we'd encountered the past two nights, the ground around the Beaver Pond lean-to was overloaded with a plentiful selection of prime hardwood trees, which were all accessible within a few minutes' stroll from the shelter. It didn't take long, and the walk through the woods without a backpack felt wonderfully refreshing. I also found a few "artifacts" (meaning old junk) from the days when fishermen used to fly in with their full loads of cargo and supplies. The woods are still loaded with this stuff if you know where to look.

While we were setting up for our evening meal and fire, we were joined by a lone thru-hiker by the name of Erik. A resident of Seattle, he had previously lived in Rochester and had also attended RIT for his college degree. It felt like having another local friend along for the night. Erik declined the offer to join us in the lean-to, opting instead to pitch his tent in the clearing above the shelter. He did promise to stop down to share the fire later on, so we looked forward to his company.

It would be our last night in the woods, and we found ourselves wishing for a true clearing of the skies that might expose a worthy sunset. And wonder of wonders, our wishes were answered; about an hour before dusk the clouds parted and the sun appeared in all its glory, painting the remaining clouds and the upper reaches of Goodluck Mountain with an orange-reddish glow. It was truly one for the ages, and we took it as a good omen for the following day.

The evening turned out to be as good as the sunset, with the possible exception of my dinner. Tonight's selection was sweet and sour chicken with rice, and it just didn't live up to its advertising. As a matter of fact, I knew I didn't care for it before I even sampled my first bite, as I had grown tired of this entrée on my first trip into the woods earlier in the summer. It was only by mistake that this meal had found its way into my food pack. I had intended to bring along spaghetti with meat sauce for the final night, but had erred in my packing. Over half of the chicken remained uneaten, and I substituted an extra dessert to finish satisfying my appetite.

As we dined on our freeze-dried delicacies, Erik stopped down to share the evening fire. He was an incredibly nice fellow. I asked if he usually hiked long distances solo like this.

"No, as a matter of fact, I didn't even start off on this trip by myself," he explained. "My buddy was going to hike the entire trail with me, right up to Lake Placid. But he developed some nasty blisters in the first few days on the trail. He tried forcing himself to push through it, but by the time we got to Piseco he could barely walk. So he's taking a few days off and then hoping to meet up with me again in Blue Mountain Lake."

I winced at the thought of attempting to walk 134 miles with open blisters—not a recipe for an enjoyable long-distance hike. Thankfully, I'd never been susceptible to blisters, but I do know how much they can hurt, especially once they rupture in the wrong place. It can definitely ruin a pleasant hike and send almost anyone home early.

The fire was difficult to get started that night as everything was wet, including the tinder. I'm not sure if I should be ashamed of this or not, but I relied on using several of those chemical fire-starter rolls that advertise a guaranteed fire even in the rain. Since carrying a butane-fueled stove has eliminated my need to carry a supply of white gas, it's the only artificial help I have to rely on. But it works, so that is what I used. Within ten minutes I had a blaze crackling away, which in turn would dry out some of the other wet firewood.

Erik didn't stick around the fire for long, instead deciding to call it an early evening. Casey and I were left to sit on the front log of the lean-to and stare into the diminishing flames. It was approaching "sack time," but we were both enjoying the fire and the conversation, so we decided to sit and feed the blaze just a little longer.

It was just about the time when the last vestiges of daylight were being squeezed from the skies when we saw it. It was a barely detectible movement on the left side of the fireplace, yet we both noticed it simultaneously. It sprinted briefly into view before pausing and then darting back again into the shade of some sawed-off logs.

The mouse!

For some reason I've never been able to determine, some lean-tos have resident mice while others do not. Most of the ones on other lakes in the area are devoid of these tiny rodents, while Cedar Lakes seems to harbor a bumper crop. I've never known a mouse personally, so I haven't been able to ask them about the logic behind their choice of living accommodations. But for whatever reason, the Beaver Pond lean-to on Cedar Lakes has always had more than its fair share. They tend to come out after sunset and commence mining their way into backpack pockets, stuff sacks, and even bags that are hung from bear-proof trees. They know just how to get to the bag and then gnaw their way in.

This particular mouse attempted another foray out from the fireplace, obviously en route for the lean-to. But Casey and I blinded him with beams from our flashlights, using both the lights to triangulate his position and send him scurrying once again for safety. He wanted "in" to our lean-to, but it had become a game to us. Shut off the flashlights until he reappeared, and then hit him with both beams until he retreated. We repeated this over and over again, laughing each time he leapt backwards into the shadows. It really wasn't that funny, but at nine at night on the shore of Cedar Lakes it was the best entertainment we had at our disposal. Finally, after about fifteen minutes and at least that many attempts, our rodent friend decided that this activity simply wasn't worth the effort. We saw him suddenly veer off and scamper into the woods, presumably heading towards wherever he called home. It was the last we would see of him that night; he never returned to the shelter to dig into any of our supplies. I guess that means we won.

The final topic of conversation around the campfire that evening was our own longevity and our ability to repeat hikes such as this in the future. I was amazed at just how much we had in common regarding our outlooks and ambitions. We agreed that this had been a very, very hard week, and that our desire to repeat such a trip was greatly diminished at best.

"That dunking in the river kind of did me in," admitted Casey, "although the rest of the hike was pretty hard too. The conditions back here simply do not favor the older hiker. It's hard getting though all that mess and muck. It's almost like the Department of Environmental Conservation has given up on the trail system, especially anything that is not part of the Northville-Placid Trail. And even that's horrible in places."

"I know what you mean," I agreed. "I know there's no money left to hire a trail crew. But it seems like they could at least tackle the worst of it, like those stream crossings back there. That's almost inexcusable. They're just asking for trouble, especially if someone is hiking alone and gets hurt. What the heck would they do?"

The questions went unanswered as the conversation quietly subsided, each of us mesmerized by the flames dancing from between the fireplace logs. It was a magical time of night, and we both enjoyed its hypnotic appeal.

As we climbed into our sleeping bags that last night, I knew we both realized that we had been through a lot that day and had somehow emerged relatively unscathed for all the rigors we'd experienced. Tomorrow would be another long day. We'd have more mud to navigate, slippery "stringer" logs to traverse, the funhouse bridge to cross, as well as the tricky crossing of Grassy Brook at the base of the backside of the Blue Ridge climb. But we'd take it slowly and carefully, and even as senior citizens we'd make it out to the trailhead. It was only about six miles to the car, and we could easily achieve that no matter how many obstacles were set in our way.

With that in mind, we settled back and drifted off to sleep. Neither bears nor mice bothered us that night, and the only sounds we heard were from the solo calls of the distant loons out on the lake.

Day 3 was gone, one day to go.

Day 4—Sunday:

It was another good omen; the dawn came accompanied by the prospect of blue skies and a fully visible sun. This was something we hadn't seen that entire week, and we welcomed it wholeheartedly. Even as we enjoyed the cessation of the rain, however, we knew that the southern states were being pummeled by Hurricane Maria, and we were eager to hear the latest news on that ongoing disaster.

Getting into my well-worn hiking pants and boots, I was pleasantly surprised to find that my footwear had partially dried out, which made it much more comfortable to insert my feet and get laced up. Meanwhile, Casey removed the tattered remains of yesterday's duct tape from around his boot and replaced it with several yards of parachute cord, after which he applied a fresh layer of the ubiquitous duct tape. It was quite a sight, and he muttered under his breath while making the repairs.

As we munched on the last of our GORP and breakfast bars, Erik emerged from his tent and stopped down for a brief chat.

"How did the tent work?" I queried him. "Did you sleep all right? That looks like a pretty spacious tent for backpacking."

"Oh yes," he nodded in agreement. "It's spacious alright, although getting it set up correctly is sometimes a bit challenging. But I do wish I hadn't set it up right where I did."

"What do you mean?" I asked.

"I set the damned thing up right in front of the outhouse!"

"Yes, I did notice that last night, but I thought you knew it was there," I laughed. "I don't imagine that could have smelled too wonderful."

"It wasn't all that bad," he replied. "But there were a couple of smaller tent sites right along the path that leads out to the point. I wish I'd picked one of those."

I felt it imprudent at that point to mention that he had also erected his tent at the precise location where the majority of campers go to irrigate the ground during their middle-of-the-night excursions from the lean-to. He just didn't need to know that.

Once the packs were packed and Casey's boot had been reassembled, we re-shouldered our backpacks and hit the trail for the final time. The topic of conversation was 100 percent food, with the major focus being on the contents of the submarine sandwiches we'd have for lunch at Charlie John's store in Speculator. The very thought of that would keep us going until we hit the trailhead in six miles.

Passing by the final half mile of Cedar Lakes always brings back sentimental feelings, as that is where I started my life as a ranger in 1979. Walking past the sight of the original Cedar Lakes caretaker's cabin, we could still see where the foundation had stood back in the early 1970s. This station had been burned out several years before I came to live in the West Canadas, so it held less meaning for me than its companion station at West Lake. But John Remias had spoken of it often, and his wife had shown me a great many pictures of the site when it was in its heyday. The doorway to the root cellar still stands intact, and numerous cast-iron parts of the stove are scattered about the area.

The "new" lean-to on Cedar Lakes (which is now almost thirty years old) is beginning to show its age. It too was unoccupied, and I marveled at the difference between our wilderness area and some of the more well-used territories. I hoped the West Canada Lakes never changed, but remained a quiet, remote forest where humans were few and far between. In my opinion, overcrowded wilderness ceases to be wilderness and quickly loses its character.

As we proceeded farther up the lake, we passed the site

where the original Cedar Lakes Lean-to #1 had stood. It was the spot where I had spent my first night in the woods as a ranger, and it was there that I had received my initiation to the "local fisherman versus modern hiker" debate. I will never forget the folks with whom I shared the lean-to that night. They are like permanent family, the image of their faces eternally engraved in my memory.

We marched on.

The original dam is now almost completely gone. Only the old-timers remember the lake as it was back then, significantly higher than present-day levels. Numerous bays and inlets existed on the fringes of the main body of water that are now completely dry. At one point, a few hundred yards up from the dam, it looks as though you could almost walk across the water on the tops of flat rocks that are barely submerged, although this is probably not completely true. Still, the old lake isn't what it used to be, and it saddens me.

We signed into the trail register, noting that we were the first ones to pass through that morning. Then we turned east and onto the trail that would cross the outlet of Cedar Lakes and lead us onto the Old Military Road, diverging from the Northville-Placid Trail. From then on we could expect to see almost no one along the way, as it was Sunday afternoon and any weekend campers would be heading out of the woods rather than in.

As tired as we were, we soon found ourselves flying along the trail at speeds we hadn't attained all weekend. The trail climbed higher and dipped lower, but throughout it remained relatively dry, and we could not believe our good fortune. Casey had predicted that we'd make it out of the woods in time for lunch, but I hadn't believed him. Now, I was beginning to think that we had a chance.

In about an hour, we reached the first of the "stringers," which are long, thick logs which had been cut in half lengthwise and then laid onto pilings as a way to traverse spots in the trail that had become too flooded to repair. These always made me nervous, especially those distances where there was only one stringer on which to balance instead of two. It was hard enough at my age to maintain my footing when I could have a pair of the wooden beams on which to plant my feet. But being afforded only a single plank tested my abilities, and I found myself inching along until I reached the other side. There were three of these sections along the way, but I surprised myself at navigating across the devices with very little difficulty.

The next encounter with the obstacle course came once we reached the "funhouse bridge." It was absolutely nuts, and it really did resemble the kind of thing you'd see at a haunted-house carnival ride. It featured rotted planking that stuck up at crazy angles, exposed rusty nails, and numerous missing boards, and the entire bridge tilted at an angle of about thirty to forty degrees. One of these days someone isn't going to make it across, which will lead to trouble, as the water in the creek appears to be over head level. But for now it is still holding, and we both managed to cross it while maintaining our balance and composure.

Once across, we were able to resume our rapid pace and quickly arrived at the last crossing of Grassy Brook. This one was also a bit tricky, although nothing like what we'd already faced. There had been a series of bridges crossing this waterway back when I lived in the woods, and the remnants of the last span still stood on the opposing banks of the brook. But there were enough decent stones that were closely spaced to make simple work of this crossing, even for a couple of old-timers like us. Even if we missed a step and fell in, the water would only come up to the lower calf, which was far from threatening. Within a couple minutes we were both across safely, still with dry feet.

OK. Only one last hill to climb, and then the long descent back to the trailhead. There were no more stream crossings or crazy bridges to cross. Only one hill and one-and-a-half miles left to go.

"Why don't you scoot on ahead?" I asked Casey, looking at the imposing hill ahead of us. "I know I'm going to take a couple breaks along the way to the top of Blue Ridge, but I'll catch up to you on top."

"OK," he agreed. "I want to take my pack off once we get up there and take a longer rest anyway, so I'll meet you on top."

The path from the Grassy Brook crossing to the height of ground where the trail to Pillsbury Lake diverges to the right is only about a quarter-mile long, but entirely uphill at a fairly steep grade. My endurance had already been worn thin by the past four days on the trail, so I took it very slowly, taking breaks as needed to allow my heartbeat to return to an acceptable rate. It seemed to take a long time before I crested the ridge and saw Casey sitting next to the trail sign, swigging water from his canteen. It would be all downhill from there.

Coming down the major declines of Blue Ridge, including "Sonofabitch Hill," I was reminded that descending a lengthy hill can be tougher on leg muscles than the original uphill climb. The slope kept going and going, and my calf muscles and feet were protesting the movement the entire time. Casey went out in front by about twenty yards as he was in better shape than me, although I stayed close throughout the final mile.

Finally, my hiking partner turned around with a big smile, both arms raised with the thumbs-up sign, and announced, "We're here!" And so we were.

As we headed away from the trailhead parking lot, now relying on all-wheel drive rather than duct-tape-repaired boots, many subjects were discussed. We both agreed that the trails had degraded significantly in too many places to repair without a full-time crew that was dedicated to this region alone. And that, we knew with certainty, would never happen in today's economic environment.

We also concurred that the truly memorable aspects of the West Canada Lakes Wilderness Area had endured the test of time. The views from our favorite lean-tos had not changed, the midnight songs of the loons remained just as hauntingly memorable, and there was still very little in the world that could compare with an Adirondack sunset.

Quoting the words of Adirondack author William Chapman White: "As a man tramps the woods to the lake, he knows he will find pines and lilies, blue heron and golden shiners, shadows on the rocks and the glint of light on the wavelets, just as they were in the summer of 1354, as they will be in 2054 and beyond. He can stand on a rock by the shore and be in a past he could not have known, in a future he will never see. He can be a part of time that was and time yet to come." (William Chapman White, 1954)

Finally, we agreed that, while we would certainly return to do some lean-to-camping stays of two or three days, hopefully at Beaver Pond, our days of station-to-station hiking were over. It was just getting too painful due to the variety of ailments and injuries we now experienced, and the prospect of completing any lengthy hike (such as the entire Northville-Placid Trail) had long since gone by the wayside.

Now that we were out of the woods, everything seemed wonderful, although at that moment I wouldn't have traded that car seat for all the views and bonfires in the entire north woods. We had indeed completed the final descent.

About the Author

Larry Weill has led a career that is as diverse and interesting as the subjects in his books. An avid outdoorsman, he has hiked and climbed extensively throughout the Adirondacks and the Northeast since his days as a wilderness park ranger. He has also worked as a financial planner, a technical writer, a technical trainer for Xerox Corporation, and a career naval officer. A self-avowed "people watcher," Weill has a knack for observing and describing the many amusing habits and traits of the people he meets. He is the author of *Excuse Me, Sir... Your Socks are on Fire*, about his days as a wilderness park ranger in the West Canada Lakes Wilderness of New York State. His later books, *Pardon Me, Sir... There's a Moose in Your Tent* and *Forgive Me, Ma'am... Bears Don't Wear Blue*, have entertained a new generation of Adirondack enthusiasts and generated a renewed interest in the concept of wilderness camping in New York's largest state park. His most recent works, *Adirondack Trail of Gold* and *In Marcy's Shadow*, have charted Weill's move into the genre of historical fiction. Weill lives in Rochester, New York, with his wife and younger daughter. They vacation and hike in the Adirondacks annually.